Who Killed
Mister Moonlight?

Who Killed Mister Moonlight? Bauhaus Black Magick and Benediction
David J. Haskins

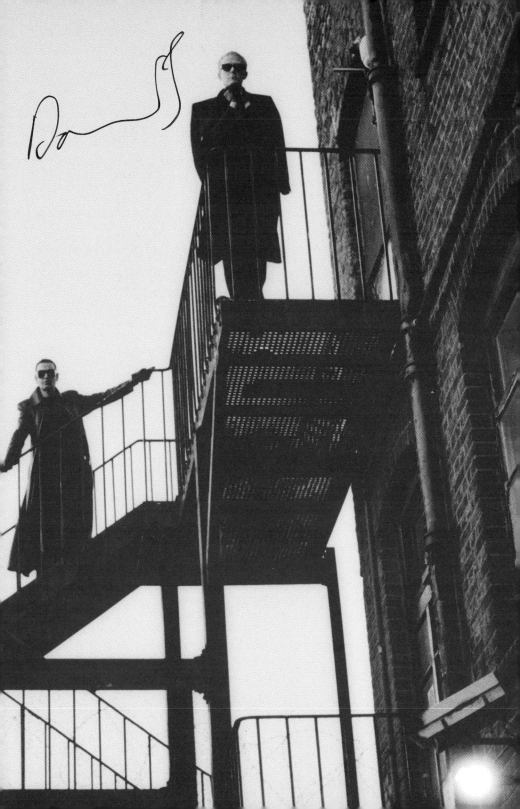

For Annie

In memoriam
Derek Spencer Tompkins
1925–2013

Who Killed
Mister Moonlight?
Bauhaus
Black Magick
and Benediction
David J. Haskins

A Jawbone book
First edition 2014
Published in the UK and the USA by
Jawbone Press
2a Union Court,
20–22 Union Road,
London SW4 6JP,
England
www.jawbonepress.com

ISBN 978-1-908279-66-8

EDITOR Tom Seabrook
JACKET DESIGN Mark Case

Printed by Everbest Printing Co Ltd, China

1 2 3 4 5 18 17 16 15 14

A free download of an unreleased acoustic version
of 'Who Killed Mister Moonlight?' recorded in
2007 by David J. with Mister Uncertain on piano
and Tom Vos on violin is available here:
www.davidjonline.com/mr-moonlight

Contents

In many ways, Bauhaus were the darkest and deadliest of Britain's post-punk pioneers. Seeing them live in London the week *In The Flat Field* came out is an experience I'll never forget. Instead of overkill, they were the masters of underkill and spine-tingling tension. Then they got famous. Now, David J. Haskins reflects on both personal and collective evolution and how to rise from the ashes the right way when a truly great band breaks up. And to think it all started in a vacuum, far away from the lights of London, in a sleepy market town in the Midlands. It's amazing how far people can go when they're not afraid of their own intelligence, curiosity, and new ideas. I don't think he's done, either. Jello Biafra

Bauhaus was like a hard cock in a dimly lit room filled with vampires. This book is told firsthand by one of the reckless. few that created such an important and unusual genre of music. Their odd, witchy songs snaked themselves all the way from whence they came into my temporal lobe and impacted on what I ended up becoming as an artist. Marilyn Manson

This is mesmerizing writing with a sense of humour with a bite and attention to detail so vivid you're there! This personal and bold accounting of frequently outrageous events will inform and enthral those who love an engaging life story (as well as music history buffs) with its many powerful behind-the-scenes explosions, but the book really gets into high gear in the final sublime metaphysical chapters. An enthralling read. Jarboe

It's been well over thirty years since I've seen David in person, but reading his wildly vivid memoir makes 1982 feel like yesterday. Eloquent and Smart. A great read. Gavin Friday

This book offers a fascinating glimpse into the musical and artistic development of David J. Haskins, from his involvement with Bauhaus and the counterculture underground to his stoned immaculate forays into the occult. At times insightful, sometimes shocking, often hilarious, a delightful book. Brendan Perry (Dead Can Dance)

The bats may have left the bell tower, but David J. Haskins has reached deep and down, dredging up musty skeletons long thought buried for this blacklit rock'n'roll romp through the birth of a new music, dark and mysterious. Sharpen your fangs, light the candles, and dig in to this scrumptious gothic feast.
Shade Rupe, author of *Dark Stars Rising*

I knew David J. Haskins to be a fantastic musician and visual artist, but it turns out that he is also a gifted writer with a sharp style and sly wit. *Who Killed Mister Moonlight?* is not just a revealing account of the evolution of Bauhaus and Love And Rockets— peppered with stories about David's interactions with The Clash, John Lydon, Joy Division, Iggy Pop, Rick Rubin, and other heroes of mine—but an electric journey through the struggles and tensions of the creative process. David J. has a dark side, but he's no one-dimensional goth, his shades of black manifest in remarkably varied ways in his art, and in his writing, as wicked black humour. What is most compelling about this book is the way David articulates the inspirations, irritations, triumphs, and defeats that are inherent to creativity … the alchemy of turning black thoughts into white light. Shepard Fairey

Captivating and charming, David J. Haskins's witty memoir is a must read for anyone who was ever in a band, went to art school, or danced like a New Wave slut to 'Bela Lugosi's Dead'!
Ann Magnuson

This is not merely a legendary rock'n'roll story but an epic creator's journey of a man who is not only a master musician and storyteller but also a master magician. A man who knows that music and art are magic, and that magic can and will destroy what destroys us. This book kills fascists.
Steven Johnson Leyba, artist and author of *Coyote Satan Amerika* and *The Trickster's Torah*

Another sorry tale of how ego, drugs, and black magic (and I don't mean the chocolates) destroyed another great band. It made me sad. Peter Hook

Foreword
by Jeremy Reed

David J.'s memorably inventive personal and musical documentation of his times employs a parallel-processing narration of band histories, notably his trademark Bauhaus and Love And Rockets identities, together with a synchronistic overlap into occult left-path magic that has by chancy accident and cultivated ritual run contemporaneous with his intensely wired creative energies, opening highly idiosyncratic pathways into four decades of music, from the optimally disruptive late 70s to the continuous edge-pushing present.

I live in an off-limits unvisitable Hampstead basement, niched on a loop, where I write all day, sub-level, in a space compacted with books. My first inerasable memory of David was walking down the S-curved residential hill to meet him at the Magdala pub, where he was seated outside, drinking a Guinness at noon, the obsidian drink looking like it was cuffed with a Zelda Fitzgerald demimonde mink collar. We'd planned to work together, and I instantly liked his singularly intense focus, as though there was no obstacle between how he conceived of an objective and how he executed it, just an energised, realisable dissolve.

In this book, David's unstoppable resolve to connect with people to whom he feels psychic affinities has him fortuitously visit William Burroughs in Kansas, and Brion Gysin in Paris—by instinctual radar, sighting him on a balcony, wearing a Moroccan djellaba—as well as receiving into his company the lugubrious, druggy ex-Velvet Nico, armed with a large bottle of mescal, limes, and salts, in London.

Graduating from Nene College of Art in Northampton, David's musical trajectory, inspired initially by seeing the ripping anarchic energies of punk terrorists like The Sex Pistols and The Clash assault the tiny 100 Club in London's Oxford Street, fed into the repurposed gothic indie of Bauhaus, and the cult acclaim surrounding edge-walking unapologetically broody tracks like 'Bela Lugosi's Dead', 'In The Flat Field', and the deconstructive remake of Marc Bolan's 'Telegram Sam.' The drug-fuelled, highly contentious inner politics of the band's conflicting sensibilities, their breakups, crack-ups, reunions, and final disintegration in 2006 are all charted here as explosively implosive; not with the linear regularity of most band chronicles, but with David's own inspired facility to deregulate time into the significant episodic snapshots that memory processes and stores. There's no bitterness here, either, no recriminatory blame, but rather the sensitive appraisal of individual psychologies. Peter Murphy's fireball paranoia and Daniel Ash's self-destructive propensities are seen as their exaggerated and uncompromising realities, rather than as deficits to band community. This generosity strikes me as a lesson to most rock autobiographies, in which the protagonist invariably sets out to settle old scores to vindicate his star qualities. David's parallel journey— his pathway into travelling the astral plane, or accessing the occult gateways signposted by the likes of Aleister Crowley, Kenneth Grant, and Robert Anton Wilson, and psychedelic journeyers like Timothy Leary and Terence McKenna—has given him an expanded overview on the nature of his creative resources as a musician, and how these energies interact with the psychic senders he contacts.

How refreshing it is to read a music book that is not an ego-drenched mantra of ME but an account of personal development in the light of contemporaries who have coloured the way forward, written in high-octane descriptive prose with a real aptitude for strong, detailed characterisation.

If a big part of David's identity is of course pioneering music, then he's aware his creative expression is an integrant of his personality and a phenomenon conditioned by the times. No other art form in the past fifty years has had so much money thrown at it for so little, so much fame, fandom, and media attention, in the way that poetry, fiction, and non-celebrity art hasn't, or taken it for granted as its right to arrogate over cultural taste. It's David's transcendent side which gets above this; his awareness of the whole counterculture thrust collaterally shattering the tectonic plates over which music dances.

Explanations Disclaimers and Plaudits

Bauhaus was a band of outsiders. Mutant misfits. Strangers in a factory town. Bonded by music, rebellion, and a desire to escape, we dared to live out a brave and quixotic dream, only to fly too close to a screaming black sun and die on the Icarus wing.

Black Magick with a *k*, and not without tears. I believe that this kind of sorcery was perpetrated against me and my circle with devastating results. I have never utilised the black arts but instead have always leaned toward a whiter shade of juju that has always been conducted in a positive, benevolent spirit and focused on the attainment of spiritual/ creative advancement, help for others, and, on occasion, a 'get out of jail free' card (so, OK, 'off-white magick', I'll grant you).

Benediction came in the form of two spiritual awakenings and an exorcism of sorts. All of which are described in detail in this book. 'Benediction' is also exemplified by Bethesda, the Angel of the Healing Waters. We used an image of the statue of Bethesda in New York's Central Park as the cover for the final Bauhaus album, *Go Away White*, which was eventually released on our own independent label in 2008. Bethesda is symbolic of holy saving grace, catharsis, and spiritual healing. I consider myself blessed to have known her, and while writing this book I have also been blessed by the friendship and invaluable support and assistance of the following: Ann Greenaway, my wife, best friend, soulmate, original proofreader, muse, and whip-cracker. Andrew J. Brooksbank, invaluable 'tenacious truffle pig' adept in the unearthing of minutia and obscure facts. Also: Jello Biafra, Black Francis, Kyle Burkhart, Circle23, Kerry Colonna, Anton Corbijn, Antony, John Cornelius, Fin Costello, Ken Eros, Perry Farrell, Cathryn Farnsworth, Shepard Fairey, Pat Fish, Gavin Friday, Peter Hook, Melinda Gebbie, Marc Geiger, Dawn Hurwitz, Harry Isles, Jarboe, Mitch Jenkins, Robert Kaechele, Mary Jo Kaczka, Peter Kent, Steven Johnson Leyba, Judy Lyon, Ann Magnuson, Marilyn Manson, Darwin Meiners, Mick Mercer, Eugene Merinov, Richard Metzger, Lynda Mortensen, Alan Moore, the late, great Brendan Mullen, Blair Murphy, Gabor Nemeth, Adam Parfey, Brendan Perry, Richard Peterson, John A. Rivers, Mavis Tompkins, Jeremy Reed, Howard Rosenburg, Shade Rupe, Scott Saw, Thomas Jerome Seabrook, Suzi Skelton, Stella Watts, Damien Youth.

David J. Haskins
June 2014

PROLOGUE
Gestation
1961–78

'You look like a star but you're still on the dole.'
Mott The Hoople, 'All The Way To Memphis'

Nineteen sixty-one was the year of the Berlin Wall, the Bay of Pigs, and The Beatles' first gig at the Cavern. It was also the year that I met Daniel Ash. We were both four years old and reluctant attendees of Miss Cherry's kindergarten, an institution specialising in cruel and unusual punishment for the under fives. We both had our little knuckles rapped, were made to stand in the corner or sit in the high chair for refusing to eat things that we found unpalatable, and we would throw hurt and conciliatory looks at each other in righteous indignation over our unfair plight. We bonded fairly early on as fellow rebels against draconian authority, and the medium of our outraged expression was music. The instrumentation was limited to the contents of the school percussion box, but while the triangle and wood block are not really the instruments on which to vent livid frustration, it all served a purpose. Bonded, rebellious, and musical we would remain.

Following this seminal meeting, Daniel and I would not see each other again for some thirteen years. The location of our reunion was another educational institution, albeit one of a far more liberal bent. In 1974, Nene College of Art in Northampton was a laboratory for avant-garde experimentation and the furtive exploration of mind-altering substances, a crucible of non-conformity populated by freaks, weirdoes, and assorted misfits. Naturally, we both felt right at home.

It was here that I had my first drug experience. The Grant projector is a tool that enables designers to enlarge or reduce images by placing them on a glass platform in front of an adjustable lens. The image is projected onto a transparent surface so that it can then be traced over. A large canvas hood shuts out the surrounding light. There was one kid who would always be hogging the Grant. One time, when I decided to lean over his shoulder to investigate, I discovered that he was rolling joints. He gave me a conspiratorial wink and suggested we sneak off down to the basement for a smoke.

The effect of the drug was instant and intense: a feeling of inner warmth suffused my body, and my mind was softly bent. In this altered state, the only place that I could think of going was the library at the top of the building. (I certainly could not go back to class!) I floated up the steps and had the distinct impression that stone was turning to marshmallow.

Time was out of whack and slowing down. Inside the reading room, I slumped down at one of the big wooden tables. Looking up at the bookshelves, I noticed that the books were breathing, their spines having turned from card and leather to living flesh. I slowly realised that this breathing corresponded with my own. Eventually, I hauled myself up, ventured over to the outsized art books, and pulled out a large tome. The complete works of Hieronymus Bosch. Fascinated, I poured over these lurid phantasmagorical depictions as they writhed and came to life before my dilated pupils. When I saw the Grant-hog the next day and enquired as to what the hell it was that we had been smoking, he told me that it was opium.

* * *

Daniel and I were taking different courses. We had yet to strike up a conversation, but we would always nod as we passed each other in the corridor. It was a tentative gesture of mutual recognition prompted in part by the fact that we both eschewed flares in favour of drainpipe trousers (a rarity in those days).

One day I spotted those skinny black jeans—incongruously and somewhat unnervingly combined with an Afghan overcoat—striding down the high street as I was driving into town in my old Morris Minor. I was interested to see that Daniel was carrying a guitar case. I pulled up alongside him and offered him a lift. He was on his way to band practice. MI5 were an almost all-black funk band (Daniel's being the single white face) who were just starting to make a name for themselves locally. Daniel invited me along to the session. They were a pretty tight little combo, but most impressive of all was Daniel's natural feel and flair for the guitar.

'Ay, Danny, man,' one of his bandmates began. 'We got this idea, yeah? Look, we got this wicked gas mask, man. Why don't you wear it, innit?'

This suggestion turned out to be the clincher that prompted his voluntary departure from the ranks of MI5. At this time, I was in a band that went by the name Grab A Shadow. My little brother Kevin was on drums, with Dave Stretton and Dave 'X' Exton on lead and rhythm guitar, respectively. I played bass and shared vocal duties with the other Daves. (A running joke was that whenever anyone called out 'Dave', at least two if not three of us would answer.)

Prior to forming this group, Stretton, Kevin, and I were in a band called Jam with another school friend, Roger Rideout on lead guitar and vocals. Weekends would find us driving up north—Birmingham, Doncaster, Manchester, Leeds—to play the working men's clubs. Typically, we would come on between a drag act or a lewd comedian and the bingo.

X was my best friend at school, a tall, blonde, handsome bastard, sharp as a scalpel, and with a strong rebellious streak. It was he who turned me on to iconoclastic, rebellious writers such as Burroughs, Ginsberg, Kerouac, Cohen, Rimbaud, Baudelaire, and the like. We had similar tastes in music, too. We were both Bowie nuts, and would stay behind after art class, painting obsessive portraits of our hero while listening to *Hunky Dory* or *Ziggy Stardust*. This voluntary extracurricular activity seemed to upset the school's blockhead bullies, who would shatter our reverie with brutal invasions, kicking over easels and stomping on tubes of paint with their metal-studded brogues. Oddly, they would never lay a finger on our trembling skinny frames. I think they were secretly afraid of us.

After the bullies' noisy, belching departure, we would crank up 'The

Bewlay Brothers' and sink back into reverie. When Bowie announced that he would be appearing at the Hammersmith Odeon in London (for what would turn out to be the legendary 'retirement' concert) we applied for two tickets but received only one. Gutted, we ceremoniously ripped up the single pass, and our bond was sealed forever.

A couple of years later, X and I would make regular forays down to London in order to catch some of the bands on the burgeoning pub-rock circuit, the boozers in question being the likes of the Nashville in West Kensington, the Greyhound in Fulham, the Bull & Gate in Kentish Town, and our favourite, the Hope & Anchor on Upper Street, Islington. It was at this old haunt that we caught acts like The Stranglers, Eddie & The Hot Rods, Ducks Deluxe, Nick Lowe, The Kursaal Flyers, and on one memorable occasion, Kilburn & The Highroads, fronted by Ian Dury. Not wanting to miss anything, we arrived early for this gig and ventured down to the basement, only to find Mr Dury and his towering minder-cum-roadie Spider setting up.

'Can I 'elp you, lads?' came the incongruously deep, roaring voice from Dury's tiny frame.

'Uh, sorry, no, uh … I think we're a bit early.'

'Spider, would you kindly escort these young gentlemen from the premises?' Dury boomed.

'It's OK, we're going!'

The Hope & Anchor had a great jukebox upstairs, and so lost in it were we that we missed the Kilburns' first set. We were well and truly present for the second, and as the band ambled on we were quite awed by their misfit strangeness. The drummer was a black man on crutches, the bassist was a midget, the keyboard player a giant, and on sax was an albino with a Teddy Boy quiff and wraparound shades. And then there was Dury, now kitted out in a classic comic-book convict's outfit, all green with black arrows plus matching cap, which was tilted at a rakish angle. He had a single razor-blade earring stuck to the side of his profusely sweating face and wore a black leather glove on his wizened left hand (he had contracted polio when he was kid, and his left side was severely affected).

We had not heard the band until now, only heard *about* them, and when they launched into the opening number we were bowled over by the sheer ferocity of the sound, not to mention Dury's tremendous gravelly voice. And the lyrics were something else: tumbling cascades of clever wordplay, Cockney rhyming slang, and cheeky innuendo detailing the spicy lives of London's miscreants, criminals, and wide boys.

Kilburn & The Highroads instantly became our second favourite band on the scene. Numero uno, without doubt, was Dr Feelgood. The first time we saw this lot was at the old Marquee Club in Wardour Street. The opening act was a band called Flip City, fronted by a skinny, bespectacled guy in drainpipe jeans and white T-shirt who sang his heart out to a very disinterested group of barflies. X and I thought he was great. The following year he would resurface as Elvis Costello. The Feelgoods, meanwhile, looked like small-time gangsters with their shabby suits, skinny ties, and surly scowls. The drummer was known as The Big Figure, which suited him to a *T*. There was 'Sparko' on the bass, Lee Brilleaux barking out the vocals and blowing a mean blues harp, and on black Telecaster guitar was the incredible Wilko Johnson, who bore an unsettling resemblance to Tony Perkins in *Psycho*, but with a pudding-basin haircut. He would maintain a rock-steady choppy staccato rhythm until it came time for a solo, whereupon he would suddenly explode, holding his instrument like a machine gun and letting rip with a blistering volley of notes—this while zigzagging around the stage like an electrocuted animal. (The idea of amphetamine abuse was not out of the question.)

We were right down the front for this one, and the close proximity to all that wired energy was utterly thrilling, although it did have its downside, as throughout the set we were frequently showered by Mr Brilleaux's copious sweat. Either way, we could not get enough of this riot on eight legs.

Whenever we were in London we would scour the independent record stores for obscure American treasures on imported vinyl: The MC5, The Stooges, The Flaming Groovies, Jonathan Richman & The Modern Lovers, The Velvet Underground, Patti Smith, The New York Dolls (whose exciting appearance on *The Old Grey Whistle Test* was a key moment for us both). Another big record for us was *Nuggets*, Lenny Kaye's great compilation of 60s garage rock. These hard-to-find platters were like tablets from the mountain, and back in our candlelit teenage bedrooms we would pore over their grooves and bask in revelation. Just around the corner, rising on the event horizon like a huge convoy loaded with high explosives, was punk, and we would soon discover that—contrary to our sense that we were part of a marginalised minority—there was a whole generation being inspired by the same sounds. A generation that was sick to the gills of all the overblown, overwrought, and overpaid rock bands belching out their irrelevant crap ad nauseam. Revolution was in the air!

When the Ramones came to London in 1976 to play their first UK gig at the Roundhouse in Camden Town, we were there, right down near the front of the stage. They were like a cartoon come to life, the perfect rock'n'roll band in their uniform black leather biker jackets, ripped drainpipe jeans, and grown-out mop-tops. The music was ultra-simple, tough bubble-gum punk rock, with no song lasting longer than three minutes (and most of them done in two). At one point, during 'Beat On The Brat', they handed out dozens of miniature wooden baseball bats. We were well and truly coshed! It was at this gig that I first saw kids wearing charity-shop clothes that had been ripped apart and then reassembled and festooned with safety pins.

I had left art school that year, and like most of my contemporaries, I was signing on the dole. Each week I would receive a cheque for thirteen quid, which would not go very far at all, so I foolishly took to artfully altering the amount with a biro, changing the *1* to a *2*. I got away with it for a few weeks, but then one morning down at the unemployment centre I was pulled out of line and told to wait in an office. After a nerve-wracking fifteen minutes or so, a small grey man entered the small grey room and informed me that certain discrepancies concerning my weekly cheque had been discovered. He then asked if I had anything to say about it.

My heart was in my throat. I'd been nicked! I had to own up. They gave me a verbal wrist-slapping, and the extra funds that I had illegally claimed were docked from my future handouts.

Every now and again I would be offered work and would reluctantly drag myself off to some insufferably tedious dead-end job. Still, the small boost in income was always welcome. The local sawmill was a rough one, though. On my first day, I enquired after the profusion of six-inch nails—sharpened to a vicious point—that sat atop most of the workstations. I was informed that these were for the extraction of splinters—'Cos you're gonna get a lot of 'em!' We had to wear oil-filled headphones to shut out the cacophonous noise, and sawdust would inevitably get trapped between the slimy inner part of the phones and the ears, which was extremely irritating, especially in the steaming summer heat. Several long-time workers were missing digits. I lasted all of one week.

My longest stretch of torture was six weeks at Jaybeam Aerials. I worked on a machine that bent two-foot-long pieces of aluminium at right angles. After eight hours of doing this, to the imbecilic strains of daytime 'Wonderful' Radio 1, I was going round the bend. Still, only another 232 hours to go. I could not get my head around the fact that some of these poor bastards had been working in this factory for thirty fucking years.

Another awful job was at a meat pie factory. It was my job to scoop out globs of pink, gristly meat from a huge vat and use it to encase the hard-boiled eggs that would continually roll by on a rubber conveyor belt. Sometimes, passing employees would vent their disgust by spitting in the vat. Scotch eggs somehow lost their dubious appeal after that. Then there was my two-week stint as an ice-cream man. The van would be constantly full of angry wasps, and one time I nearly crashed the bloody thing during a particularly frenzied attack. This vehicle had a wind-up music box that played 'The Teddy Bears' Picnic'. I would find mild amusement in letting it run down so that it sounded like a funeral dirge.

Speaking of funerals, I quickly learned that you had to be very careful about where you parked. The 'ice-cream mafia' was all too real, and if you pulled up onto some demarcated patch there would be hell to pay. It was not uncommon for Mister Softy to end up torched and in flames. It was my responsibility to return the van at the end of the day and attach the vehicle to a generator. This would keep the thing refrigerated, so that the ice cream wouldn't melt. One time, I decided to skive off and call in to see my mum for a cup of tea. After an hour or so, I returned to the van, inserted the key in the door … and it promptly snapped off in the lock. I had an hour to get the van back to the depot before the soft scoop became very soft indeed. I had no other recourse than to hire a rescue vehicle. We made it back just in time, but the cost of the tow truck was docked from my wages, and as I was paid on commission I ended up owing the company the sum of £2.10.

One of the worst jobs I had was at a sheet-metal-dipping factory. This was in the middle of an especially bitter winter. The temperature would go from one extreme to another. The heat inside was intense, and there was an odious reek of sulphur as the huge metal sheets were dunked in acid, but when deliveries arrived the huge doors would roll up, letting in a great gust of icy wind. We had to run out and offload the truck, our fingers sticking to the copper in the cold. Then it was back to Hell. Again, some of the other workers had been there for years. Unimaginable! It certainly made you appreciate how lucky you were. One poor fellow had been there for twenty-five years. He was clearly mentally challenged, and bore an unsettling resemblance to Boris Karloff. He had the unnerving habit of creeping up behind you and then suddenly whispering 'I drive Leyland cars!' loudly in your ear before slopping off again.

I lasted four hours at the factory before being quickly replaced by Daniel Ash. When he turned up, the manager remarked, 'Another one from the art school, is it? Well, I hope you last longer than the last one!' He did—two weeks, in fact. Stoic chap.

Another somewhat incongruous place of shared employment was a building site, although I followed Daniel this time. It was hard work. I had to break up rocks, load them into a wheelbarrow, and then cart it over to the other side of the site, where the rubble would be used as filler. At lunch time I would sometimes join the others—most of whom were Irish navvies—at a nearby pub, where they would think nothing of downing five or six pints of Guinness before returning to work. I would knock back a couple and be pretty buzzed upon my return. The booze fired the lads up, and they would set about demolishing brick walls and stone pillars with great gusto. Needless to say, I did not fit in, and occasionally my choice of reading matter—Camus and Sartre, rather than the *Sun*—was brought into suspicious question. ('What ya reading dere den, lad?') After two weeks the foreman gave me and two other weedy student types the old heave-ho.

These spells of not-so-gainful employment were interspersed with yet more time on the dole. Eventually however, I found more suitable work as a graphic designer at a firm specialising in rip-off football club merchandise. It was my task to subtly alter the clubs' logos in order to evade prosecution for plagiarism. The biggest perk of this job was the lovely Ann Greenaway, head of human resources and personal assistant to the boss. She was a beautiful, willowy twenty-eight-year-old former model with a vivacious personality and radiant smile that lit up any room she entered. I wanted to possess her—but so did the boss!

This state of affairs would ultimately result in my departure from the firm. My final day there played out like a silly French farce. I had been on the payroll for some six months, and had been sleeping with our shared object of desire for the last three. When her other would-be suitor found out he was none too pleased. I worked in a small office with two other guys. It was like a long corridor, with doors at either end. On that last day, the doors were flung open and slammed shut many times over as my irate employer stormed through in a mad rage, followed by a highly strung and flustered Annie.

'What the hell's going on?' my co-worker Ian exclaimed. I could have told him, but I didn't. Eventually, Annie made a broadcast over the PA, requesting my presence in reception.

'Sorry!' she said. 'You've got to leave! Hand in your notice! Don't ask why now. I'll explain later. Just GO!'

I obediently followed my orders and left, never to return. Ten years later, having eventually gotten over the incident, and his infatuation with my future wife, my former boss would become the manager of my band, Love And Rockets. He was a charming man with a wicked sense of humour, and he became a good friend.

* * *

One balmy Indian summer night in that eventful year of 1976, I took my brother Kevin down to the 100 Club in London to see a new band. I was following up on a Xeroxed flyer taped to a wall in the Hope & Anchor. The Sex Pistols had arrived, and things would never be the same again.

The dingy little bar was packed with rambunctious proto-punks. There was quite a bit of jostling going on, and a couple of kids were pogoing to the support band, Stinky Toys, who were pretty awful. I grabbed a couple of beers, and as I was heading back over to Kevin, the bevvies and I were nearly sent flying when some idiot suddenly propelled himself backward and barged into my side. I shot him a 'what the fuck?' look and was met with a manic scowl and a sharp downward glance. I followed the trajectory of those optical daggers and saw that my assailant was wielding a motorcycle chain, at which point I made a sick grin and moved on. I would later recognise this ruffian as one Sid Vicious.

Also on the bill that night was a magnificent seminal version of The Clash that included the gaunt guitarist Keith Levine (later of PiL) alongside the impossibly cool and handsome Paul Simonon on bass, solid Terry Chimes on drums, rock'n'roll incarnate Mick Jones on lead guitar, and the electrifying Joe Strummer on rhythm guitar. They looked amazing in paint-splattered and stencilled high-collared shirts and straight-legged zippered pants. They also had little shards of coloured lighting gel safety-pinned here and there.

At one point, while a guitar string was being changed, Strummer held up a small transistor radio to the mic. He turned the dial and randomly tuned to a news report about the latest IRA bombing. The soundman had the wherewithal to stick some dub-style echo on it, and suddenly it was the sound of the zeitgeist. And then—*ONETWOTHREEFOUR!*—they exploded back into vital action once again.

We recognised Mick Jones as the cool-as-fuck dandy we'd often seen on trips to check out the latest hot bands on the London pub-rock scene. Another familiar face at those early 70s gigs was John Lydon, reinvented on the 100 Club stage that night as Johnny Rotten when his band shambled on and launched into a pulverising 'Anarchy In The UK'.

Contained in the scrawny vessel of Rotten was all the seething rage, aggression, and spiked inspiration of a generation, distilled to its white-hot essence. Hunched and twisted, Richard III in bandage/bondage drag, his aura crackled with a blistering electrical charge as, clasping the mic stand with both hands, arms outstretched and ratty head sunk low, he glared at the rabble before him, imperious and undeterred as a storm of spittle rained down.

The Pistols' sound came as a primal roar bursting from the guts of the great dark beast that had been festering in the cellars of the nation during the bleakest months of the recent past. There was mass unemployment and deep recession, and Margaret Thatcher had taken over the Conservative Party and was poised to squeeze the lifeblood from the working class. In the Queen's jubilee year, the filthy London streets were full of garbage; traffic was getting worse, and the resulting pollution coated your skin with grime and stung your eyes. All this, and rock'n'roll had turned into a pantomime horse in a powdered wig—until the Pistols came along.

At one point during that galvanising gig, Kevin and I looked at each other with the same wild-eyed grin. It was the night we decided to form our own punk band. Back in Northampton, we called once again on X (Grab A Shadow having recently split up in a blue funk of disenchantment with the local music scene, and rock music in general). He was already in the loop and on his way to the barbers. All we had to do now was find a singer.

The half-Latvian, half-Scottish Janis Zakis arrived at our rehearsal room (a small office above my parents' newsagent and tobacconists) looking like punk rock perfection. He had shaved his head and burnt off the stubble with a cigarette lighter! He wore a rough smear of bright red lipstick, an extra long, python-like multi coloured *Dr Who* scarf, and a mad glint in his baby blue eyes. He unravelled the python and made an announcement.

OK. I've got this lyric. It's called 'Explosion', and it's about oral sex. You boys play me some music. OK, let's go! One-two-three-four!

Silence.

Come on, yer fuckers! Let's GO!

We all looked at each other, gobsmacked. The young try-out was certainly not short on chutzpah! I suggested that we play an instrumental version of a three-chord tune that we had been working on prior to the arrival of this steaming force of nature.

'Uh, OK, uh … Janis, give us the count-in again.'

'That's more like it! One-two-three-four!'

Of course, he got the job, and I renamed him 'Vince Venom'. Two weeks later we played our first gig, as The Submerged 10th, at the Racehorse pub in Abington Square. Every punk rocker in town was there—all four of them! Annie Greenaway was also in attendance, and was a little freaked out by my 'other life'.

For starters, Janis decided to empty half of his pint of lager over the head of some poor fellow in a suit who was trying to have a conversation with a lady friend. The drenched victim rose from his seat, all set to lay one on his assailant, when the mad bastard poured the remaining drink over his own head, sprayed himself from head to crotch with shaving cream, and mashed All-Bran cereal into chest. (Always a good ploy.) This act of surreal madness seemed to defuse the situation, and a punch-up was allayed.

Janis counted us into the first song. The set was made up of three-chord originals I had penned—two-minute ditties with 'au courant' titles like 'Dole Queue', 'All Fucked Up', and '9 to 5'—plus covers such as The Seeds' 'Pushin' Too Hard' (culled from *Nuggets*), the Velvets' 'Run Run Run', and an amphetamine-kicked version of Petula Clark's 'Downtown', performed with a suitably sarcastic twist.

We played two more shows after the Racehorse. The plugs were literally pulled at the last of them, and Janis decided to go off and become a gypsy, playing the accordion while wandering through Eastern Europe. Unimaginably, he would resurface years later as the deputy headmaster of an exclusive private school for boys. Rather than look for another singer—and who could replace Vince Venom?!—X and I decided to share the vocals and beef up the instrumentation with the addition of another guitarist.

Daniel Ash was the first one to come to mind. He had seen the Pistols on TV and was suitably impressed. He *got it*, and he was in. I discovered that Daniel's taste in music had much in common with my own. Apart from the twin touchstones of Bowie and Iggy, he was also into Roxy Music, and I was impressed that he had been in attendance at their concert at the Rainbow in London in 1973, and also when Lou Reed did his rock'n'roll animal thing live at the same venue that same year. Lou's Bowie-produced *Transformer* LP was a huge album for both of us. And then there was our shared love of Marc Bolan and T.Rex. (I had been a fully paid up member of the T.Rex fan club—the only one I ever joined.) And if that wasn't enough, the first record Daniel ever bought was 'Double Barrel', an early-70s reggae cut by Dave & Ansel Collins— the same as me![1]

Apart from the Trojan Records reggae roster, Daniel and I were into artists like Scott Walker and Jacques Brel, both of whom had been brought to our attention by Bowie, who spoke glowingly about them in interviews. It was a dazzling constellation of inspirational stars, but the one that burned brightest was Bowie himself. Like me, Dan had been floored by Bowie's performance of 'Starman' on *Top Of The Pops*. It was a monumental event for kids of our age. In 1972, England was so utterly drab and grey. Bowie's visitation was a startling explosion of colour and excitement—a galvanising shock of beauty.

Along with the addition of Daniel came a new name and a shift in musical direction. As The Craze, we began to lean more in the direction of twisted post-punk power-pop. We played a few gigs on the usual pub/ college circuit, and on one occasion, Daniel broached the idea of having an old friend of his come up and join us to sing the soul classic 'Knock On Wood'. That friend's name was Peter Murphy. We gave Daniel the OK, but apparently when Peter turned up at the gig he hated the band (now renamed Jack Plug & The Sockettes) and opted out after an attack of nerves.

By the end of 1978, the band had split up, and punk was all but over too. I moved to London for a spell and sniffed around the post-punk scene for a few months before getting an offer to go to Germany to play on US air bases with a disco/funk band. It was a pretty good paycheque, so I accepted, but before leaving I received a phone call from Daniel. He wanted me to come over and check out the new group that he had just formed with my brother Kevin on drums, Chris Barber on bass, and that 'stage-shy' school friend of his.

'I'd really like your opinion, Dave,' he said. 'I think that Pete has something special, and we've been writing together.'

They were just about to start playing when I arrived at the small mobile classroom at a teacher-training college that served as their rehearsal space. We nodded to each other, and Daniel counted us in. Peter looked amazing. He had a preternatural beauty: high, chiselled cheekbones, pale skin, piercing blue eyes. He had his dirty blonde hair slicked back like a 1920s matinee idol. He moved with an elegant grace, and then there was that voice—a booming baritone that would soar to a stratospheric 'character' soprano at the drop of a cymbal. He had a pronounced stammer when he spoke, but it disappeared completely when he sang.[2]

The music that they made together was stark, stripped down, and jagged, with Daniel's razor-tone guitar sculpting diamond-sharp shapes in the cold air. I had never wanted to be a part of anything so badly, but I decided not to voice this desire as I knew this was Daniel's baby, and that he would be very wary of having me come in and take over the pram.

After thirty minutes or so, the band took a break, and Daniel came over to ask what I thought of Peter.

'Solid gold!' I whispered. 'Solid gold!'

* * *

It was a week before I was due to travel to Germany. I was in the back room, trying to nail the bassline to 'Boogie Nights', when Daniel came a-knockin' on wood. It was sheeting down with rain, and he stood on my doorstep like a drowned crow.

Once inside, Daniel said that things weren't working out with Chris, and would I be interested in joining his group? He left me with a tape of some demos, and I told him that I would let him know within forty-eight hours. Of course I wanted to shout *YES!* there and then, but I had my commitment to the other band. I immediately called up Dave Henderson, the bandleader, and explained the situation. He very graciously gave his blessing for me to stay behind. The experience of playing with them had proved useful, however, and some of those disco basslines would find their way into our music in the months to come, albeit in a decidedly ironic context.

The first thing that I brought to the group was not a note but a name. It had struck me that in the stark quality of the band's sound there was an affinity with the ideal of the Staatliches Bauhaus in Weimar, the school of architecture and art founded in 1919, which held that form was function and any superfluous embellishment should be stripped away in favour of elegant design. It was the opposite of the Gothic ideal (the irony of which would be lost on me for at least another year). Bauhaus 1919 was my suggested moniker, and everyone seemed to like it immediately.

We crammed in as much rehearsal time as we could over the next two weeks. We were still using the mobile classroom at the teacher-training college. The Pretenders were due to play in the union hall one night, so we decided to play a guerrilla-style gig. We carried our amps across the parking lot and set up in the corner, uninvited. We plugged in and blasted away until the union staff pulled the plugs. By all accounts Chrissie Hynde was not at all pleased that this gang of upstarts had cut into her band's set time.

Strictly speaking, this was our true live debut, but our first real 'semi-pro' gig was at the Cromwell pub the following week. Come the big night, we still had a very limited repertoire, and consequently played 'Raw Power' four times, starting and ending both of our sets with The Stooges' raucous beasty.

Leo Casey—the hottest girl in town—was there in her leopard-skin and black leather, getting down on the smelly pub carpet and literally taking up Peter's invitation to 'bite my hip' (the chorus lyric to our new song, uh, 'Bite My Hip'). The bite-marks remained for days, and Peter would proudly show them off to all and sundry at the drop of a pair of Levi's.

At the end of the night we were paid twenty quid and, buzzed on beer and music, we felt quite elated as we loaded out our gear in the snow. Nineteen seventy-nine felt like it was going to be an eventful year.

PART ONE
Fornicating In
The Gods
1979–83

In this world there are two tragedies. One is
not getting what one wants, and the other
is getting it.
Oscar Wilde

CHAPTER ONE
Children Of
The Night

Midnight. The room was illuminated by the blue flicker of the TV. Outside, snow fell in a soft, slow drift. The coal fire crackled and spat, its embers all aglow. On the screen, an old black-and-white creepy, the beautiful pale girl recoiling in horror as the elegant vampire moved in for the seductive kill.

Daniel saw it too, and this kicked off a conversion about all the old Dracula movies that we had loved since our youth. (Daniel's strict mother had banned him from seeing them, which naturally lent an added illicit thrill to his sneaked viewings.) We talked about all the vampires: the suave Christopher Lee; the hideous Max Shreck as the original, terrifying *Nosferatu*; the effective latter-day portrayal by Klaus Kinsky in Herzog's atmospheric version of the tale; Carl Theodor Dreyer's early silent masterpiece *Vampyr*; and then there was Bela Lugosi.

At the time, I had an excruciatingly boring job in a warehouse, packing up wholesale goods for delivery. I always had pockets full of address labels, and they came in handy on this occasion when I was suddenly seized by inspiration on the bicycle ride home.

White on white, translucent
Black cape's back
On the rack
Bela Lugosi's dead

By the time I got home, I had the whole thing scrawled out on the backs of those yellow labels. I couldn't wait to take it to band practice that night. We had just acquired the use of a room above a photographer's studio in Horsemarket Street, at the corner of Gold Street in Northampton. This came via the auspices of Graham Bentley, who was Daniel's dad's accountant at the time and had taken an immediate interest in the band when Daniel played him some rough demos. His brother-in-law rented the studio below, and Graham had somehow persuaded the poor unsuspecting fellow that it would be a good idea to have a bunch of reprobate would-be musicians occupy the upstairs space.

We decked out the dingy room with black plastic bin liners and low lighting (including a UV strip and strobe) and consequently felt at home, like bats in a cave. I handed the lyric sheet to Peter and strapped on the bass. Daniel said that he had come up with an idea: three ascending chords that utilised the trick of playing semi-barré chords but leaving the top two strings open. The chord progression was stolen from Gary Glitter's 'Rock And Roll (Parts 1 And 2)'. Kevin started to play a bossa-nova rhythm. (He had been taking lessons from an old jazz guy, and this was one of the two beats that he knew!) I underpinned the whole thing with a simple descending bassline. Peter started to sing, and it was a kind of miracle as we all just fell in with each other.

It was as if we had been playing this strange song for years. All the parts fitted perfectly into place, and all of a sudden we had a fully formed nine-minute epic on our hands. Magic out of the blue! After that first run-through we all looked at each other and started to laugh.

'Let's do it again!' Daniel said excitedly—and so we did.

We debuted the song—our first four-way collaboration—at our next gig, on January 3 at the Romany pub in Kingsthorpe, much to the bemusement of the middle-aged golfers who had strayed in from the links across the road. A couple of weeks later, we entered Beck Studios in Wellingborough to record the track along with four other originals.

This, our first recording session, was presided over and engineered by the studio's owner, Derek Tompkins, who appeared through a thick fog of cigarette smoke at the rear of the narrow control room. He was carrying a can of air freshener, which he proceeded to spray with liberal abandon. He then swallowed several aspirin, which he washed down with coffee from a flask.

A tall, slender man in his mid-fifties with lank silver-grey hair, carpet slippers, and a pronounced stutter, Tompkins had built the eight-track studio himself and, acquainted as he was with its home-made idiosyncrasies, he would occasionally disappear under the mixing console, pliers and screwdriver in hand, to fix some snag or other. At one point during the session, we came into the control room to discover him laid out flat on his back with his legs sticking out from under the desk.

'It's all been too much for Derek!' Daniel laughed.

Derek's background in recording mostly consisted of working with Irish show bands, folk duos, comedy acts like The Barron Knights, and the crooner Frank Ifield. He did have very good ears, though, and he was certainly open-minded. Plus the fact that he was not some young hipster but someone from outside our own scene held great appeal. The studio itself had a very homely feel with its warm and funky red-and-brown carpet, comfy old couch, a coffee table which was dominated by Derek's huge exploding ashtray, and a little kitchen for brewing up tea.

When it came to the recording of 'Bela', Derek quickly miked up the drum kit and amps and then simply rolled tape as we played the track through—one live take, vocals and all, and that take was The One. (It was the first time that Peter had ever sung into a studio mic.) Derek then showed Daniel how to use his marvellous analogue delay unit, which was operated by a slider that increased or decreased the effect. Derek had recorded several reggae artists, and he was correct in recognising that there was a dub aspect to 'Bela'. He told us that when it came to recording reggae artists, he would just leave them to it, and he decided to do the same with us.[1]

By the end of the three-hour session we had five tracks recorded and mixed. Alongside 'Bela', the other songs were 'Boys', 'Harry', 'Bite My Hip', and 'Some Faces'. Before wrapping up, Derek wanted to do one edit on 'Bela' in order to lose a bum note played by yours truly, which induced a now laughable state of panic in me as he wielded a razor blade and spliced the tape.

'Hey!' I blurted out. 'What the hell are you doing?'

'Wha-wha-wha-wha-what am I doing?' he replied. 'I'm ma-ma-ma-ma-making you sound like you c-c-c-can play that b-b-b-b-bloody thing!'

Derek smiled and made the necessary cut.

*   *   *

Our next gig was booked by Peter—the first and last time he would act in this capacity. It was a lunchtime show at the Wellingborough Railway Working Men's Club, a large wooden building populated by railway workers and their spouses, plus lots of young children running riot around the long Formica tables. The manager, a portly old fellow, would intermittently interrupt our set by marching onstage and bellowing, 'Oi! Oi! Oi! What yer tryin' to do? Blow the bloody 'ouse down?' which became a running in-joke catchphrase for years following.

We were booked to play two sets. After the first, the manager took us aside.

'Look,' he said, 'I know you lads like yer rock'n'roll, but we've got lots of old-'uns in 'ere, so you would do well to play some standards. Something they know and can tap along to, all right lads?'

With that, Peter's career as a booking agent was over.

The Racecourse Pavilion was a more fitting location for our next show, it being an old Edwardian building with an air of crumbling elegance. It was situated in a large park, formerly home to a racetrack that had been the scene of several brutal murders. ('Vampire Killer Gets Life' was one memorable headline in the local press.) Per head of population, Northampton had one of the highest rates of violent crime in the UK. It was in this seedy building that my friends Alan Moore (soon to become the renowned master of the graphic novel) and the wonderfully strange Pickle had held an irregular irregular event they called The Deadly Fun Hippodrome.[2]

We played three shows at this venue, and it was here that the crowd grew exponentially, as our sound cohered and our sense of dress style evolved. We would never discuss what we were going to wear onstage— the look of the band just came together organically. We would frequent antique stores, rummaging through piles of moth-eaten Victorian velvet (in both the ladies and gentlemen's departments), while occasional raids of girlfriends' closets were also fairly common, and so too Oxfam charity shops, where in those days you could often pick up the odd stylish bargain. There was still a hangover from the punk days—ultra-skinny black jeans and winkle-picker boots were still very much 'in'—which we complemented with eyeliner and eye-shadow, and sometimes a smear of dark lipstick. We also loved the look of some of the German expressionist films from the 1920s: Conrad Veidt, in the role of Cesare the somnambulist in *The Cabinet Of Doctor Caligari*, was as much of a style icon to us as was Bryan Ferry, and we would promptly stick his image on the back of our first single. (The image on the front cover was taken from the 1926 D.W. Griffith film *The Sorrows Of Satan*.)

Peter was the most 'dandified' member of the band, and I can recall a couple of incidents where his flamboyant sartorial style was the cause of several raised eyebrows in the streets of conservative Northampton. I once got on a bus with him as two middle-aged women gasped, one then saying to the other, 'Well! Get a load of 'im!'

'Yes,' Peter retorted, 'I'm sure that you would like to get a load of me, but frankly, you really don't stand a chance!'

On another occasion, again while riding the bus, he responded to the stares from the huddle of dowdy passengers with the classic Withnail-esque line, 'It's all right, I'm on the stage!'[3]

It wasn't just his outré dress style: it was also a matter of carriage and deportment, very straight-backed, with a self-assured imperial stride that would announce to all and sundry that *His Majesty* had arrived. Some of this sartorial style was captured on film by Graham Bentley, who by now had established himself as our resident video documentarian and lighting engineer. At the time, video was a very new technology, and Graham was one of the few people in the UK who owned a video camera. He would film our gigs and also some studio performances, which we then used as demos to show to record labels. We were on video before we were on audiotape.

As a lighting engineer, Graham was an innovative artist, quite brilliant in his use of stark white lighting, which perfectly reflected the band's aesthetic and stark musical stance. These lights were actually industrial rigs, usually used to illuminate buildings. When aimed at a small stage, the effect was very intense. He would also create clever devices of his own, such as a huge custom-built strobe made from the guts of an old washing machine.

There were only a few bands on the scene at the time to whom we related. Joy Division, Pere Ubu, Devo, Gang Of Four, Cabaret Voltaire, and The Pop Group come to mind. We went to see the latter demonstrate their wild collision of post-punk anarchy with dissonant neo-beatnik free jazz at St Martin-in-the-Fields church in Trafalgar Square, London. The Pop Group were quite magnificent, but I had an unfortunate run-in with the band's singer, Mark Stewart, after the show, when I met him backstage and told him I really liked what they were doing.

'Liked?' he sneered, reeking of ex-public-schoolboy condescension.

'Yeah, I really enjoyed it.'

'*Enjooooooyed?*'

'Uh … yes, I enjoyed it, you know, uh, fun … in the right way, I think?'

'The right way? Enjoyed? What? Fun? Ugh!'

It was at this point that I turned on my heels, seething, and left. What a jerk![4]

* * *

There was another more auspicious meeting at the Pop Group event, as it was here that we were approached by the organisers of the ultra-hip Final Solution events, who had put on that night's concert. They always put together complementary bills, and they were interested in working with Bauhaus 1919 (soon shortened simply to Bauhaus). We had an acetate of 'Bela' in the car with us, which we gave to them as a sampler. They, in turn, passed it on to Pete Stennett, the owner of Small Wonder Records, an independent label run out of a small shop in Walthamstow, East London.

Pete invited us down to the shop and, when we arrived, pulled down the blind and hung the 'closed' sign on the door. He then turned the lights down low and put on the acetate of 'Bela' with the sound turned up. When it had finished, he told us how much he loved it, and that he would like to release it on his label. The deal would be a 50–50 split.

We were elated. Pete then produced a large bag of marijuana from behind a life-size cardboard cut-out of Elvis Costello (whose debut album, *My Aim Is True*, had just been released on Stiff Records) that he had standing in the window.

After a while, we noticed that Peter was missing. It turned out that he had had an adverse reaction to the grass, and having been suddenly seized by a black wave of paranoia, had taken to hiding in an upstairs storeroom.

For the B-side to 'Bela', we rerecorded 'Boys' in a London studio. There was a strong smell of burning in the place, apparently the result of the engineer's chair having been set on fire by The Damned during a previous session—and this while the poor chap was still sitting in it! Pete Stennett came in with us, and after we had laid down the main track he wisely suggested that we run through our live set with a single mic set up ('just to get it down for posterity, lads').[5]

Around this time we paid a visit to Dial House, a large sixteenth-century farmhouse in Epping Forest, southwest Essex, then occupied by the anarcho-punk revolutionaries Crass. Graham had become pally with them, their whole alternative DIY way of living resonating strongly with his own. I have to say, their noble stance of resistance against the hypocritical powers-that-be was admirable.

We traipsed through the mud and wiped off our boots before going into the farmhouse, which was immaculate inside: very ordered and spare. Crass were their own little cottage industry, writing and printing books, making T-shirts and black, military-style clothes, and manufacturing their own records. They had previously been with Small Wonder, but their first record, *The Feeding Of The 5000*, had caused a lot of controversy, which ultimately resulted in them setting up their own Crass Records label. The album included a track called 'Asylum' that was deemed to be blasphemous by the workers at the record-pressing plant, who refused to have anything to do with it. Consequently, the record was released with a two-minute silent gap where 'Asylum' had once been. It was given the ironic title 'The Sound Of Free Speech'. Good people.

* * *

True to their word, our benefactors at Final Solution provided us with our biggest gig so far when they put us on the bill with Throbbing Gristle for an event at the Guildhall in Northampton. Every black-clad hipster-beetle crawled out of the woodwork for that one. Also in attendance—and feeling extremely out of place—were my parents, my mum in her best white mink stole and my dad in a suit and kipper tie.

'We thought we would just pop in and see the boys before going on to the Connie [Conservative] Club,' my mum informed Annie. They stayed for two songs. I saw my dad the following day. 'Well, I have to say, they're a bit peculiar, that lot that follow your band,' he told me. 'They all look like bloody corpses!'

I can only wonder as to what my dad would have made of Throbbing Gristle, had he chosen to stay. In 1979, TG were living out their own personal industrial revolution, and they came with a strong edgy mystique. They looked like the Gestapo, in black leather military-style gear. Their frontman was the odd, charismatic, and decidedly creepy Genesis P. Orridge. During load-in, I was standing outside the hall when I heard a terrific crash. Two cars had smashed head-on into each other across the street.

Genesis came running out to observe the twisted carnage.

'Wow, those things really change their shape when they collide!' he explained. He introduced himself, we shook hands, and then he went back inside. It was an oddly dispassionate and curiously detached observation on his part.

During TG's set, Daniel and I went and stood in the crowd, near the front of the stage. It was very strange: the band were producing this great roaring wall of extreme noise, and yet we both felt ebullient. At the end of their set, they quietly packed away their equipment as the house lights came up. It was a very humble, understated ending to an anti-rock'n'roll show. (We knew that we would never find ourselves doing that!)

Later, we asked Genesis about the incongruous high we had felt during the performance, and he remarked that it could have been something to do with the negative ion generators that they used onstage. He then showed us these huge industrial machines, which charged the air in such a way that it feels like the aftermath of an electrical storm.

We all went out and bought smaller versions of the same thing the next day.

* * *

By now, we had set our sights on London, and the pay-to-play circuit, where you would always come out with a financial loss but hopefully a strategic gain. Our first gig was at the Music Machine on a bill topped by the neo-psychedelic group The Teardrop Explodes. The Nashville pub was next, and this night was distinguished by the presence of Lemmy from Motörhead, who promptly tried to make off with my Annie. Fortunately she declined his backstage overture to 'slip away into the night'.

This gig was followed by an appearance at the hallowed Marquee club. Our small following was starting to grow. In attendance was the manager of Siouxsie & The Banshees, who tried to poach Daniel away from our ranks as he was looking for a replacement for Banshees guitarist John McKay, who had just left the band. His manner was somewhat underhand, all furtive whispers and slimy handshake. Daniel declined without having to think too hard about it.

Another guileful attendee of the same gig was one Michael Mason, who was impressed enough to approach us with an offer of management. We set up a meeting with him at his suburban home the following week. After running through all the wonderful advantages of having him at the helm of our career, he asked us if there was anything we didn't like, to which Peter responded, 'Yes, I don't like your trousers!'

Mason tried to laugh it off, but he was visibly shaken, and actually went upstairs to change. He returned wearing a pair of jeans instead of the hideous orange-brown leather pants that had so upset our singer. He then had the audacity to tell us of his idea for a new look for the band.

'Picture this! Dan and Pete, you two have like, black hair, and always wear white, and the bruvers, Dave and Kev, what if they were to dye their barnets white, and then wear black? Wotcha fink?'

'I think we'd look like a bloody chessboard!' I told him.

That night, on the way back to Northampton, my old Ford Cortina broke down for good. Consequently, the four of us spent the night in the car, playing our only compilation tape over and over while smoking dog-ends retrieved from the ashtray. It was so cold that Daniel climbed into the faux-sheepskin seat cover to keep warm. He looked like an emaciated poodle. In the early morning we wiped the steamed-up windows to peer out at office workers on their way to work, and they, in turn, glanced back in at us with bemused disgust (if not horror). It was not a good omen.

Despite this, we foolishly signed a letter that stated that Mason would be our manager for a trial period of six months. Over the next couple of weeks, we were courted by our wide-boy manager and his charming sidekick, Martin Gordon (formerly of the 70s new-wave pop band Radio Stars), who would take us out on the town to upscale London nightclubs such as Legends and Monkberry's. The champagne and cocaine would flow; Michael would always have a large bottle full to the brim with little blue tabs of speed, and Peter and Daniel would follow him into the bathroom like dogs at heel.

Chemical persuasion was not enough, however, and when the six months were up, our association with Mr Mason was over. We had to sign another letter to make the cessation legal, and this had to be done by a certain date. Of course, we let it drift, and if it hadn't been for Annie rushing over to the Avon cosmetics factory where we were all temporarily employed at the time, we would have missed the boat and found ourselves in a potential legal pickle. Fortunately, Annie stuck the document under our perfume-filled noses in time, and the necessary signatures were applied.

By now, we had developed a bit of a taste for the high life to which our erstwhile would-be manager had introduced us, and we would return to the chic clubs on our own and blag our way in. We were back on the dole, broke but dressed to kill.

On one occasion, Daniel and Peter were at Legends, flirting with a couple of aging gay American businessmen who were plying them with drinks in an obvious effort to get them into bed. Peter ended up going back to an expensively appointed flat in Knightsbridge. Silk robes were laid out, a bubble bath was run, cologne sprayed and lotion applied. Despite all this, the amorous attentions of his would-be seducer were miraculously avoided, and our pretty boy escaped unmolested. He had a disturbing surprise a couple of weeks later, however, when he received a phone call from his slighted sugar-daddy. His mother took the call and then shouted upstairs, 'Peter, there's a Dan Silver on the phone for you. He sounds like he's an American.' Peter emphatically waved her away.

Mrs Murphy's son would shortly take further evasive action and vacate the family home to move into a terraced house in Adams Avenue (number 37) with Daniel and me. The landlord was a mad Irishman, Mr Corr, who would pinch the pennies when it came to home improvements. He told us that the reason the threadbare carpet did not extend to the edge of the floor was so that 'you boys can puke up in the corners when you have your parties, and then it'll be easier to clean up'. The place had no heating, and we would all wear our army greatcoats indoors and huddle around a single bar electric heater in the kitchen. We would cook up mounds of potatoes in a big pot and live off that and cheap beer from the local off-licence (or 'the offy', as it was affectionately known).

One night, we were sitting around the table sharing a joint after partaking of another exquisite meal (mash'n'hash) when our first single, 'Bela Lugosi's Dead', came on the radio. The DJ who played it, John Peel, was the most influential in the country, and had been established as such for many years. We would listen to his late-night show on the BBC whenever we could. He was always ahead of the curve, and his genuine enthusiasm and great wit made for a wonderful show. We were over the moon when he gave 'Bela' a spin. We decided there and then that we would drive down to the BBC studios in London the following night and present a copy of our follow up single, 'Dark Entries', to him. (The single was set to be released early in the New Year, but we had included a snippet of a live version of the track on the B-side of 'Bela' as a little teaser.) Upon reaching our destination, we told the receptionist that we were there to see John Peel. She asked if he was expecting us. We said no but he *had* been playing our record, and we *had* met him once when we both appeared on the same bill at a pub in Wollaston. She smiled sweetly at our touching naivety and advised us to wait, telling us she would see what she could do.

Broadcasting House is a vast, circular establishment, like a cross between a cathedral and an old bank. There we perched, hyper-attentive to anyone who came through the doors. Eventually, the lady at the desk called us over: she was on the phone to Peel's producer, John Waters, and he had told her that we could come up.

All of the lights in the studio were off apart from a single angle-poise lamp, which illuminated the twin decks on which the great man was spinning vinyl. 'Whoops! I think we'll try that again … at the right speed this time!' we heard him say, the familiar warm drone followed by a typically self-deprecating chuckle.[6]

As the record played, Peel silently beckoned us to come in and take a seat. BBC-issue paper cups were handed out, and he generously shared his bottle of very good red wine. For the rest of the night, he would make various oblique on-air references to our presence without ever revealing the name of our band.

At one point, I remarked on a photo of Kenny Dalglish, the celebrated Liverpool FC and Scotland footballer, which he had framed and positioned directly above his desk. 'No one has ever touched that picture,' he said, as he lined up another disc, 'and there would be hell to pay if they ever did!'

Come midnight, we handed Peel our own seven-inch record, thanked him for his great hospitality, and bid a fond farewell. He played 'Dark Entries' the following night. A few weeks later, we were invited to record a session for his show. This was a big deal for us—a 'Peel session' could put a new band very firmly on the map. We carefully chose four tracks to best represent our sound. The challenge now was to record and mix them in eight hours. This proved to be a valuable exercise. Having that kind of time restraint made for a highly spontaneous and vital-sounding recording. There was no time to fuss and over think. It was a lesson that we took on board to the extent that we would self-impose similar restrictions on our own recording sessions in the future.

* * *

We finished up the year by playing more London gigs, during one of which Peter, much to our consternation, turned his back to the crowd and raised his hips while looking over his shoulder in the classic *lordosis* pose employed by female animals in heat. He then proceeded to pull down his pants and present his thong-clad backside to the audience while announcing, 'We are now stars!' From here on, his behaviour would become increasingly more bizarre and perplexing.

When Peter first joined the band, he had had no experience (unlike the rest of us) of 'paying his dues'. Those years of slogging away in dives and dank cellars served to give us a grounding that acted as true ballast when success finally arrived. Prior to the band's formation, he had worked as a commercial printer and only ever fantasised about a life in music. When fame arrived, it came hard and fast, and it has to be said that it went to the boy's head. Peter came from a poor, working-class family, and now, lionised by his loving parents and siblings, his already huge and fragile ego would be pumped up all the more. The golden boy could do no wrong.

That ego was inflated further when we signed a new deal with Axis Records, which would shortly become 4AD due to another business having already registered the name Axis. Geoff Travis at Rough Trade Records had passed our demo to Peter Kent, who ran the burgeoning label with Ivo Watts-Russell, once again out of an independent record store, this time Beggars Banquet in Earls Court. The store shared its name with a larger independent label, the owners of which had backed the new boys, granting them carte blanche to sign any artists who complied with their artsy taste.

We took an immediate liking to Peter and Ivo. Peter was a tall, elegant man with the bearing of a slightly camp theatrical impresario, Ivo an astute and outspoken hipster with a nice line in beautiful silk shirts (with the top button always done up, the weirdo!). They released our second single, 'Dark Entries', in January 1980. The title came from a paperback collection of horror stories by Robert Aickman that I had found in a thrift store. Peter took that title and gave it a wicked punning twist with his evocative lyric, a decadent tale spun from the threads of Oscar Wilde's *Dorian Gray* and set it in the underworld of modern day Soho.

This colourful and seedy area of London became the backdrop to our residency at Billy's in Dean Street. The dingy little club was a seething cauldron for the witches' brew that would eventually be labelled 'goth' and would soon host the infamous Batcave nights. During the course of our five shows at the venue, we saw the audience evolve and establish its own code, in terms both of dress and attitude.

Black was of course the only way to go: the colour of night and death, and always the distinguishing mark of those who wished to stand outside of the norm, from existentialists to beatniks to goths. It is the flag of morbidity under which the anarchic troops of apolitical revolt rally before storming the barricades of convention. The nineteenth-century decadents believed that it required a highly refined sensibility to truly appreciate and savour the delights of sensual sadness and the beautiful phosphorescence of decay. The goths would no doubt agree. In their disdain for the vulgar and their celebration of all that is wan, delicate, and slowly dying, they were and still are the true descendants of those poets of exquisite unease.

On one of those rainy Soho nights, we were visited by an icon of this as-yet-unnamed melancholic subculture when Ian Curtis appeared at the end of a set during which a wild and abandoned Murphy had laid waste to a wall of mirrors. We had always felt that there was a sympathetic resonance between Joy Division and us. The tall, gangly singer told us that he had come with Factory Records boss Tony Wilson, who had apparently left after the first number as he strongly objected to bands that wore make-up.

'It were 'is fooking loss, man,' he told us. 'He really missed out tonight. Fook him. He's a cunt, anyway!'

Ian said he thought the gig was great, that both our singles were excellent, and that he had been hoping that Joy Division's recent recording sessions (for *Closer*) would coincide with one of our live shows.

Many years later, I would get chills when reading of this desire in Ian's own hand, in a letter to his mistress, Annik Honore, a copy of which had been lent to me (with the rest of Ian's letters) by Michael Stock, the screenwriter and would-be director of an early biopic about Ian.[7] Although Ian was cheery and warm that night at Billy's, I remember a look in his watery blue eyes that was so sad and haunted. Three months later, he hung himself in his kitchen.

On May 3, we played a gig at the Russell Club in Manchester. Joy Division bassist Peter Hook was there, helping us load out our gear, as he often would. After we had packed up, we went out with Peter and his manager, Rob Gretton. The band had recently released a limited edition single on the Sordide Sentimentale label consisting of 'Atmosphere' on one side and 'Dead Souls' on the other. It was only available in France, so I had been unable to find a copy. I mentioned this to Rob, and he very kindly said that he would send me one. It turned up on my doormat, two weeks later, the day after Ian's death.

I had never heard 'Atmosphere' before. I slipped the seven-inch out of the beautiful, elaborate sleeve, which featured a painting of hooded monks on a mist-shrouded mountain by the artist Jean-François Jamoul. There was also a striking photograph of the band by Anton Corbijn. In light of the tragedy, the majestic track was almost unbearably poignant. With some trepidation, and a tear in my eye, I called Rob to thank him and to commiserate over the terrible news. He could hardly speak.

Following our stint at Billy's, we staged a two-night stand across town at the Rock Garden in Covent Garden. We wanted to do something different for these gigs, and we came up with the idea of Peter in effect making his entrance twice. This was achieved by setting up a large TV monitor, centre stage, to show a blown-up image of the singer's head as he sang the opening 'Double Dare' via a video link to the dressing room. It was very effective, and when he actually appeared for real at the end of the track, the audience went nuts.

Back in those days we would come offstage completely wiped out and drenched in sweat, having put everything we had into those intense ninety minutes. We were possessed of a kind of quixotic romanticism, feeling as if we were teetering on a stratospheric precipice, ever willing to take a giant leap into the dark. It was a kind of inspired madness, intensified by adolescent arrogance, ridiculous hubris, and a telescoped sense of impending catastrophe. We felt that we were destined to spark a revolution and sacrifice all on the altar of art, and there was a sense that on any given night that *this could be IT*—namely the cataclysmic event where art spills over into death, and in that moment returns to art again, our future forged in blood, white light, and the glittering darkness. Then again, we were just another rock'n'roll band making a pit-stop at Watford Junction services, ordering saveloy, egg, and chips, plus a packet of Silk Cut with a book of matches for the bus ride home.

In addition to the 4AD band In Camera, we had another special guest at our first night at the Rock Garden: Guy Forester, an outrageous, Wildeian aesthete and friend of the band who staged a kind of twisted puppet show featuring the re-animation of various road-kill, much to the delight of the punky members of the crowd, although some in the audience were so disgusted that they were physically sick. (I remember Daniel turning to me during the act and saying, 'I don't like this. It's so perverse!')

Guy had been introduced to us by Peter's girlfriend, Joanna Woodward. They were both art students, and they exerted an enormous influence on the impressionable Peter, turning him on to avant-garde art, literature, and European film. It was something of a ménage à trois in which the upper-middle-class Joanna and Guy would delight in shining their working-class, diamond-in-the-rough protégé. Peter made an arty film with Joanna entitled *The Grid*, in which he appeared as a kind of elemental pixie sprite occupying a fantastical grid-like landscape. We would show this as the support feature on our first headlining tour. Joanna would go on to become a celebrated filmmaker.

Another important association formed during this period—and from the opposite end of the social strata—was with Peter 'Plug' Edwards, a meat-and-potatoes working-class Londoner with a taste for a pint and a punch-up. Both proclivities became apparent on our first meeting with him after Beggars Banquet recommended him to us as a first-rate front-of-house sound engineer. This introduction took place at a party that was held for Gary Numan at the end of his highly successful *Pleasure Principle* tour. Plug, whose former employees were the bloke-y beer-swilling band The Lurkers, recalls being somewhat taken aback by 'this limp skinny hand in a black net glove coming out for a shake'. The other hand was holding a long-stemmed flute of Bucks Fizz.

'Peter meet Plug. Plug, Peter.'

Plug tentatively connected with the elegant Murphy fingers as one might the ravaged paw of a leper.

Shortly after this awkward introduction, we were sitting at our table in the corner, somewhat disconcerted by this seemingly ill-fitting choice of crew when all hell broke loose. Plug had punched the DJ, who had apparently turned his nose up at his repeated request of, 'Oi, mate! Play some Stones!' The disk jockey (Peter Kent's brother) retaliated by socking Plug in the jaw. The turntables and mixer then crashed to the floor as the two set about each other while 'security' tried to pull them apart.

We looked at each other in consternation. But despite this altercation, we ended up taking Plug on, and we never regretted it for a minute. He turned out to be a lovely man with a huge heart and a willingness to expand his craft as the band evolved through the stages of the next three years.

* * *

Job demarcation can sometimes be a tricky thing, especially when the lines of definition are not drawn up early on. In the early days of the band, there was some vying for the position of manager. Like the rest of us, Graham Bentley had been put on a £50-a-week retainer by Beggars Banquet. We had agreed to this as he was doing considerably more than simply designing and operating our light show. He had provided us with our rehearsal space, was booking gigs, and was promoting us as well. But we never viewed him as our 'manager' as such.

Peter Kent, meanwhile, was keen to represent the band in this capacity, so we decided to give him a try. As he would be taking over all of Graham's duties, except for operating the lights, we deemed it fair that he should be paid the fifty quid, not Graham. (Graham would be paid separately for doing the lights.) This cut Graham to the core, and he wrote us a very long, bitter letter about it, but we were adamant in our decision. Graham never really got over it, though, and our relations with him were somewhat strained from then on, which was a shame because he had been there from the start, and he was a genius at what he did best—namely, live lighting.

The rift with Graham would widen further when he wanted to have his mixing desk set up on the stage, as opposed to at the side. At the same time, he had started to wear badly applied make-up, and stage costumes similar to Daniel's.

'Graham,' I recall saying at one point, 'why don't you do the gigs on your own, and we can go out front and shine lights on you?' It was all getting to be a bit much!

In the meantime, Peter Kent did arrange some of our tours, and also came out on the road for a while, but it didn't quite gel, so we were back to being manager-less for a while.

* * *

For our next recording session, back at Beck Studios, we worked up a drastic deconstruction of T.Rex's 'Telegram Sam': very angular, stripped to the bone, sharp-edged and punchy. We also recorded an early version of 'Terror Couple Kill Colonel', the title of which came from a newspaper headline. The story concerned the assassination of an army colonel 'in his West German home'.

We would soon see the interiors of many a West German home when we embarked on our first tour of Europe. The hospitality we encountered there was overwhelming. Complete strangers would welcome us with open arms and deli trays, smorgasbords of cold cuts, delicious cheese, and wine. Back then, West Germany had a thriving economy, and it was clearly evident that the standard of living there was a hell of a lot better than in England. The audiences were very enthusiastic, too, and we established many friendships that would last for years to come. In Holland, rather than stay in hotels, we would hole up at places run by various anarchist/punk collectives who were also the promoters of most of the gigs. There was a highly structured alternative lifestyle in action. We did find it amusing and somewhat ironic, however, that some of these revolutionaries were funded by the very government they were railing against.

Despite our cynicism in this regard, we returned to the UK with our eyes opened, stimulated by a broadened experience of independent life outside of our own green and unpleasant land. Over the next few months, we got to know that miserable little island pretty well as we travelled its motorways from bottom to top and back again, this time to play in larger venues as support to ex-Buzzcocks singer Howard Devoto's new band Magazine.

We had taken on a new roadie for this jaunt, a guy called Gerard, who we soon realised was Mohawk head over Cuban heels in love with Peter. We would catch him gazing dreamily at the singer's profile, and would often have to remind him that there was equipment to load in, so lost was he in his star-struck infatuation. It all reached an unpleasant head when, drunk to the gills on Bell's whisky, Gerard confronted Devoto backstage at Tiffany's in Glasgow and berated him about his undeserved position as bill topper.

'Peter is twice the singer you are,' Gerard screamed, pushing Devoto into a corner of the small dressing room, 'and he's *soooo* beautiful. You're ugly, and you can't sing.'

'That may be your opinion,' the quietly spoken yet seething Devoto replied, 'but then your opinion doesn't really count, does it?!'

That night, we covered a comatose Gerard in Indian take-away leftovers as he lay slumped in his Y-fronts on the floor of our shared hotel room. Two days later, I would find myself similarly unconscious on the stage of London's Lyceum Ballroom. We had played the same venue the previous month as part of a special tribute night to Gary Glitter. Before the soundcheck, Daniel and I came across the shiny one's dressing room, which resembled a dazzling Aladdin's cave, chock full of over-the-top costumes.

'Hello lads! Admiring the frocks?'

The man himself had followed us into the room. A pleasant little chat ensued, and we cheekily dropped a pinch of his early hit 'Do You Want To Touch Me' into our set that night.[8]

The return event had an inauspicious start as, having just walked onstage, I realised that I had no guitar cable. The opening song was 'Double Dare', which I always started, but tonight I was without sound. I shouted over to Glenn Campling, our roadie at the time, but I failed to get his attention. Daniel saw my predicament and started to make some feedback noise while Peter paced the stage. The lighting as usual was very low, with the stage lit only by the slow pulse of a strobe.

The Lyceum has an unusually high stage, and as I was calling out to the monitor mixer, who was situated at the side, several feet below the stage floor, I lost sight of the perimeter and went plummeting down. I landed on my back in the pitch dark. (I have to confess that I had been imbibing quite heavily before taking the stage, which only contributed to this mishap.) The crowd were making a right racket, and it suddenly occurred to me how ridiculous this all was. I started to crack up with laughter, and when the monitor man came over to assist, I could barely get the words out.

'I've got no fuckin' lead!'

A pair of security guards picked me up and deposited me back on the stage. Mr Campling had finally located a cable and plugged me in. I immediately plucked the opening notes, and the song—after an extremely protracted, ad-libbed overture—was underway.

For this gig, Peter had one of those old-style mic stands with a heavy lead base. At the climax of the last song, 'Dark Entries', he swung it in a circular motion above his head and then let it fly. It smashed into my head, shattering my shades, and *BANG!* I was out cold.

The next thing I knew, I was being carried up the many flights of stairs to the top of the building and into Magazine's dressing room. The Mancunian band passed me on their way to the stage, making various exclamations along the lines of *Fookin' 'ell! Look at the state of 'im, Jesus Christ! Poor Fooker*, and simply *Wow!*

With some trepidation, I felt my forehead and was alarmed by the cartoon-like bump that seemed to be growing under my fingers. I was laid out on a table in the deserted dressing room, holding a cold compress to my head. At the end of the night, when I finally made it back down to our own dressing room, the perpetrator of my injury was getting ready to leave. I waited for some kind of apology or expression of concern, but none was forthcoming. That hurt more than the cracked head.

The penultimate gig on the tour was at Guildford University. There was a third band on the bill that night, Crisis, who had a big skinhead following—despite the fact that they were associated with the Anti-Nazi League. Anyway, the thugs were out in force that night, and by the time we came on they were lit and looking for trouble. They pushed their way to the front, poleaxing any poor, wan goths who happened to be in their way. A storm of gob rained down on us, and especially on Peter. He immediately ripped off his shirt, grabbed a floor light, shone it into our assailants' faces, and stared them down.

While all of this was going on, the rest of us vamped on the intro to 'Bela Lugosi's Dead'. We kept it going for a long time, standing our ground, and eventually the idiots backed off and barged their way back through the crowd. Our relief was shortlived, however, as they returned ten minutes later, the spittle having now been replaced with piss. The bastards had apparently come armed with water pistols, which they had urinated into, and now, on a pre-arranged cue, they let rip. The strobes were on, and I could see this slow motion golden cascade falling dangerously over the electrical cables and amps.

Our regular crowd were horrified. More fights broke out. The security guards had apparently thrown in the towel. The vile skins pushed closer to the stage to get a better aim. We stood our ground, Peter assuming a crucifixion pose, dripping with piss and phlegm. This war of attrition continued, and finally victory was achieved as the skins left. Our defiance had either earned their respect or, more likely, 'freaked them the fuck out', as one attendee put it. I walked into the toilets at the end of the night, and it was like a scene out of *The Shining*. There was blood all over the mirrors and in the white alabaster sinks, and broken glass covered the tiled floor.

Despite these rigors of the road, the tour served us well. 'Bela' was top of the indie Top 40—and would remain on the chart for the next two years—and 'Entries' was chasing its heels. A third single would soon be needed in order to keep the momentum going, and so we set about recording 'Terror Couple Kill Colonel' at Southern Studios in Wood Lane, London, on June 17. The session gave us an opportunity to get a feel for the studio, which had been suggested by 4AD as the place for us to make our first album. It had a kind of isolated *das bunker* feel to it, which we liked, and consequently we booked it, ready to embark on the recording of *In The Flat Field* the following month.

* * *

Tony Cook, the engineer at Southern, had the right kind of open-minded attitude, and did not balk at our spontaneous 'leap in the dark' approach to the recording process, which involved things like utilising a prepared-piano technique on 'Nerves', rigging the instrument out with sets of keys, tin cans, and strips of metal, which were laid across the exposed piano wires to achieve the spooky sound effects heard on the recording.

One day, I came into the studio to find Peter sitting at the piano, picking out a plaintive descending melody. Without saying a word, I sat next to him and played a simple counterpoint. Tony rolled tape, and we had the start of what would become 'Crowds', an acerbic diatribe on the fickleness of fame. Daniel arrived and instantly laid down a nicely understated guitar part. Peter wrote the lyric on the spot and recorded his vocal straight away. Done!

A lot of the inspiration for Peter's lyrics came from the potent Catholic imagery that had so disturbed him and Daniel at school, all of which would now be recontextualised into gothic melodrama. This was no fashionable pose: 'goth' culture did not yet exist , and this was, in fact, a form of genuine expression, and an attempt to exorcise the deeply entrenched head-fuck that had been laid on Peter and his poor impressionable schoolmates by the priests and teachers of St Mary's School For Boys. The crippling indoctrination of notions such as one's soul becoming increasingly blackened due to improper actions and thoughts; that, if they were unable to change their evil ways, those black-souled boys would burn in hell for all eternity; that all sensory pleasure was wrong and should be denied.

Daniel would say that he felt a great wave of poisonous guilt when listening to dub reggae, as anything that made you feel that good must be a product of the devil! ('In fear of dub' indeed!) Thankfully, Kevin and I attended an easy-going Church of England school and had an agnostic father and a lapsed-Catholic mother, so we were never at the mercy of such qualms.

One song that vehemently questioned these received beliefs, but one that we could not capture on tape to our satisfaction, was 'Double Dare'. Our benchmark was the leviathan version that we had recorded for our Peel session, which crackled and sparked with dark magic. In the end, we negotiated a deal with the BBC to use that recording. 'A God In An Alcove' was another personal favourite, its lurching, propulsive syncopation framing the story of a fallen idol. 'Dive'—originally entitled 'Kamikaze Dive'—was an up-tempo paean to the delights of nightclubbing.

'Spy In The Cab' was a stark slice of paranoia, this mental state having been induced in the song's speed-freak truck-driver protagonist by the installation of a tachometer. My bass part consisted of a single-note bleep. Kevin had acquired a Synare 3 analogue electronic drum, which was shaped like a flying saucer and used to great effect on this track as well as others on the album. This very modern instrument became part of our signature sound. The only other drummer we knew of who had one was Stephen Morris of Joy Division.

'Small Talk Stinks' featured fuzz bass, and at the time I used to have this FX box gaffer-taped to my bass, as it was operated by a switch rather than a pedal. Looking back on my lyric for this, it now seems quite preposterous. Oh, the intense intolerance of youth! 'St Vitus Dance' was a taut, frenetic freak-out sparked off by another new acquisition, a Bass Balls foot pedal that created a swirling maelstrom of phased noise.

'Stigmata Martyr' again drew on Peter's Catholic upbringing, specifically the supernatural phenomena of the title, and featured some rather satanic backward chanting to boot.

The album's title track was a sprawling epic inspired—if that's the word—by the quotidian mundaneness of life in Northampton, and the desire to escape that 'flat' existence. Peter's interesting lyric drew on Greek mythology, referencing Theseus and the labyrinth, but there was another mythic figure with whom we would soon feel an affinity: the androgynous god of wine, excess, and ecstatic madness, Dionysus.

CHAPTER TWO
New York's A Go-Go And Everything Tastes Nice

The elevator doors slid open to reveal a statuesque youth, naked except for a gold lamé thong and matching body paint. He was flanked by two beautiful young girls, who were similarly semi-naked and daubed, but in metallic blue rather than gold. The girls had matching electric-blue feather boas draped around their necks.

The boy offered up a small silver platter of white powder. My two front teeth were already numb, so I declined. He smiled, blew an extravagant kiss, and strolled on into the buzzing club, shadowed by the females. Soon, they were lost in a Fellini-esque parade of flaming creatures—proto-club-kids reinventing themselves as the glittering stars of their own science-fiction art-house head movie.

Cocaine concentrates the upper register into laser-beam-sharp focus. I think that's why the music of the 80s was so biased toward the top end. When you are high on blow, you love to hear that clean, white-light treble slicing like a scalpel with cold, clinical precision. All the edges are made sharper, and the UV lights somehow articulate this state of the senses. It is the frigid purple/blue/silver/white end of the colour spectrum that resonates. It's a high-octane sex rush, and a nightclub—especially a nightclub in New York City in 1980—becomes charged with the frisson of erotic possibility.

Our cramped and filthy room back at the Iroquois Hotel was another matter entirely. The four of us shared these tiny quarters with Peter Kent (acting as tour manager) and a legion of fat black cockroaches. When you switched on the room's single, garish neon light, there they would be, spread over the walls and beds for just a split second and then gone. They say that if you see one then you have a lot. We saw a great many. In the wee small hours, the light would go off, and we would listen as they made this weird clicking sound while foraging for scraps. We would try to ignore them, burying our heads under the bleached sheets, but eventually someone would crack and the light would come on. They would be all over the beds, and then would suddenly vanish again. The light would go off, and the whole dread cycle would start over. I once woke up with one of the vile things in my ear. A very disturbing experience, I can tell you!

The Iroquois had been the notorious haunt of the likes of James Dean and, later, The Clash. It was the archetypal low-rent rock'n'roll hotel. It had a pleasingly dingy bar, which sometimes featured a greasy-looking old man in a well-worn tuxedo playing off-key standards on a cheesy organ. We loved him.

One our first day in town, the four of us were sitting at the bar, pinching ourselves but failing to wake up from the dream of being in New York. The whole great pulsating beautiful beast of the city was there, just outside the revolving door, and loaded with the exciting promise of hedonic pursuits. We were the only patrons until a small, wiry man with huge blue eyes sauntered in and pulled up a stool. He ordered a beer and sat with a straight back as our conversation stopped sharply. We started to nudge each other with our elbows, while making surreptitious sideways nods in the direction of, yes, Iggy Pop.

'Hi guys, how's it goin'?' That unmistakable dark brown baritone. He introduced him self as 'Jim'.

We nodded, smiled nervously, and spat out our own names. Soon, we were sharing a beer with one of our biggest inspirations—and in New York Fucking City, at that! Iggy Pop was the first American we had met, and he was an angry American, on the warpath as he told us about the recent death of a beautiful cellist who had been raped and murdered a few blocks from the hotel. He bristled with righteous indignation as he described what he would do to the murderer if he could only get his hands on the 'motherfucker'.

We narrowed our eyes, nodded, and gulped our drinks.

'So, what's the name of the band?' he asked.

'Bauhaus,' I replied.

'Oh, like German? Weimar?'

'Yeah.'

'Cool! So, you guys playing a gig or what?'

We told him that this was our first time in the States, and that we were there to play a handful of dates, two of which were in NYC: one the following night, at a club called Tier 3, and another at Danceteria, six days later, after we'd taken in Toronto and Chicago. He said that he was leaving town that day but would be back for the second of our shows and would come down to check us out. 'Let's see if you're as good as you think you are.'

We asked Iggy if he was staying at the hotel, and when he answered in the affirmative, Peter got up from his stool and—to everyone's astonishment—proceeded to tickle his ribs while telling him that he would be more than welcome to come to his room.

'Come on, Iggy,' he said, 'I know you want to!'

After Peter had gone, a flustered Iggy Pop remarked, 'Wow, that's some fresh kid you've got there! Some fresh kid! Man, is he always like that?'

We told him that Peter had probably acted in such an over-the-top manner because he was nervous about meeting one of his idols. Iggy shook his head from side to side, still looking quite shocked and not that convinced.

Twenty-four hours later, 'the fresh kid', Kevin, and I ventured out on a club crawl, riding in boxy yellow cabs through the warm Manhattan night. Despite our protestations—'Come on, we're in fuckin' New York City, we've got a night off, we've got a bunch of dollars in our pockets, and you're gonna stay behind to prop up this seedy bar?'—Daniel insisted on staying back at the Iroquois. He would not be moved. In the hungover morning of the next day, we were all set to chide him for being such a wallflower and missing a great night out when he totally trumped us by coolly mentioning that, just after we had left, Iggy had come into the bar and invited him up to his suite, where they shared drinks with the Ig's beautiful girlfriend and one Mick Ronson while listening to cuts from

Mr Pop's new album. Come the small hours, they politely requested that Daniel leave, as they intended to do some 'dangerous drugs'.

In those days, Times Square was also dangerous. Dangerous, dazzling, and dirty. The blazing neon shamelessly trumpeting smut. Down on 48th Street was the notorious Pussycat porno cinema, an electric picture palace of lascivious dreams. I had to venture inside. The lobby was surprisingly plush and glitzy, with crimson carpeting, velveteen fixtures, and crystal chandeliers. It was also air-conditioned. The inner sanctum was enormous, and sparsely populated, with plumes of blue cigarette smoke spiralling up from the occupied seats, seventy-foot hirsute vaginas in vivid 33mm ablaze on the screen in front of them.

Less salubrious were the extremely seedy smaller cinemas that lined the streets from 42nd to 48th. Upon entering, one's olfactory sense was assailed by a pervasive stench of rancid sperm as the 7th Avenue whores cruised the sticky aisles, hooking for hand-jobs. These rat holes were often adjacent to the 'hot-sheet' hotels that rented rooms by the hour. ('Couples welcome!')

I would wallow in this glorious squalor and sniff out the dimly lit dive bars in the area. One time, I was imbibing in one of these dodgy establishments when I became aware of ecstatic groans coming from behind me. With some trepidation, I turned around to see a small cubicle with a shabby curtain drawn across it, the noises of sex issuing from behind. Another time, I was walking fast down 44th Street (you always walked at a pace down there) when an old homeless grifter slammed into me, his brown paper bag falling to the sidewalk, smashing the liquor bottle inside. He raised merry hell, claiming that I was responsible. *How many times had he pulled this one?* I wondered. I told him to get lost and walked away. He stood there for a while but then gave chase, screaming out, 'Hey, asshole! You owe me!'

I finally managed to lose the bastard by dashing into a hotel and exiting through a side door. It was a pretty sketchy scene, but I still preferred it back then, when that area of town had so much gritty character, all of which is now long gone since the lamentable Disneyfication of the twenty-first century.

* * *

Chicago was an important port of call for the band as the city's Wax Trax! label, run by Jim Nash and Danny Flesher, had been instrumental in spreading the word about Bauhaus and was very interested in licensing the band in the States. They promoted our first Chicago gig at Space Place, and they also had an ultra-hip indie record store, inviting us to browse the aisles and pick out some records on which they would give us a nice fat discount. To my eternal shame, I have to confess that even after this generosity had been extended, I still found myself slipping a bunch of albums into my bag—rare and expensive spoken-word recordings featuring the likes of William S. Burroughs, Allen Ginsberg, and Patti Smith. When it came to records and books, I had always had rather sticky fingers. I had previously 'half-inched' some choice discs from the DJ at Billy's, and my bookshelf was stocked with art books stolen from the art school library or second-hand shops. Shameful—and, in the case of Wax Trax!, also extremely stupid!

The final gig of the tour was at Danceteria. It was the biggest and best club in Manhattan at the time, and we had a great turn out. Word had obviously circulated following our initial dive-bar appearance a few days earlier, our tactical ploy having achieved the desired result. We were on form that night, and there was a palpable charge in the air. Throughout the gig there was one guy down the front in a black leather biker's jacket, continually bating Peter, making obscene gestures and shouting out challenges to which the latter rose, dishing it back out and apparently relishing the battle. The heckler turned out to be Iggy Pop! True to his word, he had come to the show, and soon after we came offstage, the door burst open, and there he was.

'Hey guys!' he began. 'That was fuckin' great! I was passing by in a car and I saw the name out front, then I remembered you guys in the bar, so I told the driver to pull over but to keep the engine runnin', 'cos chances were you kids would be shit. But I stayed till the end, and he's still out there, so that's the story, man!'

The following afternoon, I made my way down to Greenwich Village for some last-minute record shopping before we flew home. I bought a

John Lennon bootleg at Bleecker Bob's, where I learnt that, had I arrived ten minutes earlier, I would have seen Mr Lennon himself rummaging through the crates.

'Yeah, he comes in here all the time,' Bob told me, 'and ya know, he's this skinny little guy. It's funny, 'cos ya tend to think of John Lennon as, like, this big guy, right? But he ain't big at all. Skinny little guy!' (Three months later, I would be devastated by the news that Lennon had been shot and killed outside his apartment building.)

While I was in the shop, I spotted a bootleg of one of our gigs in the UK. When I told Bob that, as I was in the band, I should be given it for free, he replied, 'Oh yeah? And how ya gonna prove that, buddy?'

I held the sleeve—which featured a photo of the band—up next to my mug for Bob to compare and contrast.

'Oh, OK,' he said. 'Then I guess I can't sell it to ya!' With that, he handed the vinyl over, gratis. Nice man!

* * *

Upon our return to the UK, we filmed our first music video, for our new single 'Telegram Sam'. The atmospheric location was an old haunted Victorian swimming baths in Fulham. The film, directed by Mick Calvert (himself assisted by 'Punk Dread' Don Letts), captures some of the energy and certainly the aesthetic of the band at the time, with Peter swinging around on a large metal chain we had discovered hanging from the ceiling in the boiler room.

The B-side of the single was a cover I had suggested, of John Cale's 'Rose Garden Funeral Of Sores', which would become a highlight and staple of our live set for many years to come. We first played it on our UK tour that autumn, and it developed into a nice little piece of stark theatre, with Peter striking a Nijinsky pose and then performing a sort of bastardised version of 'Prélude à l'après-midi d'un faune' as the strobe lights snapped. During Daniel's electrifying guitar solo, the two would play out a psychosexual drama in contest for stage domination—and possibly the affection of the nymphs—although the fact that the whole performance was charged with homoeroticism cannot be denied.

The penultimate show of the tour was a homecoming at Northampton's Theatre Royal, a lovely old Victorian building, all tromp-l'oeil, gilt, and red velvet. My granddad had been Errol Flynn's chauffeur during the randy swashbuckler's run in rep at this place in the 1930s. Ours was to be the establishment's first and last rock concert. We had a wonderful night there, with the old-time grandeur of the place providing a fitting backdrop to our theatrical presentation. The show sold out in minutes. Consequently, we requested a return gig at Christmas. The theatre manager's memorable written response was less than enthusiastic, turning us down due to the unsuitability of both music and audience, two members of which the theatre staff had apparently been shocked to discover 'fornicating in the gods'![1]

Our final date was a Final Solution gig at London University with Mass and Tuxedomoon, the latter a fascinating experimental group from San Francisco. They used film to great effect, with lots of small projectors set up on the stage, aimed in different directions, with the images falling on the band and various sheets that were pegged to scaffolding. The music was electronic-based, but they also employed a clarinet (fed through a bunch of effects pedals) and atmospheric guitar to create a sound infused with mystery.

Although this tour was intended to coincide with the release of *In The Flat Field*, the album did not hit the shops until the following month, due to the fact that our negotiations with the BBC and the Musicians' Union to use the Peel session version of 'Double Dare' took longer to resolve than anticipated. Despite this, the tour made an impression, and the album sold well, topping the independent charts.

* * *

It was always either Daniel or I who would come up with the sleeve designs. *Flat Field* was one of mine, and featured a black-and-white photograph by Duane Michals entitled 'Homage to Purvis de Chavannes', taken from a postcard I had picked up in Brussels on our European tour. It's funny, but it never occurred to us that the image of a naked man blowing a long, phallic horn would be considered controversial.

The reaction to the music itself was also extreme. The stance that we struck in the early 80s was very much against the grain of the times. There was a prevalent attitude of down-to-earth humbleness, whereas we were reaching for the stars and wholly unapologetic when it came to glamour. We exalted in our pretentiousness, believing in 'the lie that tells the truth' over the very English notion of mundane enslavement to the station into which you happen to have been born. Fuck that!

There was often a subtle wink there, too, but it was lost on a lot of people. We once spoke about the band's sense of humour in an interview, and at our next gig the crowd was chanting, 'Sense of humour! Sense of humour!' over and over, which was itself rather amusing. As far as the London-based music press was concerned, though, we had never 'joined the club'. We refused to court their affections, and we even made them pay full price to attend our gigs (which was unheard of). Consequently, what ensued was a war of attrition in which we were cast as the *bête noire*. There was even one damning review in the *Melody Maker* that referred in great detail to a gig that we never actually played.

The press reaction to *Flat Field*, then, was predictably negative. The fanzines showered us with praise, however, and our fan base continued to grow. Interest in Europe had also grown, so we embarked on a return trip to Belgium, Holland, and Germany. The support slot on this short jaunt was filled by the extraordinary Z'EV. We were always very selective in our choice of 'special guests', and we endeavoured to find artists who were different from the expected norm (that is, not another boring rock band). Z'EV fit the bill to a *T*. Peter Kent and Ivo had shown us a video of him performing with his homemade percussion setup, which consisted, in the main, of multiple large plastic containers and pieces of metal strung together with ropes. These objects were swung around and flayed with punishing intensity. Z'EV also used every part of the building in which the performance took place, playing the floor, the walls, pillars, staircases, and so on. The rhythms were intense, building to a cacophony, and the graceful physicality of this performance was most impressive.

Z'EV was something of an alchemist, too, with a great knowledge of Kabbalistic Gematria and magick. He knew how to induce trance states through precision drumming. And he also liked his drugs. At the start of the tour, we had just made it over the border from Belgium into Holland when Z'EV, who was travelling with us in a mini bus, realised that he had failed to get his passport stamped. He insisted that we pull over, as he really wanted to get that international ink. He was a small, wiry, gaunt, rat-faced man with a sallow complexion and an ever-present growth of salt-and-pepper stubble, punky orange spiked hair, and a jangle of earrings. He had great style, but it was the look of a renegade druggy artist, and as we were all aware of the fact that he had a fairly large amount of cocaine stuffed inside a condom and inserted in that place where the sun don't shine, we were naturally nervous. We waited in the bus for what seemed like an eternity, until Z'EV finally returned, grinning from ear to ear, with US passport in hand and the blow still up his arse. A perturbed Peter Kent put the pedal very firmly to the metal, and we were off.

Z'EV was only with us for a few more dates, however, as he had a bitter falling out with Plug, and one day called for the van to be pulled over so that he could get off for good.

'Fuckin' English!' he announced. 'Piss 'n' fuckin' moan, man! Piss 'n' fuckin' moan!' We missed him. (Really.)

Our first Dutch gig was at the legendary Paradiso in Amsterdam. Initially, we were quite amazed and delighted by the liberal attitude to cannabis, which was for sale in the club's shop. They had many varieties of dope, all laid out on the counter for inspection: hashish like large blocks of chocolate in silver foil; Moroccan black and Lebanese gold; sticky buds of sparkling sensimilla. A stoner's paradise—Paradiso indeed! The downside of this was that the audience was so zonked that they all laid down on the floor like a crash of clubbed seals. Only one big guy in a beaten-up biker jacket had any life in him. He was the only person who was actually standing when we played.

Peter started to slag off the hippies, and they did at least manage to muster a degree of half-hearted retaliation, but the whole experience was frustrating, and we looked forward to arriving in Germany, where we knew that the audiences would be sharp, on their feet, and up for it. Before we crossed the border, however, we had three more Dutch gigs to play. Annie had joined me in Amsterdam, and she stayed on for Eindhoven the following day. Graham had arranged for us all to stay that night in a disused windmill, its filthy floor strewn with even filthier-looking sleeping bags. My discerning lady took one look at the place and informed me that she would be checking into a hotel on her credit card. I could either stay with the boys or come with her—my choice.

'Are you sure you want to do that?' I sheepishly enquired.

'Oh yes, I'm sure!' came the predictable reply. The hotel was lovely!

The following morning, I kissed Annie a fond farewell, and the bus made its way to Nijmegen, where the audience there was somewhat more alert than those of the previous two nights. Then, finally, we made it to Germany.

Rattinger Hof, in the industrial city of Düsseldorf, was certainly a 'live' venue. The earthing system was completely shot, and consequently anything metal—including the pillars, the scaffolding, and parts of the stage—was live. We had all been getting shocks throughout the soundcheck, but we were told that everything would be fixed by the time we came to play. It wasn't. The club was packed with hard-core punks who became decidedly fractious as we abandoned the stage for the third time that night. Missiles were hurled, bottles smashed against the PA, and some in the crowd were demanding their money back. We were herded out of our dressing room by the club staff and into something resembling a closet as a full-on riot ensued. When we asked why we had to abandon the other room, we were told that the crowd would assume that's where we'd be, so would attack there first!

Our brave roadie, Bob Edwards, was still on the stage, kicking disgruntled Germans out of the way as they made a grab for our equipment. Eventually, the police arrived in force, and we were escorted round the back of the building to our van, which had been pummelled by the mob. There were large dents all over it, graffiti was sprayed over the paintwork, and the windows were smashed. We had to make the long drive to Berlin that night for our gig the next day. It was late November and bitterly cold. We taped transparent plastic sheeting over the gaping holes and hit the road.

There was a blizzard that night, so we had to drive down the autobahn as slowly as possible. By the time we arrived in Berlin's Turkish Quarter, Neukölln, we were tired, miserable, and freezing cold. Rather than traipse around looking for somewhere to stay, we decided to sleep in the broken bandwagon (in those days, we would often wing it as far as accommodation was concerned, and would either end up crashing at someone's place or book into a cheap hotel at the eleventh hour).

The club we were due to play at, SO36, had a reputation as a rough and wild psychobilly hangout, and tonight they were out in force. The heckling started the minute we hit the stage. The fact that we had been flirting with some of the greasy boys' girlfriends did not help the situation. Throat-cutting gestures were thrown in our direction, which prompted Peter and Daniel to blow kisses at the bequiffed and pissed in the audience. Once again, German blood was coming to the boil, and by the end of the set, furniture was being thrown. There was no dressing room as such, just a space behind the curtain, piled up with chairs, so we had to squat there once we had left the stage.

It was then that we realised that Peter was still out there. We all took a peek through the curtain, and there he was, assuming the old crucifixion pose and singing a glossolalic a-capella extension of the 'Spiritus Sanctus' ending of 'Stigmata Martyr' while chair legs, ash trays, and beer bottles flew all around him. It was insane, and strangely beautiful.

We were finally spirited away to a safe house overlooking the Berlin Wall, where we buoyed our flagging souls with beer and schnapps. Our kind host was the owner of a hip clothing store called Blue Moon, which specialised in high-quality leather apparel. We were taken to this establishment the next day and told that we could each choose one item each for free. After saying our auf wiedersehens we headed over toward Den Hague.

After a few minutes, Murphy peeled off his jeans to reveal a pair of expensive-looking black leather trousers that he had purloined to match his freebie biker's cap. As I had engaged in similar criminal activity in Chicago earlier in the year, I could not be too vocal in my criticism, but Daniel was disgusted, and he let Peter know it. (A couple of weeks later, we received an excruciating letter from the owner of the shop, who made clear how upset he was that after all his hospitality, we had ripped him off. This was deeply embarrassing—and very annoying, in that the blame was levelled at all of us.)

By the time we reached The Hague, I was exhausted. I went out for a walk, and I had the oddest sensation that the ancient, tram-lined streets were melting. My vision was distorted, and I was in desperate need of some shut-eye. I made it back to the small hotel, where Daniel and Peter rushed up to me, imploring me to take a deep sniff of something or other that they had in a small vial. They insisted I would love the experience.

Foolishly, I closed my eyes and inhaled. It was like being coshed with a chemical blackjack. I felt a rush of blood to the brain, saw red then black, and immediately collapsed. Daniel and Peter were cackling like idiots as I pulled myself up and made it to my door. I pushed them aside and crashed onto the bed as my head pounded and throbbed.

More 'fun with poppers' was had the following night on our drive back from the final gig in Rotterdam. The giggling duo of Daniel and Peter once again produced a bottle of the stuff, having decided that it would be a very good idea to stick it under Kevin's nose as he was sleeping. Aroused crudely and rudely from his repose, my brother exploded into life, arms flailing wildly. The bottle was upset, spilling the entire contents all over the vehicle. Peter Kent was sufficiently affected that he drove us off the road and into a field. We all clambered out and gave the culprits a stern tongue-lashing. We had to stomp around in the cold until the fumes had sufficiently cleared so that we could continue on our journey.

The atmosphere for the rest of the trip was dark and heavy. I buried my nose in a book: *Satori In Paris* by Jack Kerouac. 'Satori' is a concept in Zen Buddhism that describes a moment of sudden spiritual illumination. In his book, Kerouac applies this to his own ecstatic experience in the French capital, describing the revelation as the 'kick in the eye'. This phrase would inspire the title of our next single, and the funk-driven track would point the way to the next evolutionary stage of the band.

* * *

The first thing that we did in January of 1981 was move from 4AD to the parent label, Beggars Banquet, thrilled by the offer of a long-term contract that we would later bitterly regret signing (and which 4AD's Ivo Watts-Russell would once compare to the shameful rip-offs experienced by the old bluesmen back in the 50s). We had basically signed away all our publishing in perpetuity—that means 'forever', punk![2] Still, we were now on a recoupable fifty quid a week, which was a lot better than the twenty that we had been getting on the dole. (Yeah, sure! Suckers!)

That year, our star was in the ascendant, and it did feel that we had outgrown 4AD. Beggars Banquet had enjoyed considerable commercial success with Gary Numan, and was now looking for the next big breaker. Significantly, it also had the money to assist in that desired outcome.

In January, we recorded 'Kick In The Eye' at Jam Studios in London. We had just acquired a new Wasp synthesizer, and this great little touch-sensitive instrument was put to nice, off-kilter effect on the track, adding a touch of sci-fi weirdness to the up-tempo rhythmic funk. Daniel's previous employment in the ranks of the funky MI5 proved useful when he dropped back into that mode for the guitar part. All in all, it was an inspired session in which we also recorded a totally improvised instrumental, 'Satori', that alluded obliquely to the A-side. Built around insistent drums, congas, and a snaking synth line, it put one in mind of a long journey upstream through a hot fetid jungle.

Our next live dates were back in the USA. First, we did a quick wham-bam-thank-you-mam five-date East Coast run (including a date in Washington, DC, at the 9:30 Club, with a little starter band called R.E.M. as support) and then a return the following month for a more extensive, coke-fuelled tour which culminated in one wonderfully crazy week in my beloved New York City.

Living here is like living in a TV set
With all the colour, contrast and sound turned up full
The location of the on/off switch
Long lost in the blur of a consumer haze
But I know where it is
See it in the dark
CLICK!

I wrote this in my hotel room during that stay, but sometimes I wanted to 'keep the TV on all night'. This place was about as far from Northampton and the *Flat Field* as was possible, and at this particular time it was going through something of a renaissance, especially in the art world.

The art was coming from the streets and below them. In those days, the subway was a spectacular gallery in motion as spray-painted trains sped by, emblazoned with bold graffiti. The walls above ground provided an illegal canvas for the nascent art stars. Daniel and I were both haunted by Richard Hambleton's powerful shadow figures, which lurked beneath the awnings of the East Village and SoHo.

Some of these street artists were beginning to emerge as serious contenders. Jean-Michel Basquiat and Keith Haring were starting to make a big splash alongside Julian Schnabel, Kenny Scharf, and other neo-expressionistic painters. Andy Warhol still presided over this milieu as a kind of working patron saint, although he was in great danger of being eclipsed by the new, street-born talent. New galleries were springing up all over SoHo, and the young artists were claiming unprecedented prices for their large vibrant works. This vibrancy was a true reflection of the electric energy of the city. The club scene was thriving, and evolving into another colourful mirror of the zeitgeist. The black flowers of the 'No Wave' scene were starting to bloom through the cracks in the gum-caked sidewalk, and everything was art.

One of the bands on the bill with us during this time was Arto Lindsey's DNA. We were impressed by their unconventional approach, Lindsey whacking the strings of his electric guitar with a drumstick in a percussive assault (an effect Daniel would steal and then make his own). They had the same irreverent, anti-musician approach as us, and we felt an affinity with their stark visual style, too. James Chance & The Contortions were another group who caught our attention. They were like an angular post-punk bizarro James Brown & The Famous Flames. The Lounge Lizards' 'fake jazz' also held appeal. It was all very East Village art-damage, and we soaked it all up like a sponge in the filthy Hudson.

On March 12, we appeared on a TV show, *New York Bandstand*. They wanted us to mime to 'Kick In The Eye' and 'Stigmata Martyr'. We told them that we would prefer to play live, but they were not set up for that, so when the cameras rolled, we decided to take the piss, not even bothering to play at times. The audience was made up of cherry-picked trendies who were encouraged to dance at all times. There was also an interview, conducted by an ultra-preppy presenter, whom Peter threw off track with his repeated references to Daniel's huge testicles.

We played three New York gigs, all at different venues—the Peppermint Lounge (which became a favourite post-gig haunt), Privates, and the Rock Lounge—and hopped over to New Jersey to play at Trenton City Gardens. These shows went a long way to cementing our reputation in the Big A.

I used to love going out and wandering the streets during the day. One time, I was down near St Mark's when a fuzzy-faced fellow in a multi-coloured woolly hat stopped me on the corner.

'I got ya pegged as a musician, man!' he began, holding out his leathery old paw for a shake. 'Bass player?'

I told him that he was right and asked if he knew my band. He didn't, he said, but he could just tell. Then he introduced himself as Tuli—Tuli Kupferberg from The Fuggs!

'Takes one to know one, man! You have yerself a good one!'

Another time I was down in this same sketchy neighbourhood turned out to be anything but a good one. I wanted to score some dope and heard someone grunt the word 'hash'. This being something of a rarity in the States in those days—and definitely my drug du jour—my ears pricked up. A filthy looking individual in a greasy leather jacket and long, ratty goatee nodded toward a darkened awning. When I got the shit home it turned out to be something other than as advertised, and in fact resembled one of those crumbly rubber erasers mixed with road tar.

The next day I happened to see the same sleazy dealer on the street. In anger, I reproached him about the rip-off, and the next thing I knew, he'd pushed me into an alley and I had a six-inch blade at my throat.

'You wanna fuck with me, asshole? You wanna fuck with me?'

I answered timidly in the negative, and—thanks be to the blessed patron saint of idiots—he lowered the glinting knife. I eased out and off.

'*Asshole!*'

The expletive resounded in the street behind me. I did not look back. Lesson well and truly learned.

We had a new tour manager for this Stateside jaunt. His name was Harry Isles, and we were very impressed with his thoroughness in all aspects of the job. He was also an articulate, cultured man, a part-time art teacher, and was very together, with just the right kind of sensitive, easy-going disposition. By the end of the tour, we'd decided that he would make a great business manager, and when we offered him the job, he accepted (albeit with a typically self-deprecating 'Are you sure about this?').

Upon our return to England, we played another Final Solution gig at Heaven, a club under the arches beneath Charing Cross station in London that usually hosted hard-core gay dance nights. Also on the bill that night were Clock DVA, who made a big impression on me. They had one track, '4 Hours', that Z'EV had turned me onto, and which was dynamite. (I would later cover it on a solo record.) Joining them were Torso, a highly physical dance troupe. One of their pieces was a slow-motion fight sequence that was like a scene from a punk-rock *West Side Story* and had the crowd going wild.

We took the stage on a high tide of energy. Toward the end of the set, Peter tauntingly enquired of the audience, 'Are you expecting something weird?' With that, the power went down, and it stayed down for some time. By the time it was finally restored, the atmosphere in the place had changed. It had become charged with a glinting, violent edge, and we reacted to this, delivering a storming encore of 'Muscle In Plastic' and 'St Vitus Dance'.

Whenever we had a London gig like this, we would all pile into Daniel's old Jag the night before and drive south down the M1 with the stereo blasting. It's a wonder we ever made it, as Daniel, acting as chauffeur, would crack open a can of extra strong Carlsberg Special Brew lager at the start of the journey, and once it was half empty would proceed to refill it with cognac—this being the first of several of these awful cocktails. He would then repeat this dangerous activity on the drive home the next day.

This hedonistic behaviour could be viewed as relatively tame, however, when compared to that of our next touring companions. Enter The Birthday Party. This extraordinary band of firebrands was actually third on the bill, preceding Vic Godard and The Subway Sect, but if such hierarchies were based on musical accomplishment alone, they should have been topping it. Whenever we could, we would go out into the crowd to watch them deliver some of the most devastating performances we had ever seen, although 'performance' is not really appropriate, as this was more like shamanic catharsis, with a young Nick Cave hurling himself across the stage and often into the crowd with total fucked-up abandon while stocky bassist Tracy Pew danced around his cowboy hat, the elegantly emaciated Roland S. Howard—cigarette permanently dangling from his lips—shot out staccato metallic shards of noise from his low-slung guitar, Mick Harvey on rhythm guitar played the part of grounded lieutenant and Phil Calvert accentuated the extreme dynamics with his sometimes frenetic, sometimes pared down drumming. The sound was wild and anarchic, taking off on fierce unexpected trajectories, lurching this way and that, but always with everyone going at the same time and in the same direction.

By now, as a band, Bauhaus were very hit or miss. We would hardly ever rehearse. We liked to think that this was the best way to maintain an exciting edge, but often it backfired and we were just plain sloppy. Seeing The Birthday Party go out and deliver, night after night, certainly made us pull up our fishnets. This was a band, though, that was tight in more ways than one. Sharing the same seedy hotels, we would join them in the bar on occasion, and they would think nothing of downing half a dozen pints each with whisky chasers before the gig. They would be boozing all through their set, then back to propping up the bar until it closed. In the morning, we would see them knocking back cans of larger before setting off on the drive to the next town. And though we were not aware of it at the time, Nick and Roland were also shooting smack.

By this stage in our career, Bauhaus had built up a fanatical cult following, with many of the regular faces—Millie, Basildon John, Middlesbrough Mick, Peter 'Luton' Hosier—becoming very familiar to us. This ragged bunch would travel all over the UK and Europe to catch as many live shows as they could on a non-existent budget. We assisted them in this endeavour by always putting them on our guest list. When we played the Top Rank in Reading, they were all there to help carry in the PA and speedily set it up after the crew arrived late due to their van having sustained three punctures en route. The large speakers were stacked on tables with crash barriers placed around them. The security was made up of scary-looking bruisers, including one behemoth who had just been released from jail for committing GBH.

Before we went on, Peter was approached by the management and told to be very careful with the precariously positioned PA. (He had taken, during this tour, to climbing all over the speakers, leaping from one to another and throwing himself back onto the stage, much to the fans' delight.) He promised to be good, but as soon as he came on his first act was to push the ex-con off the front of the stage and then command the audience to break down the barriers. The whole of the left speaker column came crashing down onto the crowd. Miraculously, no one was hurt, although the jettisoned security guard had plans to change that, and was waiting for Peter to emerge from the stage door at the end of the night. Fortunately, the management tipped us the wink, and we slipped out sharply through the front door instead.

For this tour we were staying either in cheap hotels or B&Bs. Our stop-over in Leeds was highly amusing, as the hard-core Scottish punk band The Exploited were being held captive by the owner of the B&B we were staying at. Apparently their manager had absconded with all the tour money, and they were unable to pay the bill. The disgruntled proprietor had them in lockdown until the funds turned up. The poor buggers asked us imploringly if we would bring back a crate of brown ale for them as they had run out, to which we complied as they seemed so pathetic. Never has a band been so aptly named!

On the last night of the tour, at the Corn Exchange in Cambridge, Kevin and a couple of the roadies decided to pull a prank by storming onstage during The Birthday Party's set and plastering them with shaving cream pies. It made me cringe. So unimaginative! The Aussies retaliated by rushing Peter, mid-song, wrestling him to the floor, and drawing a huge erect penis on his torso. Undeterred, Murphy spent the rest of the gig lovingly masturbating the 'Magic Marker' prick. For the encore we invited Nick and the boys back on to join us for a cover of the Peggy Lee classic 'Fever'. The song inevitably developed into a slow-burning duel, which, it has to be said, those badass fuckers from down-under won hands down.

It also has to be stated that I was not entirely innocent of pranksterism that night. I had the drunken inspiration to set up what appeared to be a thick line of coke on a mirror in the dimly lit backstage area, but which in reality was salt. Peter came offstage and immediately snorted it, then shook his head as the tears came and his nose began to run the Olympics.

I felt pretty bad about that little stunt, and decided that flowers were in order. That and some Kleenex.

CHAPTER THREE
From Weimar
To Walthamstow

The envelope bore a Walthamstow postmark. It was from Pete Stennett at Small Wonder Records. Inside, along with a brief note from Pete, was a letter from a Ben Israel. He had originally sent this missive to John Peel, care of the BBC, and they in turn, had passed it on to Pete, whereupon he had forwarded it to me.

Ben had heard 'Bela Lugosi's Dead' on Peel's show and had told his friend about it. That friend was one René Halkett, a septuagenarian former student at the original Bauhaus school in Weimar in the 1920s, who was somewhat intrigued that the name of Bauhaus should be applied to something other than his old stomping ground. (He did stomp—sometimes on top of a piano, while firing a pistol—but that's another story.) Upon receiving the letter, I fired off an immediate response, and a long correspondence ensued.

My first visit to 8 Chapel Street in Camelford, Cornwall, will abide as a cherished memory for the rest of my days. The small house was situated at the top of a steep hill in the centre of the charmingly craggy village. I was greeted at the door by a young man (Mr Israel), and a not-so-young gentleman dressed in various shades of khaki (the great man himself.) I was welcomed warmly and ushered into the front room.

This little cave was exclusively coloured in the same sepia tones as its owner. Thick clumps of cobweb clung to the dim corners. Archaic musical instruments, Javanese puppets, and masks hung from the walls. Row upon row of books—many of them first editions, all turned brown with age—lined the old wooden shelves. Newspaper cuttings and thumbnail sketches were pinned to the antique cabinets. There were old photographs on the mantle, including one of René's beautiful wife in her youth, standing on the deck of a sailing boat. (On a later visit, he would show me his 'grey paintings', which hauntingly depict her tragic descent into schizophrenia.) There was also a colourful, mosaic-topped coffee table, on which sat a large ashtray overflowing with stubbed-out Black Cat cigarettes.

I would be regaled with all manner of wonderful tales in this tiny room, René spinning out the lustrous yarn of story, long into the night. He would tell me about the artistic life in Weimar in the 1920s, his meetings with the likes of Bertolt Brecht, Anna Pavlova, Vaslav Nijinsky, and most of the original French surrealists. (Breton, he said, was an ass.) He also spoke of his work with the British Secret Service during World War II. (He had been a recorder at the Nuremberg trials, too, but he would never talk about that.) Then there was his life in London at the height of the psychedelic 60s, and his fondness for the spirit of that colourful age. He told me of his great love for the theatre, glider planes, and how he had actually died on three separate occasions!

It would be I—nearly fifty years his junior—who would tire first and slope off to the draughty back room to sleep, my dreams percolating with the wild swirl of anecdotes newly minted on my mind. Back home, I would look forward to the arrival of one of the master's long letters, distinctive both for their fascinating insights and roguish humour as well as the idiosyncratic errors resulting from the faulty mechanics of René's antiquated, broken-down typewriter and failing eyesight (he was blind in one eye and severely myopic in the other).

On the occasion of our meeting at London's Paddington Station in 1981, for an interview with the *NME*—René having travelled up from Camelford and I down from Northampton—we were most amused to find that we were dressed exactly alike, he in his beautiful camelhair overcoat and flat woollen cap, worn at a rakish angle, and I in an inferior herringbone tweed version of the same with a Kangol hat. Anton Corbijn, the photographer, remarked that we looked as if we were in a band.

We were there to talk about our recorded collaboration, a double A-side single that had just been released by 4AD records. At my suggestion,

René had sent me a tape of three spoken-word pieces with the idea that I would choose two and set them to music. I played the tape constantly for a couple of weeks in order to become familiar with the rhythm of the words and then set about the creation of a suitable soundscape. For 'Nothing', the main melody was played on a miniature pocket calculator; for 'Armour', I used a very basic drum machine, the Wasp synthesizer, acoustic piano, and bass guitar.

I had Ivo from 4AD over one evening and played the two tracks to him. I asked if he would be interested in putting them out, and he gave me an immediate and very positive thumbs-up. Years later, when the idea came up to rerelease the single on CD to coincide with the occasion of its twentieth anniversary, I decided I'd like to include some additional material if possible. I dug out the original cassette tape that René had sent in 1980. The unaccompanied spoken word versions of 'Nothing' and 'Armour' would make for an interesting inclusion, I thought, and then there was this other unused track, a long narrative piece that René had recorded as well because, he wrote in an accompanying note, it happened to be in the same folder as the other two poems, 'and there was all that lovely tape on side two'.

I had not played this tape in years. The third piece, 'The New God', was an intriguing fable told in that wonderfully rich and expressive voice. It was time to make a new collaborative recording. Just as before, I played the tape over and over until it became a part of me. The choice of instrumentation was obvious.

After René died, in 1983, I inherited the marvellous luta—a cross between a guitar and a lute that dates back to the mid-nineteenth century—that used to hang on the wall of his study. René had left all of his possessions (apart from his papers, which went to his biographer, Ian Fell) to Sally Holden, the proprietor of the North Cornwall Museum & Gallery, with the instruction that she was to keep, sell, or gift as she saw fit. I was thrilled when she invited me down to pick up the luta and view all of the paintings, drawings, and etchings that were in her care.

The day I arrived, Sally took me to the gallery, where she had set out René's life's work for a private view. She left me alone with the works, telling me to take my time. He had shown some of the pictures to me before, but at this retrospective viewing, I was suddenly in the presence of practically every work that he had ever made. It was overwhelming. After much deliberation, I left with the drawing that we had used for the cover of our record, which depicted an elaborate surrealistic music machine, plus a small etching of a Minotaur and a self-portrait of René playing the luta—a fitting companion piece to the prized instrument itself. Sally set an extremely fair price for the art, and I can only say that René left his worldly wares in very good hands.

On the eve of my departure from Camelford, I decided to take a stroll, and I was suddenly arrested by a compulsion to follow a certain trail. It was very odd; I felt that René was directing me. I ended up in a field full of chomping cows and consequently a vast spread of cowpats. On closer examination, I discovered that there were a great many psilocybin liberty-cap mushrooms sprouting from the bovine deposits. In fact, the field was full of them. I remembered one conversation I had had with René, where he told me that he had always wanted to have a psychedelic drug experience but had not even smoked marijuana, as he did not want to compromise one of his best friends, the local bobby, who would often make off-duty house calls. In that instant, I felt that he was urging me to collect the mushrooms, so I did.

When I returned home to Northampton, I sat in my study with the luta, now newly hung on the wall. I made a pot of tea from one hundred of the mushrooms and drank it down. I had a distinct feeling that the luta's former owner was present at that moment, and as if to announce the fact, all six of the instrument's strings rang out loudly, apparently strummed by an invisible spectral hand. For the next hour, I had what I can only describe as an intense spiritual communion with the ghost of René Halkett. I felt him moving around the room, and although I could not see him, I knew exactly where he was. I received a telepathic message from him, telling me that he had directed me to the mushrooms, their ingestion allowing me access to the particular subtle realm that we now occupied. The general feeling imparted was one of sacred peace and harmony.

Suddenly, there was an almighty crack—like the sound of breaking glass, but greatly amplified. I had some old Victorian lantern slides in a box near to the fire, and my first rational assumption was that they had cracked in the heat, although the volume of the mysterious noise was far greater than the sound that this would have produced. I examined the slides, and they were all intact. There was a strong smell of ozone in the room, and the air seemed charged, as it might after an electrical storm. René had left the building.

He did not return until the day I entered Barry Paul's studio in North Hollywood to record the music for 'The New God'. Now, as I played René's luta for the first time, I felt the same warm spectral presence. I always felt that I would use the instrument on something, but that it would have to be something special, something worthy of its history and association. 'The New God' was that piece.

Before René died, Ivo and I were very interested in putting together another record with him, an extended work that would build on the interest created by the first disc. Mr Murphy also visited him in Camelford, and was keen to be involved. Although René liked the idea, the proposed project caused him a lot of frustration, as his rapidly failing health prevented him from realising anything that he considered worthwhile. His last letters were full of this frustration, and betrayed a deeply sad bewilderment.

This very special man now lives on in his paintings, drawings, and words, but most of all in the memories of the many friends who were blessed to have known him. He is greatly missed.

CHAPTER FOUR
White Lines
And Wanderlust

In September of 1981, we played two festivals that helped to establish our footing on the upper slopes of the indie-rock mountain: Futurama at Bingley Hall in Stafford, and Daze Of Future Past at the Queens Hall in Leeds.

The former featured the excellent, spiky Gang Of Four at the top of the bill, with us second (plus seventeen acts on before us), with the line-up for the second day including one of the most interesting bands of the era: The Virgin Prunes, fronted by Gavin Friday and Guggi, two fascinating shamanic misfits who would act out their little psychosexual dramas and create edgy compelling theatre with only a chair, a cigarette, a candle, and a bag of flour at their disposal. Gavin would utilise the full potential of the stage space, stalking it like some wrath-child while the strange yet charismatic blonde Guggi would invest a mannequin in a wedding dress with potent eerie life. We were impressed enough that we invited the Prunes to be our special guests on our next tour.

The Daze of Future Past festival had Echo & The Bunnymen in the top slot, with the electrifying American band The Cramps second on the bill and Bauhaus in third place. The Cramps' singer, the exotically named Lux Interior, distinguished himself by simultaneously exposing himself and vomiting onstage. Six other bands preceded us.

Our set for these gigs was based around the new album, *Mask*, that we had just finished recording. The music was taut and punchy, with a lot more emphasis placed on the drums, percussion, and bass, and the sound was a lot fuller, sharper, and more defined than that of our previous album.

The late-night sessions for the album took place mostly at Playground Recording Studios and to a lesser degree Jam Studios, both in London, and were fuelled by white powder. They were subject to some surprise visitations. Late one evening, the studio buzzer crackled into life, and when we enquired as to who was at the door, we heard the name Nico, uttered with a strong Teutonic accent. We thought it was a joke.

'Yeah, sure,' said Daniel, 'and I'm Lou Reed!'

'No,' the disembodied voice insisted, 'it is really *meeee*, Nico!'

We conceded and buzzed her in, and it was indeed the Velvets' chanteuse! Apparently, Peter had met up with her a few weeks prior, and had told her where we were recording. She had come armed with a large bottle of mescal, plus some limes and salt. She immediately demonstrated how to put those three elements together to pleasing effect.

I had finished my takes, so she and I snuggled up in a corner, a strange chemical smell detectable under her heady perfume, and her long dark hair brushing my cheek as we entered into a whispered conversation about New York in the 60s. I had tentatively raised the subject and she, rather surprisingly, seemed to be in the mood to reminisce. She told me that her favourite Velvet Underground song was 'I'll Be Your Mirror', and how she didn't really care for 'Femme Fatale'—especially since Lou Reed would not pronounce 'femme' correctly.[1]

Another midnight caller was Billy MacKenzie, the talented but troubled singer from The Associates. He too came bearing gifts: a school satchel full of best Bolivian cocaine, which was duly chopped and snorted. (In those days, the razor blade used for splicing audiotape had a duel purpose.) The song we were recording at the time was the title track, 'Mask', and I can still recall with crystal clarity overdubbing the echoed bass part and using a metal bottleneck to achieve the cascade effect that comes in at the point where Daniel's acoustic twelve-string part starts. Hearing these sounds in ultra-sharp coke-intensified focus through headphones produced an ecstatic heart-bursting emotion on the edge of orgasmic release.[2]

For the early sessions at the Playground, we worked with a co-producer, Mike Hedges. He was a good mixer but a bit over-fond of effects and multi-layering for our taste. We ended up taking over the reins and did the final mix at Jam, with the personable Kenny Jones engineering.

One day, I turned up at the studio, grabbed the first piece of paper that I could find, and wrote down a transcript of a haunting dream I had had the previous night. When I turned the paper over, I saw that Peter had written something on the other side. When I asked him what it was, he told me that it was a dream that he had had. It was so synchronistic, and we took it as a sign that we should immediately utilise this reportage of the subconscious. We improvised some music and then took turns to record our individual readings. 'Of Lilies And Remains' was the result.

Another off-the-wall experimental track that I initiated was 'David Jay,[3] Peter Murphy, Kevin Haskins, Daniel Ash'. It was made up of a sequence of 'blind' contributions to a five-minute piece in the manner of an 'exquisite corpse'.[4] Each of us was allocated one minute to record whatever we wished over a pre-programmed drumbeat, while for the final minute we each recorded two tracks without listening to what the others had put down on tape.

The flip side of this commercial suicide was 'The Passion Of Lovers', an acoustic-guitar-driven slice of gothic pop that was our most melodic track to date, and was consequently released as a single. It came in a rather wry picture sleeve featuring an image of a female praying mantis devouring its post-coital mate. The cover of the *Mask* album itself was an elaborate gatefold spread sporting a drawing by Daniel of four strange, cartoon-like characters. The following appropriately surreal sleeve notes were credited to one Brilburn Logue, which was actually a pseudonym for our friend Alan Moore (an early champion of the band who wrote the first article on Bauhaus, for *Sounds*, in 1980):

This is for when the slats of the night slam shut on you, for when the radio is broken and crackles like uranium orchids, for when the Fohn-wind rattles the telegraph wires, like a handful of bones, and this is for when dream ambulances skitter through the streets at midnight. In the amusement arcade a sailor whose muscles writhe with pornography, doubled up, is vomiting emeralds.

Elsewhere a black man with brass teeth and a swallow skin tie is laughing and laughing and offering poisoned candy floss to the children. This is for when your cuffs get caught in the cogs of an urban evening, for when your vision is frayed and you don't have any more lust. This is for the wasp-woman. This is for the torturers' wives with their thumbs blue as billiard chalk. This is for all the mathematicians who got mixed up in the dream gang. This is for when you get caught in a sleep-riot, this is for when your jism turns to platinum, for when the television is full of murder, for when the sky is out of order, for when your room is crawling with cheap poetry. This is for when your veins are singing with indigo, for when the radiator is full of fever, for when your sex is full of voodoo, for when your clothes are imaginary, for when your kitchen is dead. This is for when your flesh creeps and never comes back.

* * *

In keeping with our surrealist leanings, we would also apply the 'exquisite corpse' idea to an experimental film, *Consequences*, to be shown on tour in place of a support band. For this, we were each allocated an amount of time to film whatever we wished. The four sections were then spliced together at random.

Kevin's section comes first: a little film-noir episode that shows the most accomplished use of the language of film and features a rather disturbing nightmare sequence set to an off-kilter psycho-circus soundtrack that hints at his future accomplishment as a film composer. The end link section is quite clever. The eye of the paranoid Kafka-esque protagonist (played by Gordon King from the band World Of Twist) is seen in extreme close-up and is then freeze-framed. Suddenly, the film cuts to a working-class living room, where the wife is watching TV, the frozen eyeball glaring from the screen.

'Roy!' she calls out. 'Come and look at this!'

Roy, her husband, then enters and sits down in his armchair in front of the screen.

'Arrrh,' he says, 'what's all this then? Gorrrd! That's one of them bloody modern plays, innit? What a load of bloody crap! I 'ent watching that crap, that's for sure and certain!'

With this, Roy gets up and changes the channel, his sizable posterior blocking the screen.

'Ah,' he says, 'this looks a lot better.'

We cut next to Peter's segment, which shows him dressed in a white loincloth and moving through various twists and turns on the floor, the film eventually intercut with other scene, including one of Peter drawing some curtains, his outstretched arms in an echo of a still image shown next of the pope. That's followed by a looped film of someone being slapped in the face—an action that is repeated later on, with Peter as the recipient, having asked a woman to hit him. Various mundane street scenes are juxtaposed with Tibetan devil masks and a homoerotic episode focused on a banana and the Murphy rear. Toward the end, there is an almost indiscernible voice-over. One of the few lines that can be heard is 'But the play was rubbish!', which resonates interestingly with the conclusion of Kevin's section.

Daniel is up next, with a very curious offering in which he is shown dressed almost identically to Peter but covered from head to toe in white pancake make-up. He also wears a white skullcap. A pinging electronic soundtrack plays as he cavorts and prances around a room full of torn-up white paper. Next, a video synthesizer is brought into play, and the colours change throughout, as positive turns to negative and back again.

My section concludes the piece. A spectral bride (played by Annie) is presented with a mysterious box by a masked midget waiter (nine-year-old Ben, my future stepson). Gazing into the box, the bride sees an animated forest (a scratched Super 8 film projected inside the box). We then go into the forest and see a man running from (or maybe toward) something. He arrives at a desolate place, where a Bergman-esque spectre sits alone at a table playing chess. A bloody wound appears in his chest, and the man collapses backward. The bride carries the box through a dark house as a strobe light flashes. We see her discarded bridal dress; a tailor's dummy appears outside some French windows, and is replaced by the bride. She is naked, and her eyes have disappeared. (One of the characters in Kevin's section, a businessman on a train, also loses his eyes.) A distorted music box plays over the ending, which shows the bride, now dressed and back at the table, staring at a knife, which she holds in her left hand. The film ends with a close-up on her eyes, reflected in the blade—another echo of Kevin's part of the film, which also ends with a close-up of an eye.

Watching this again, all these years later, it has to be said that the whole thing is extremely self-indulgent and overlong. Suffer the *Consequences* indeed!

The 'Mask' video was a lot more successful, despite being shot on the fly, and a shoestring budget. It was set in a condemned factory, situated just across the road from Northampton's county police station. This proximity to the law did not deter us from illegally breaking in one cold autumn night to power up the lights with car batteries and roll film. In fact, the illicit nature of the situation lent a delicious edge to the shoot. We improvised around the loose idea of a ritualistic resurrection, with Peter lain out like a corpse on a wooden slab. Each of us would administer some kind of shamanistic voodoo to assist in the raising of the dead. The place was freezing cold, dank, and dripping with filthy water. The lights kept going out, and we would be plunged into complete darkness until they were restored.

Once we had filmed the scenes in the factory, we set off for a second location: the woods on the grounds of the Spencer family's country estate—another illegal situation, and a potential threat to the monarchy. We did have fun that night! The finished film looked great: a fog-cloaked atmospheric drama that was redolent of a German expressionist silent horror flick. As a promotional video, it was unusual, in that 'Mask' was not a single. This was more of an art piece, and the director, Chris Collins did a brilliant job of capturing the visual essence of the band.

* * *

The *Mask* tour kicked off in Reading on October 22, 1981. The Virgin Prunes were the support for the first leg, and on the first day of the tour,

Gavin Friday and I decided to wander off to a nearby pub for a drink. Gavin was in his usual garb of fishnet tights, black dress, frock coat, and Doc Martens. He was fully made up in rouge, eyeliner, and eye-shadow, his dyed black hair scrunched up in a big top-knot above a single long dangling ear-ring, and he was carrying a black cane with an elaborate silver handle. When we walked in, it was like an old western movie scene: everything stopped, and the locals put down their pints and glared at us through mean, squinting eyes. Gavin strolled up to the bar and stared straight back; the locals sheepishly returned to their drinks. He just had this aura that suggested it would be a very big mistake to fuck with him.

In Manchester, we played at a club called Fagin's, which was ironically named, as we had all of our suitcases stolen from the van during our soundcheck. The gig was being promoted by one Alan Wise, who proved to be a bit of a character. He was a large man in a small trilby hat and a colourful splash of jazzy kipper tie. He had a rather florid manner, which he would utilise to beguile when things were going south. When I happened to complain that there was no washbasin in the dressing room, I was met with a grand theatrical sweep of the arm: 'But this is Bohemia! There's no art without dirt!' He then ambled off and returned with a steel mop bucket. 'There you go, lad, you can use use this!' We decided to bathe back at the hotel.

Mr Wise had also taken Nico under his wing in a managerial capacity. She turned up after soundcheck and requested that she play a song with us. We were elated by this, and Daniel and I went back to the hotel to work out the Velvets' 'I'm Waiting For The Man'. I had to stick my bass in the bathroom sink to amplify it. The performance was recorded, and later released on our *Covers* EP. One thing that got my goat, though, was Peter insisting on singing 'I'm waiting for my girl' in response to Nico's 'man'. This really fucked with the meaning of the song—which is about a junkie waiting for his dealer—and frankly made me cringe. Still, it did not deter Nico from contacting us a few days later to request that Bauhaus perform as her backing band on her next tour—a prospect that we seriously considered for about half an hour, before deciding that it would never work.

The following night we were in Glasgow, at a club called Nitemoves. There was an unruly element in the crowd who did their best to goad Peter, continually hurling harsh, impenetrable utterances, and he simply was not in the mood. As I had already found out, in Peter's hands, the mic stand could become a very dangerous weapon. That evening, it became a bludgeon and a spear, as he laid into the hecklers with violent precision. Skulls were cracked and blood was spilt. The police were called in, and Peter was promptly arrested as soon as he came offstage. He was driven to the station and slung in jail, still wearing his white stage make-up, eyeliner, sheer black body-stocking, tights, and pixie boots. The other rough inmates who shared his cell were apparently too disturbed by this alien presence to start anything. Peter, meanwhile, was quietly terrified. He was arraigned overnight, and he had to be in court first thing the following morning, where he was charged with GBH, convicted, and made to pay a fine.

It was not the first time this had happened. On our first headlining tour the previous year, we were playing at Rafters in Manchester when some idiot in the crowd threw a glass at the stage. It shattered in front of Peter, who then booted the fragments back into the audience. A shard hit some poor unfortunate in the face. Blood flowed, the cops were called, and off to clink went Mr Murphy. His girlfriend, Joanna Woodward, was horrified to receive the news of this latest violent incident. She delivered an ultimatum: cut out the violence or suffer the consequences.

Joanna was in attendance at our next gig, at Nottingham's Rock City. As usual, she was resplendent in little white bobby socks, black patent leather Mary Jane shoes, a white ballerina's tutu, and white lace evening gloves, with various ribbons and bows of a pastel hue tumbling from her big poodle puff of platinum-blonde hair. This ultra-feminine image needs to be borne in mind when considering the scene that follows. During the gig, Peter's mic stand once again morphed into a spear and was rammed with full force into the head of a kid at the front of the stage. There was a sickening explosion of blood, and I can recall shooting a look at Daniel, who had also seen the whole thing. His returned expression said it all: we were horrified.

We came off at the end of the set with the crowd going mad, chanting and banging on the walls, demanding we return for an encore. This rapturous noise continued for ages, as we all let Peter know the extent of our repulsion. Eventually, Harry Isles came in and told us that we had to go back out, as the club feared a riot. After placating these demands, the atmosphere in the narrow dressing room was thick with a dull, heavy silence. Suddenly, the door burst open and in thundered little Joanna. Without saying a word, she promptly kicked Peter in the balls—a storm-trooper-style high kick, delivered with every reserve of strength she could muster.

Murphy collapsed on the floor in agony as Joanna turned sharply on her heels and left, slamming the door behind her. The door was still shaking when Harry opened it again to stick his head in and nervously inform us that the fellow who had been assaulted wished to see his assailant. Surprisingly, Peter agreed—after catching his breath—and the kid was let in. We feared the worst, but ironically, all he wanted was for Peter to sign his blood-splattered Bauhaus T-shirt!

'That was the best gig I've ever seen!' he blurted.

The penultimate show of the tour was at the Hammersmith Palais in London. This night was also notable for the inclusion on the bill of a group of punk-rock street performers called The Beech Buoys, who performed as our special guests. I had caught their act in Edinburgh, where we had played two gigs just prior to the tour, and had spontaneously invited them to open for us. The troupe's leader was Neil Bartlett, who would go on to become an innovative provocateur of avant-garde theatre before receiving an OBE for services to the arts in 2000. As Neil remarked following the show, it was something of a 'baptism by fire', as they were mercilessly heckled and almost bottled off the stage.

The Beech Buoys weren't the only ones to experience violence at this show. As a jape, our lighting engineer Graham had surreptitiously chained and padlocked Kevin's leg to his drum stool, which meant he had to hobble off the stage at the end with the thing still attached. My brother reacted by throwing a cymbal at the prankster. There was blood!

A European tour followed. Annie came over for the Amsterdam

gig, as did Daniel's girlfriend Kate. We were playing once again at the Paradiso. We had a day off beforehand, and I went out in search of wine, bread, and cheese to take back to the hotel to share with my beloved. I stumbled upon a wonderful shop stacked with golden slabs of cheese and told the owner I wanted something very flavourful, aged, and crumbly. He produced a few tasty samples, but not exactly what I had in mind.

Glancing up, I spied something that looked like it could be The One. It was on the very top shelf of the high-ceilinged room. When I asked if I could try it, the man immediately tried to put me off. Maybe he just didn't fancy climbing the ladder. 'No, no,' he said, 'that cheese is extremely strong. Even the locals can't take it.'

Of course, this only wetted my appetite further. Eventually, the shopkeeper acquiesced. It was delicious! I bought a bit too much, however, and there was quite a lot left over, which I was reluctant to throw out. Consequently, I took it on the bus, but this did not go down too well with the rest of band.

'For fuck's sake, David!' Daniel quite rightly exclaimed. 'Get rid of that fucking cheese! It stinks!'

The cheese made it as far as the Vera club in Groningen before I had to concede defeat and throw it out of the window.

The girls, meanwhile, had a narrow escape on their return to the UK. Their car was searched at Dover, but when the men from Customs & Excise went through it, they somehow failed to discover the block of hash stuffed inside a road map in the glove compartment. Driving away, they were convinced that it was all a trap, and that they would soon hit a roadblock that would be the harbinger of their inevitable arrest. Fortunately, this was sheer paranoia, and the mules made it safely home.

* * *

The last dates of the tour took us to Germany, where we performed as support to Echo & The Bunnymen and were reacquainted with my old best friend from my art-school days, a lunatic by the name of Paul Kingsley. He was fearless: a charming rogue who would delight in playing devil's advocate and provocateur. It was as if he had a death wish.

I once entered a pub with Paul in Northampton, which was known back then for containing some of the roughest and most violence-prone drinking establishments in the UK. There was a six-foot-two skinhead standing at the bar, a space around him that spoke of fearful respect. You could practically smell the menace emanating from him. Kingsley strolled up to him and stood very, very close. The skin's shoulders were rising in animal response; you could tell that he was getting ready to swing—to which Kingsley responded by stroking the guy's shaved head.

'What the fack do ya think yer fackin' doin?' the skin intoned, without turning.

'I'm buying you a fuckin' drink, mate!' Kingsley replied.

The skin accepted, and after taking a big gulp, he looked Kingsley in the eye. 'There ain't many blokes what's got the bollocks to do what you just done. I reckon you must be all right, mate. Yeah, you gotta be pretty fakin' tasty, son!'

The skin then struck out with a headbutt, stopping inches in front of Kingley's skull. When Paul failed to flinch, it sealed the deal, and the bomb was defused.

'All right, nice one! Yeah?'

For the rest of the night these two maniacs were the best of pals, slapping each other on the back, making toasts, and cracking off-colour jokes. Only Kingsley could have got away with that.

In 1974, Kingsley would often join me and my band, Jam, on our trips up and down the M1 and M6. He loved to drive and would volunteer to take the wheel of the old blue box van. One occasion, he was driving us up the motorway to Doncaster when he asked our mate-cum-roadie (and sometime piano player), Simon Desborough, to take the wheel, as he felt like getting a bit of fresh air.

We were not sure what Kingsley meant by this, but we soon found out as he clambered out of the window and up onto the roof of the speeding bandwagon. We kept driving as he slithered along the roof and down the back to reappear, teetering on the rear fender, sticking a long leg out and waving at the passing traffic, which was now giving us a very wide berth—and then he was gone. We thought about pulling over to investigate but Simon, who had enough of Kingsley's capers, insisted that we drive on. ('Fuck him!')

When we arrived at the gig, Kingsley was nowhere to be seen. We stayed overnight in digs, and come the morning, we were shocked by the reappearance of Kingsley on the roof of the van. On another occasion, he and I had been down the pub at lunchtime, and were late returning to art school. He was in the driver's seat of my Morris Minor. We were waiting at a red light adjacent to the Racecourse Park.

'Fuck this!' he said, and drove over the pavement, narrowly missing two women out walking with their dogs, before proceeding to tear across the park at full speed. We arrived at the car park just as the bell was sounding. 'I knew we could make it,' he grinned.

On another occasion, however, his antics landed him in very deep shit indeed. He was managing and driving a reggae band called Far-I, which was made up of heavy-duty Rastas who had a large and expensive sound system. After one of their gigs, Kingsley dropped off the band and then kept on driving, and the next day sold the entire lot to a shop on Shaftsbury Avenue, London.[5]

Far-I were out for Kingsley's blood. He had to flee the country, and ended up in Hamburg, Germany. As a result, I had not seen him for years—not until November of 1981, when we came to play at the Markthalle in Hamburg.

I was in my hotel room when all of a sudden I heard a tapping at the window, which was very curious, as I was on the fourth floor. The heavy curtains were drawn, and when I pulled them open, there he was! He had scaled a drainpipe, and was now perched like a hideous giant crow on my window ledge. He was grinning like Mr Punch (to whom he bore an unsettling resemblance) when I carefully let him in.

'You mad bastard!' I exclaimed, as he gave me a wind-expelling bear hug. He came to our gig that night and somehow persuaded the Bunnymen that he was a top barber and that he should cut their hair. Of course, he had never cut hair in his life. His first victim—guitarist Will Sergeant, I believe—ended up with back and sides almost bald and a big candy floss bush sticking up on top. Kingsley had his eyebrows raised, with his head to one side, in anticipation of the reaction as the Bunnyman inspected the damage. I fully expected Will to land a punch on our Edward Scissorhands in the making, but after a drawn out pause, he said: 'I like it! Thanks, mate!' The rest of the band followed suit, and so the Bunnymen Barnet was born.

We all went out for a late supper after the show and sat at a long table in the cellar of a restaurant. Throughout the meal, Kingsley heckled Peter, sending him up something rotten and imitating his basso profundo. Finally, Peter got up, threw down his napkin, and left in disgust.

'That's it lads,' Kingsley announced. 'Looks like I'm your new vocalist!'

'Dave, who is this guy?' Daniel asked. I could only smile weakly and shake my head.

The following night, we had a very welcome day off in Hamburg, so we decided to visit the notorious Reeperbahn red light district. After making a pilgrimage to the Star Club—where The Beatles had cut their teeth, paid their dues, and caught the clap—we took a stroll down this boulevard of broken dreams and bed springs, furtively taking in the lascivious sights. There was a hard-edged brutality to the 'sex for sale' in Hamburg that was different to its counterparts in Amsterdam and London. Lots of whips and black leather.

We ended up in a sleazy subterranean cabaret club. The walls were lined with tacky gold strips, there was a revolving circular stage lit by old vaudeville-style floor lights (several of which were broken), a small mirror ball hung from the black ceiling, and the booths were decked out with red leatherette buttoned seats. We slid into one of these and were immediately joined by two hostesses: a tall, pockmarked brunette and a peroxide blonde with heavily mascara'd zombie eyes. They asked if we would like to buy them a drink. We hesitated for a moment, but then long red-nailed fingers were laid onto skinny leather-clad thighs, and their desired effect was achieved.

'Ya,' we said nervously.

A bottle of cheap champagne materialised suddenly and was downed in a matter of minutes, so a replacement was called for, and then another.

By this time the show had begun. An overweight buxom woman was sprawled over the rotating stage, stumpy legs akimbo. She was wearing a black feather boa, a sad forced smile, and nothing else. She masturbated with bored disinterest using a long pink dildo, and as horrible thin organ muzak played she was joined by a swarthy emaciated individual in a sailor's cap and stinky black socks, their fetid aroma blending with the funk of dead sperm to create a pungent malodour. The sailor then performed reluctant cunnilingus before engaging in a full-on fuck.

Clearly it was long past time to leave, so we asked for the bill. The total came as a jarring shock. *How much?!*

We started to pool our deutschmarks, soon discovering that we had about half the amount owed between the four of us. We questioned the figure, prompting one of the women to cock her head sharply; there, on cue, a monster was made manifest. Bruno was around 300 pounds of muscle, fat, and knuckle, and we were not about to argue with that! The brunette spat something to him in German, the only word of which that I recognised was *arschloch*.

We all looked at each other in the same sick way.

'Let's get the fuck out of here,' Daniel whispered. 'We gotta do a runner!'

Sweeping the ice bucket and empties from the table, we made a dash for the exit, with the livid Bruno in hot pursuit. We were up those steps like four skinny greyhounds released from the trap, and we did not stop sprinting until we were many blocks away. Finally, we found a quiet bar and steadied our nerves with the especially delicious imbibing that only those reprieved from death row can savour.

* * *

The tour ended in Paris—our first time there. Driving into the city at dusk, just as all the street lamps were flickering on, was magical. It had been raining, and the roads were streaked with colours reflected from all the lights.

Daniel and I were sharing a small hotel room in the Latin Quarter. A ridiculous in-joke had sprouted on this tour: variations on a bizarre theme suggesting that Daniel was engaging in sex with dogs. I made some stupid crack along these lines and he snapped, rushed across the room, and grabbed me about the throat in a stranglehold. We collapsed onto the bed and then the floor. He was red with rage and tightening his grip. I managed to wrestle free, but we were still at it when we took the stage at Le Rose Bon Bon several hours later.

The gig was recorded and released as a limited edition 45 entitled 'Satori In Paris'. You can really hear Daniel's venom on 'Hair Of The Dog' (ironically enough). By the end of the gig, the demons had been exorcised, and we all went out to some ritzy nightclub: champagne, DJs, and wall-to-wall supermodels. Vive La France!

Prone to wanderlust and enamoured of Paris, I returned to the City of Light on my own a few months later, and, with Louis Aragon's *Paris Peasant* as my guide, visited a number of surrealist haunts—or what was left of them. I also made a pilgrimage to the legendary Shakespeare & Co bookstore, unearthing many little treasures amid the crumbling alcoves, including works by Artaud, Nerval, Rimbaud, Huymans, and Gautier, among others.

The highlight of the trip was meeting the artist and author Brion Gysin.[6] I had sent him a copy of the René Halkett single, having obtained his address from Genesis P. Orridge, but had not heard back. Trusting in serendipity, I headed over to his apartment building, situated directly opposite the huge Pompidou Centre, in the hope of meeting him in person. I picked up a bottle of cheap red wine on the way and sat on a wooden bench in the large square, taking slugs and staring up at the many windows of the old towering block.

After about twenty minutes I saw a man in a Moroccan djellaba appear on one of the narrow balconies and peer out through a pair of binoculars. Gysin! I had tried to enter the building when I first arrived but it was locked, and there was no intercom. Noticing that someone was about to enter the front door, I seized the opportunity to dash over and slipped in behind him. My heart was pounding as I stood outside the great man's door.

'Yes? Can I help you?'

I told Gysin who I was and mentioned the Halkett disc.

'Oh, I have it on my desk! I haven't been able to play it, though, as I don't have a gramophone. Well, come in. I am very busy preparing for a talk, but I can give you one hour of my time. Please …'

With a gracious wave of his hand I passed over the threshold. Just as he'd said, the Halkett single was sitting on his desk, alongside a great spread of typewritten papers. The apartment was neat and orderly. I pulled up a chair and for the next sixty minutes was royally entertained over mint tea as the raconteur rolled out the anecdotes.

While in Paris with Burroughs in the early 60s, he told me, they had invented the Dream Machine in collaboration with the engineer Ian Sommerville. This was an ingenious cylindrical device with slits cut in it and a light bulb suspended inside that, when mounted on a turntable and rotated at 78 or 45rpm, would create a stroboscopic effect that would induce visions if one closed one's eyes while in close proximity to the device. I noticed one of the machines stuck in the corner of a closet. It turned out to be one of the originals that they had experimented with in the old Beat Hotel, which is where I was staying at the time. The cylinder was made of metal and inscribed on the inside with red calligraphy. I asked if I could 'have a go', only for Gysin to remind about the absence of a record player. He said that I could experience it later, in London, as a special exhibition relating to Burroughs and Gysin was shortly to be held there.[7]

Before I left the apartment, my host showed me some of his extraordinary paintings, which appeared to move the longer one stared at them. I left this urbane gentleman's abode a very satisfied pilgrim.

Coincidently, Beggars Banquet head Martin Mills was in Paris at the same time. He heard that I was there and tracked me down to offer an invitation of dinner. This I accepted, and we met at a charming little restaurant, where we dined al fresco under the stars. Martin had two other guests in tow, both of whom were French: a woman and a man with whom he was doing business.

As Martin chatted with the chap, I entered into something of a romantic tête-à-tête with the lady. We took turns drawing on the paper tablecloth with coloured crayons. I asked her to draw herself, and she produced an image of a lost girl adrift in a vast ocean full of sharks. I took her blue crayon and sketched a little boat, and she in turn, placed the girl on board. I drew a sailor standing next to her, and then a moonlit island, toward which the sailor and the little girl set sail. At the end of the meal she slipped me her phone number, with the whispered exhortation that her husband was away on business. She was very attractive, and I was sorely tempted, but my allegiance to the beauty at home won out as usual. Still, incurable romantic that I am, I held onto that tablecloth for many years to come.

* * *

Nineteen eighty-two was played out, in part, on screen—big screen and small. At the start of the year, we made our TV debut on the arty *Riverside* show. We performed 'Kick In The Eye' and 'Bela' in support of 'Searching For Satori', and the staging was impressive, utilising blue lasers and smoke to create a kind of ethereal tunnel effect in which the band appeared to be standing. Next came a Mask Ball live show at Lings Forum in Northampton, attended by both Daniel's dad and mine—a great rarity. They stayed at the back all night, drinking beer and taking the piss out of the goths, which they continued to do when they came backstage after the show. 'Well, at least you had a good-sized crowd, although most of them look half-dead!' was one comment. 'It was a bit loud! Does it have to be that loud?' was another. It was the last time either would see us play.

This hometown show served as a warm up for a special one-off gig at the Old Vic Theatre in London, which was filmed and later released as a full-length video. The performance also featured some eye-catching staging, with four huge kites painted with impressionistic faces—a concept that my clever missus had dreamed up. The gig was recorded, and several tracks were later released—alongside some songs that were taped on the *Mask* tour—on a disc that was given away with the initial run of our next studio album. The title of this live album, *Press The Eject And Give Me The Tape*, was inspired by something we heard on a confiscated cassette that had been acquired during our show at the Hammersmith Palais the previous year. You can hear the voice of a security guard saying those words just before the unfortunate bootlegger ejects the tape.[8]

Shortly after the Old Vic show, we recorded our second Peel session. By this time we were confident or foolish enough to go into the BBC Maida Vale studio with practically no preparation—just a grab bag of lyrics, the sketch of a couple of chord structures, and a lot of moxie.

'Party Of The First Part' was based around a recording that Kevin had made off the TV. It was taken from a cartoon about some ingénue character who enters into a Faustian pact with the Devil. We flew it in over a soundtrack that we made up on the spot, utilising whatever odd studio instruments were lying around, including a Hammond B3, a Wurlitzer, and an old acoustic piano. We recorded it live, improvising on an appropriately slinky Mephistophelian jazzy jam.

'Departure' featured a primitive loop over which I recorded a walking bassline and Daniel some fine dubbed-out guitar stylings. The surreal spoken word lyric was a Burroughs-esque dovetail job: the first part mine, the second Peter's, and the third Daniel's, with the three of us all mixed up together for the finale. 'The Three Shadows', meanwhile, a dark, haunting, psych-folk number, would point the way toward our next studio album.

In March we received some very exciting news when we were approached by Tony Scott, the director of a new horror film, *The Hunger*, to star David Bowie and Catherine Deneuve as vampires, with Susan Sarandon and a young Ann Magnuson among their victims. Scott had seen us on *Riverside*, and in consultation with Bowie had decided that we would be perfect for the opening scene, set in a nightclub, where the vampires are on the prowl for fresh blood.

The location for this evil seduction was one of our old haunts: Heaven. We were set up with a makeshift dressing area right next to Bowie's. There was an old, vibrantly coloured 50s jukebox there, and at one point I was making some selections when Bowie came out and politely asked if he could pick something. I was not about to say no! He chose 'Grooving With Mister Blow' and then launched into a dance with me nodding along and mentally pinching myself. Listening to this track, I was reminded of 'A New Career In A New Town' from Bowie's brilliant *Low* album. I mentioned this to him, and he smiled behind his blue tinted shades and silently put a finger to his lips.

Bowie was wearing his movie costume, a sharp dark blue shark-skin suit, and I was in the midst of admiring it when Catherine Deneuve sauntered by. I had been besotted with her for years, ever since I had seen her in *Belle de Jour* when I was about thirteen. Now in her forties, the sophisticated actress was still possessed of a jaw-dropping beauty.

'Watcha Cathy!' Mr B. exclaimed, in a broad cockney accent.

'Oh, 'allo David,' the French goddess purred, as she disappeared into her dressing room. This was going to be a good day!

When we came offstage after our first dress rehearsal, Bowie noticed that he and Daniel had on similar footwear, and called out to him, 'Oi! You've got my shoes on!' Daniel was somewhat overawed, but not to the extent of Peter, who avoided being anywhere near his hero out of sheer swooning anxiety. Bowie was actually very personable, and I got the impression that he was relating to us, 'boys in the band', more so than those from the movie world.

At the end of the day, we were hoping to say goodbye to the man but realised he had already left the set. We were feeling rather crestfallen about this when suddenly we heard running footsteps coming down the corridor. It was Bowie!

'Hey, guys, I just wanted to say goodbye. It was a pleasure working with you and I'll try to catch one of your gigs when I can. All the best! See ya!'

We shook hands, and he was off, leaving a glowing nimbus of charismatic energy in his wake. When the film was released, I went to see it in London with Daniel and Kevin. On the way to the cinema we were joking, saying that it will be all Murphy, and the rest of us won't get a look in—well, maybe an elbow and the end of a guitar, which was exactly how it turned out. Still, it was an interesting film, and it has to be said that the first fifteen minutes, in which Bauhaus appear and perform 'Bela Lugosi's Dead', are the most visceral and exciting.[9]

* * *

In April, we travelled to Italy, where the band had developed a fanatical following. We had kids doing a 'Kingsley', scaling the walls of our hotels, trying to peer into our rooms. One time, we gave them an impromptu acoustic performance, singing mock opera from the balcony as they threw roses stolen from the hotel garden.

The first date was in Palermo, Sicily, at the Teatro Dante, which was apparently operated by the Mafia. We were advised by our nervous Italian tour manager, Umberto, not to cause any trouble. We had only played in Italy once before, at a pair of festivals the previous year: one in Modena and the other in the beautiful old city of Bologna, which seemed to be full of equally beautiful women.

It was there that we met 'Red' Ronnie, a music journalist with strong leftist leanings (Bologna being a communist stronghold in those days.) We joined up with him again on our return and he travelled with us on tour to write up his report.

Ronnie was a warm, jovial man, which was exactly the opposite of how I was feeling at the time. I had fallen into something of a blue funk, the constantly overcast weather perfectly reflecting this melancholia, in great part the result of my beginning to seriously question the musical direction the band was taking. I had started to write some new material that did not fit in with Bauhaus, and which, frankly, I wanted to sing myself.[10] I was also becoming increasingly frustrated with Peter's pompous, hubristic attitude—not to mention his paranoia. In the Sicilian coastal town of Messina, I took a long walk along the desolate fog-shrouded beach listening to the Brian Eno's *Before & After Science* on my Sony Walkman—the perfect soundtrack to my melancholic musings.

The tour ended in Rome, where the ghosts of the Coliseum awaited our impudent forced entry. High on Chianti and hashish, we decided to break into the ancient amphitheatre and explore its underground chambers. The place was eerily lit by the full moon, and we felt quite delirious in the midst of all that blood-drenched history. We ran through the caliginous cryptoporticus, laughing hysterically at our own audacity.

'Hey, where's Pete?' Daniel suddenly enquired.

Peter had vanished. Then we heard a spooked cry and ran in the direction of the voice. He had stumbled and fallen, and was lying on his back under a looming scaffolding structure.

'Can you see it? Can you see it, too?'

'See what, Pete?'

'The Cross! The Cross of the Crucifixion!'

'Peter, it's just scaffolding, look! Come on, let's get back to the hotel!'

We helped the poor sod back to his feet and dusted him down before making our way to the outer wall. There was a cascade of dust and rubble as we clambered over the top. The drop was longer than expected, but we all landed safely back out on the street. A police siren cut through the still night air, and we glanced wild-eyed at each other before running off into the nascent dawn.

* * *

We returned to England to play two nights at the venerable Adelphi Theatre in London's West End. We had to negotiate very carefully in order to lock in these concerts, as the hallowed Edwardian building was not accustomed to staging 'rock' events, the management finally conceding only after we had assured them that there would no trouble with our crowd.

Both nights sold out quickly, but we would end up only playing one. As soon as we took the boards, there was a mad rush to the front of the stage. With that, the first three rows of seats—all antique wrought iron, wood, and velvet—were completely destroyed. At one point, an entire seat landed with a great crash on the stage in front of me. The following night's show was promptly cancelled, and our 'spirit' was left waiting in the wings.

The spirit was a concept that recognised the presence of a collective entity—a kind of supportive daemon that could only be evoked if we were all in tune with each other, or at least creating just the right degree of antagonistic frisson. The latter circumstance would result in the manifestation of its negative violent aspect, but better that—with its potential for transcendent exorcism—than a bland performance due to its absence.

This phenomenon was the subject of our next single, 'Spirit', which we recorded at Rockfield Studios in Monmouth, on the border with Wales, using an outside producer for the first time, Hugh Jones. After an exhausting seven days, the single came out sounding a bit too slick for our taste at the time, although listening to it now it really is a finely crafted pop interpretation.

The accompanying video, directed by our old collaborator Chris Collins, really was a disappointment. Our original idea was to have the spirit represented by a balletic male dancer, who would be painted all white. He would appear in semi-transparent form onstage to lift Murphy up and, in reference to one of the lines in the song, 'give him wings'. There would be other symbolic sequences that would subtly reference elemental magick, and at the climax of the video the stage and the band would be engulfed in flames.

What ended up on screen, however, was quite different, and it was somewhat unnerving to arrive at the location to find a bunch of actors dressed in theatrical costume—among them jugglers, clowns, and acrobats—awaiting their scenes. We asked the director what was going on, and he said that he had had an idea, pleading with us to trust him. We had been very pleased with our previous collaboration with Chris, for the 'Mask' video, so we went along with it. Due to touring commitments, however, we were not around for the editing, and when we finally saw the finished thing we were quite horrified. The director had wrongly interpreted the song as being about a bunch of spooks in a haunted theatre. It was corny.

When we told Beggars Banquet that we wanted to redo the film, they said that the budget had been exhausted. We had no other option but to pay for the re-edit out of our own pockets, to which the label agreed. Although we were restricted to working with the available footage, we did piece together something that was preferable to the original cut, but when it came time for the film to be distributed to the video jukeboxes that were popular at the time, the wrong version was sent out.

Our fickle spirit would come and go during the sessions for our next album, during which drug-fuelled paranoia would take a grip as we explored the dark themes of suicide, infanticide, decadence, apocalypse, and damnation. Yes, it's a barrel of laughs with Bauhaus, kids!

CHAPTER FIVE
Decadence

The night sky was ablaze with stars. I had never seen so many. We had just arrived at Rockfield Studios—the same place we had recorded our last single—to start work on our third album. We liked the bucolic environment, and the idea of being entrenched in a residential space was very appealing: we could dig in deep and get serious. A lot of the writing would be done in the studio, too, which was an exciting and challenging prospect.

We had persuaded our old mentor Derek Tompkins to venture out of semi-retirement and 'twiddle the knobs', and his avuncular presence and sense of humour would offer an invaluable counterbalance to the intensity of the sessions. He would rouse us night owls by banging on a conga drum in the courtyard every day.

Presiding over the madness that ensued was the spirit of the nineteenth century symbolist *poète maudit* Isidore Ducasse, aka le Comte de Lautréamont. Peter and I had been consumed by his brilliant prose poems, which told of fantastic savage acts and a desire for burning transcendence at any cost. (We were both twenty-four years old, after all.) On the inner run-off tracks of the vinyl copy of the album is a punning riddle. 'When is a door not a door?' Flip it over to read the answer: 'When it's Ducasse!'

We were held in thrall to the evil comte throughout the sessions, and one time he had us getting drunk on whisky in the wee small hours, which inspired us to rouse the understandably grumpy assistant engineer, Ted Sharp, so that the three of us could all traipse down the hill to the studio to record 'The Three Shadows, Part III', which featured Murphy sawing away on a cello and me on a violin—neither of which were instruments we could play.

Ducasse also had us smoking copious amounts of opiated black tar hashish and drinking champagne at all hours so as to induce a Rimbaudian systematic derangement of the senses. Thank God Derek was there to bring us back down to earth with a slap of sarcastic humour.

The joke was often lost on poor Peter, however. His paranoia—exacerbated by the cannabis—was reaching Kafkaesque extremes. One time, the four of us were about to drive down from our quarters at the top of the hill. Peter was at the wheel. As the rest of us were about to get in, he suddenly tore off at full speed, doors flapping, leaving us sprawled over the dirt track. He carried on driving and did not come back until nightfall. When we asked him what the hell was going on, he said he knew that we were plotting against him.

We felt genuinely concerned for the poor fellow. He was careering off the deep end, but whenever we tried to gather him back into the fold, he would lash out like a frightened cornered animal. One song recorded during these sessions was especially poignant when considered in the light (or dark) of this sad state of affairs. On 'All We Ever Wanted Was Everything', Daniel's lyric evokes nostalgic memories of a time of innocence and naive yearning. Peter sang it beautifully, emoting the bittersweet sentiment so perfectly, every word ringing true.

It was at times like this that we really did pull together, guards were dropped, and the warming fire of friendship was fuelled. The flip side was 'Paranoia, Paranoia', which was born of a dope- and booze-soaked late-night procession up to and through the little house on the hill where we were staying. Daniel, Kevin, and I were chanting, 'Paranoia, paranoia, la-de-da-de-da, paranoia, paranoia, la-de-da-de-da', unaware that Peter was in bed, recoiling in horror beneath the sheets, and thinking that this was a premeditated personal attack. We recorded the whole thing on a little tape recorder as we marched around the house, like a pack of schoolboys gone feral.[1]

'Swing The Heartache' came about after I suggested that we do a version of Scott Walker's chilling 'The Electrician', from The Walker Brothers' *Nite Flights* album. While we were working on it—at Beck Studios in London, just prior to the Rockfield sessions—it mutated into this, an original minimalist-industrial-sounding track. Another track recorded elsewhere was 'Third Uncle', our frenetic homage to Brian Eno, who had been a huge influence on the band ever since his early Roxy days. We had laid this one down at the BBC's Maida Vale studios as part of a Kid Jensen session.

Back at Rockfield, we rerecorded 'Spirit', taking it at a slower pace than the single version. It had an Old English feel that suited the subject matter, and was topped off by my baroque little harpsichord part. 'In The Night' was one of our earliest songs, a pitch-black investigation of self-loathing and suicide. 'The Three Shadows' was a three-part conceptual suite of songs inspired by our old friend Ducasse.

The final track on the record, 'Exquisite Corpse', marked a repeat of the parlour game of the same name that we had previously tried out during the recording of *Mask*, with each of us allotted one minute to do whatever we wanted while the others left the room. Kevin's contribution was particularly inspired: he seized the opportunity to stick a microphone in front of Derek's nose after he had fallen asleep at the mixing desk and recorded his heavy snoring, which he then incorporated this into a reggae-style rhythm track. The final playback of all four pieces was quite spooky, with all the disparate parts falling into place quite perfectly. Daniel had the last word, screaming out the line that would become the album's title: *The Sky's Gone Out*. He also designed the front cover, a black-and-white painting of an image that resembled the Cyclopean eye of a nihilistic god staring down at a doomed human race.

One night, after a session, we decided to consult the I Ching, the ancient Chinese book of changes and divination, whereby one throws three coins six times, with the resulting combinations of heads and tails corresponding to certain hexagrams that relate to particular conditions, prophesy, and advice. We wanted to know if the album we were working on would be a success, but when it came to the throwing of the coins we started to joke around, asking stupid questions and generally acting the goat. The first reading we received was 'Youthful Folly'. We threw again, still taking the piss, and again came the reprimand 'Youthful Folly'. This was somewhat chastening, so we sobered up as we threw the coins a third time. 'Youthful Folly' again! The book of wisdom had finally garnered our spooked respect, and I have abided by its advice ever since.

Another esoteric pursuit at this time was the Christos Phenomenon, a method for inducing an altered state of consciousness that facilitates past-life regression and 'out-of-body' astral travel. I had been reading Gerald Glaskin's book *The Christos Experiment*, which describes the technique in great detail. We would all take it in turns to lie on the floor while the others massaged the soles of both feet and the 'third eye' area in between the eyebrows. The astral traveller would zone out while concentrating on ascension, and would then be guided and asked to describe his experience.

When I tried this, I saw images of nineteenth-century soldiers marching in single file. I felt that I had been one of them: a soldier in the Napoleonic Wars. As this vision dissipated, I saw clouds drifting through the night sky. I passed through them on my way down to the ground, and then I was back outside my house in Northampton. Daniel asked me to ring the doorbell, but I baulked at this as did not want to wake anyone up. It all seemed very real at the time.

Toward the end of the sessions, Daniel and Peter spotted an undertaker polishing an old hearse while visiting the nearby village of Monmouth. It was love at first sight, and we ended up buying the poor old jalopy. After celebrating the purchase of this new Bauhausmobile, Peter decided to take the studio owner's daughter and her girlfriend for a spin down the unlit winding country roads of the Wye Valley. Drunk to the gills, he ended up driving the crate into a ditch.

Despite this incident, and much to the chagrin of our manager, Harry Isles, this clapped-out crate became the band's official touring vehicle. It was constantly breaking down, and over time, many motorists would be entertained and possibly quite disturbed by the sight of four black-clad, corpse-like figures pushing their funereal conveyance down the highways and byways of Great Britain.

* * *

'God help us, now I've seen it all!'

Northampton, 1973. My father has just seen for the first time the silver-dusted image of a naked, androgynous David Bowie that graces the inner gatefold sleeve of his *Aladdin Sane* album, newly acquired and adored by sixteen-year-old me. His distain only added to the deliciously decadent appeal.

'Is it a boy or a girl? Jesus!'

Overnight, acned adolescent shelf-stackers the length and breadth of the British Isles were transformed into fabulous androgynous creatures through the not so deft application of two-tone pantomime make-up. Sadly, the red and blue high-voltage flash that zapped across Bowie's exquisite cocaine-sculptured visage held rather less appeal when smeared onto the lardy mug of some dumpy shop boy in Bradford.

Following fast on the high-rise heels of the call to arms, guitars, and Max Factor that was *Ziggy Stardust*, this latest visual expression of our favourite space invader was something we could never have imagined, but exactly what we desired to see. Bowie had entered some wonderfully weird, schizoid, parallel dimension, and like an interstellar star-man shaman, he had brought back strange dark treasures for the tribe to wonder at and absorb.

When we decided—in an act of both earnest tribute and blatant provocation—to cover Ziggy's theme song, and needed an appropriate image for the record sleeve, I was suddenly struck by that old, electric lightening bolt from '73. Having already cheekily appropriated the original Weimar Bauhaus seal—a highly stylized rendering of a rounded human face—for our own logo, I now had the inspired notion to Bowiefy it by adding the *Aladdin Sane* flash.[2] Something clicked as soon as those two elements came together, and I sensed that we had a hit single on our hands. It was funny; up until that marriage of images, I was unsure about the commercial potential of the track. Later, when we played the song live, we utilised a back projection of the black-and-white face logo, over which the purloined blue and red lightening was superimposed to great effect.

We had recorded a rough version of 'Ziggy Stardust' during the *Mask* sessions. I was not in the studio at the time, but when I came in and heard the tape, the potential for some wicked audacity was immediately apparent. We would later record it as part of a BBC session for David Jensen. This time, we were all on board, and we nailed it to the wall. At the end of the track, you can hear Daniel shout, 'That's the one!' Similarly, at the end of that initial rough recording, Peter can be heard to exclaim, 'That's it! Next single!'

This proved to be prophetic, and the track was released in September of 1982. The accompanying video was directed by Mick Calvert and filmed in the basement of the Roundhouse in Camden, scene of a seminal Ramones gig back in 1976. We invited our followers to turn up and get in on the action—which they did, in their droves. Only the first hundred got in. The video features a caged and savage Murphy, who is eventually released and carried off into the catacomb-like bowels of the building by the black-clad throng.

The single started to move up the charts, as a result of which we were invited to appear on *Top Of The Pops*. We had been brought up on the show—it was on *TOTP* that we had seen and been wowed by Roxy Music performing 'Virginia Plain', Mott The Hoople doing 'All The Young Dudes', T.Rex bumping and grinding to 'Get It On', Slade stomping around to 'Coz I Luv You', Gary Glitter camping it up with 'Rock And Roll', and of course, Bowie himself with his paradigm-shattering rendition of 'Starman'—so it was a big deal for us to be following in those high-heeled footsteps. Despite this sense of reverence, we insisted on a special lighting setup. We told the producers that we did not want any coloured lights—coloured lights are for Christmas trees!—but rather a bank of bright white car headlamps on a vertical rack. To our delight, the producers agreed.

While I was being powdered and preened in the make-up room, I found myself sitting next to the great singer Joe Cocker. The grizzled old Yorkshireman was about to receive the same treatment from the make-up girl, until he cracked, 'I wouldn't bother if I were you, love. It's far too late for that!' We had a little party in the dressing room before we went on, blasting out Bowie, T.Rex, and The Sex Pistols on a boom box and knocking back screwdriver cocktails. We were pretty plastered by the time we got to play. Daniel and I had a last-minute idea to make the performance a bit different and memorable: at the climax of the song, we would leap into the audience. In our drunken state, however, we forgot to mention this to Peter, and he was shocked when Daniel barged into him, knocking him to the floor. It did the trick, though, and the single climbed further up the charts, eventually reaching no. 15. We relished the idea that our forthcoming album, which was loaded with transgressive decadence, would potentially now be bought by all the little girls who had picked up on the band after seeing us on *TOTP*—the innocents exposed to our dark delights!

We followed our *Top Of The Pops* appearance with a two-song set on *The Old Grey Whistle Test* (another long-running and prestigious TV show, but with a far more serious bent). We played 'Spy In The Cab' followed by 'Ziggy'. During the latter, Daniel's guitar kept cutting out, and in frustration he eventually took it off, threw it to the ground, and stormed off. He was steaming mad, but it proved to be another event that helped distinguish our performances from the ordinary. When *The Sky's Gone Out* was released in October, it shot up the national charts to the no. 3 slot. We were elated. A UK tour followed the album's release and saw us playing at the peak of our powers thus far.

* * *

Back in the spring of 1981, *Melody Maker* journalist Steve Sutherland had requested that he join the band on the road in order to write an 'in-depth appreciation of Bauhaus'. Acting very much against our better judgement, we granted permission and let the snake onto the bus. We dropped our guard and opened up to him in the naive hope that the pure intentions of the band would be reflected in ink. Predictably, however, the feature turned out to be a hatchet job.

We exacted our revenge on the *Sky's Gone Out* tour when we invited the perpetrator back for another bout. The location was to be backstage at our show at the Lyceum in London, but when the journalist turned up, we immediately escorted him onto the stage, where five chairs and five microphones on boom stands had been set up in front of the packed house.

A spotlight snapped on, and we took our seats to conduct an interview that was more like a piece of absurdist theatre. To his credit, Mr Sutherland did not back down. After a few desultory and sardonic questions and equally barbed answers, I took it upon myself to close down the proceedings by delivering a pithy statement about how ridiculous the whole interview setup was, and that by presenting it in this way, that point had been well illustrated. I then got up and walked off. The rest of the gang followed, leaving Sutherland shrugging his shoulders amid hissing cat-calls and boos from the crowd. When he finally left the stage, Sutherland approached us with the words, 'Now that that charade is over, when do I get to do the real interview?' Being a rather petulant young man, I immediately stormed out, and was somewhat disappointed then to see that Peter and Daniel actually intended to sit down and answer his questions!

This little set piece was the first of several subversive actions that we laid on the press. We once conducted an interview on closed-circuit TV monitors with a journalist from *Sounds* who was told that we were in another city, when in fact we were in the room next door. It was never written up. When we finally came face to face with our nemesis, Paul Morley from the *NME*, we pulled out a tape machine and pressed 'record' at the same time that he clicked on his own device. This seriously threw him, and I later read that it was this incident that made him rethink his career as a music journalist, and which ultimately resulted in his retirement from writing in favour of launching the ZTT record label.

Our UK tour progressed north, and our old friend Nico made herself manifest at Salford University. She was keen to sing with us again, so we dusted off 'I'm Waiting For The Man', and this time performed it in a more solid rendition than the version that had appeared on the *Covers* EP. After the gig, we repaired back to our hotel with the chanteuse in tow.

As we carried on drinking in the dark, low ceilinged bar, a somewhat inebriated Nico began to trot out a list of her lovers. 'Lou Reed luuuuurved me!' she said. 'Bob Dylan, he luuuuuuurved me! John Cale, Jackson Brown, Jim Morrison, they all luuuuuurved me!' To which she added, 'Peter is a very beautiful boy. Very beautiful.' I believe she had something of a crush!

'Yes,' I concurred, and we ordered some more drinks. She ended up sleeping in the beautiful boy's room that night, although in different beds, according to the object of desire himself. It proved to be the last time we ever saw her.

The following night, we appeared at the Birmingham Odeon, and a full-on riot ensued when we failed to provide an encore. It was an electrifying gig, one of the best that we had ever played, but the crowd were going nuts we had this long established policy that it was more effective to forgo an encore and leave 'em wanting more. Tonight, however, this strategy worked very much against us, and applause very quickly turned to aggro.

As usual, Daniel had been the stoic holdout, with the rest of us keen to go back on.

'Come on, Dan. Listen to that! They're going mad!'

'No, not doing an encore is much more potent!'

'Daniel! Let's go back on and play!'

'No, fuck 'em!'

There was no persuading him, so we escaped out the back of the venue into a waiting getaway van, but by now a large crowd of disgruntled punters appeared from around the corner. They pelted the vehicle with bricks and then climbed on the roof and started hammering down on the metal, which buckled and started to cave in. We had to get down lower and lower until we were all on the floor. The van slowly pushed through the crowd, and we were finally able to get away, although we were still followed by several speeding cars that we eventually managed to out run. Very scary!

After our show at the Royal Court Theatre in Liverpool, we all went out on the town with the writer and artist John Cornelius and the poet Adrian Henri, whom Harry used to tour-manage. Both writers had attended our show. After a bar crawl in search of Retsina, we ended up at a refurbished music hall, formally the State Ballroom but often referred to as the State. The place still had something of the old Palm Court atmosphere about it, and performing that night was the original English surrealist, art expert, writer, lecturer, jazz singer, raconteur, and bon vivant, the great George Melly, whose *Revolt Into Style* had become a favourite of mine after I purloined it from the art school library.

George was an old friend of Adrian's, and he had reserved us a table down the front. We were thoroughly entertained by his spirited and affectionate interpretations of old Bessie Smith numbers and New Orleans bordello jazz, not to mention his resplendent attire of loud red-and-orange plaid suit and broad-brimmed black fedora. After his set, the old dandy joined us at our table. He was rather taken by our appearance, and in that slow, thick plummy voice, he stated, 'Well, you're all very beautiful, I must say!'

George had Daniel pegged as Aubrey Beardsley, and Peter as Dorian Gray ('Do you have a picture in the attic?'). I was a Silver Factory-era Andy Warhol, and Kevin a 1930s matinee idol. He signed a copy of the 'Bela Lugosi' twelve-inch with the words, 'To the beautiful young people of the new Bauhaus with love and admiration from an ageing satyr.' He had previously lived up to this description of himself when a bevy of young women lined up for his autograph. He obliged, the forfeit being a prolonged French kiss with the unctuous old toad. We all looked on in fascinated horror.

Inevitably, more drinks were ordered, champagne to follow the whisky and wine, most of which was consumed by Melly and Henri, with the latter soon rendered legless. (The rest of us were totally out of our depth with these old lions, so we didn't even try to keep up.) As he mumbled lecherously about 'young flesh', George and I carried Henri out to a waiting cab and shoved him in, despite his slurred protestations and entreaty that we 'go on'.

'Come on, you pissed poet,' George slurred, as he slipped in beside his old friend. They disappeared off into the foggy night, Melly waving behind the cab window like the Queen Mother. Our other companion that night, John Cornelius would later capture this 'clash of cultures' in a painting entitled *Champagne Supernova*.

The following evening, we were at the De Montfort hall in Leicester. Peter's older brother Chris and his mates turned up that night, and there was a spontaneous rendering of Irish rebel songs in the hotel bar after the gig. The younger Murphy went along with this beery carousing, but he was secretly embarrassed. An intolerant Daniel took him to task the next day.

'Peter, why do you take part in all that? Fuck the IRA!'

'He's my brother, Dan,' Murphy replied.

The tour ended on a high with a stellar gig at the Hammersmith Palais. We decided to make the show a 'Northampton night' and invited The Jazz Butcher and Saint Anthony's Fire to join the bill. The latter group was led by our old friend Natacha Atlas, who would go on to become a renowned singer of Arabic-influenced music, and a big star on the world stage.

This tour had been unusual for us in that it was broken up into several different legs, with various different acts joining us along the way. Aside from above-mentioned locals, we also had Southern Death Cult (soon to be known as The Cult), Brilliant (whose members included Youth from Killing Joke and Jimmy Cauty, who went on to form The KLF with Bill Drummond), and gothic rockers The Dance Society. Perhaps most challenging for our audience were Incantation, who played traditional South American tribal music, and Amazulu, an all-girl reggae band.

Following the completion of the tour, we filmed an appearance on *The Oxford Road Show* in Manchester. We were scheduled to perform 'Passion Of Lovers' and 'Lagartija Nick', which was slated to be our new single, and as the show was broadcast live, we had to submit our lyrics before the show for approval by the producers. We had decided, though, that we were going to pull a version of the stunt Jimi Hendrix had played on *The Lulu Show* back in 1969, when he has band stopped their hit 'Hey Joe' mid-song and launched instead into a heavy version of Cream's 'Sunshine Of Your Love'. Our idea was to start playing the single and then, halfway through, break into a new song, 'Antonin Artaud', about the surrealist poet, actor, anarchist provocateur, which included a repeated coda of 'Those Indians wank on his bones'. The only trouble was, before we had reached that part of the song, our performance had been faded out, as the show had run over time. Much to our consternation, we also subsequently learned that the producer had superimposed a stupid schlock-horror luminous green skull over our performance.

* * *

We would revisit 'Antonin Artaud' during the winter US tour that followed, staging a performance that, in my book, encapsulated exactly what Bauhaus was all about. We had two nights booked at Cabaret Metro in Chicago, and before the second of these events we did a radio interview during which we requested that audience members bring something percussive with them to the show: anything with which to make a noise, from drum sticks to kitchen utensils.

Half the fans in attendance took us at our word, and the stage was set. We dedicated that December night in 1982 to Artaud and an attempt to raise his spirit through a ritualistic performance. For the first time ever, we opted not to play any music in the dressing room before we went on, as we wanted to meditate on the nature of what was about to take place. We wanted to break through the usual restrictions of a rock gig, where the audience is distinctly separate from the band, and desired instead to attain a state of shared transcendence. Using Artaud's concept of the Theatre of Cruelty as a touchstone, we wanted to shatter conventional perception through a violent, jarring, primitive rite, one that would go beyond 'performance' and become something shamanic, disturbing, and ultimately liberating. (We were, it has to be said, four very intense young men.)

Before we took to the stage, we each stripped to the waist and painted ourselves with white UV-sensitive paint. We came together in a circle of linked arms, breathed deeply, and gripped each other hard. The idea of a set of songs was abandoned in favour of one song only: 'Antonin Artaud'. There is a point in the piece where it moves into a bridge that consists of the repetition of two stabs of one chord, over which the words 'red fix' are sung eight times. Usually, this would last for a few seconds, but that night it was our plan to extend it indefinitely to induce a trance-like state in the audience and ourselves. Frankly, we did not know what would happen, but we wanted to take a leap in the dark.

The crowd were certainly up for it, and were making a right raucous din as we took the stage. When we reached the 'red fix' part, we locked into that jagged angular track and didn't let up for about twenty minutes.

What happened over that period was very interesting. Initially, the crowd reacted with benign amusement that quickly turned to annoyance and irritability, then anger, and finally a sort of tranced-out delirium. It was palpable to us as we played. We lost all sense of time. It was like being on some hallucinogenic drug. Peter poured bottles of water over the drum kit, the strobe was flashing, and there were these slow-motion explosions of liquid coming off the skins as Kevin pounded away. It was very trippy. Finally, we all felt the moment and nodded to Kevin to give the cue (a loud cymbal crash) to go back into the regular structure of the song. It was tight. We all hit the downbeat on the nose and carried on as if nothing unusual had ever happened. It was very effective. We left the stage at the conclusion of the song, but the stage did not leave us for the rest of the night. I was still hearing 'red fix red fix red fix' as I drifted off to dreamland, drunk on Artaud's heady, potent brew.

* * *

An inflatable plastic snowman sat incongruously on a pampered, manicured lawn under the blazing sun. Driving down the long palm tree-lined boulevards, we looked out at the opulent beauty of the houses ironically offset by the 'armed response' signs displayed in every front yard. Manson's legacy. Guns under the sun in Beverly Hills.

It was our first time in Los Angeles, and it could not have been further removed from the monotone grey drizzle of Northampton. 'This place is unreal!' Daniel remarked from the back of the van, and he was right. It was a pastel-coloured candy land populated by pretty girls in summer dresses in December, where topiary animals presided over cacti, and verdant ferns as huge cars rolled over asphalt like big metal sharks. In 1982, we were still close enough to the 60s and 70s for the automobiles to resemble rocket ships and candy flake-painted fairground rides. Everything here was expansive, the cobalt blue sky empty of clouds. They had different rules here.

On my first day in the city, I ventured out for a stroll down the famous Sunset Strip. As I was about to cross the street, a cop called out sternly to me.

'Hey, fella, want me to give you a ticket?'

That morning I had rolled up half a dozen fat joints that were now packed in a tobacco tin in my inside pocket. Paranoia kicked in.

'Eh, sorry? No, not really, uh, why?'

'You were about to cross the road on a red.'

'But there was nothing coming, no cars.'

'You tryin' to be funny?'

'No! Is it against the law? Sorry, I'm from the UK, and we cross the road whenever it's clear.'

'Is that so? Well you ain't in Europe now, buddy! Over here, we call it jaywalking, and yes: it's against the law. I'll let it go this time, but if I catch you doing it again, it'll be a different story, OK?'

'Yes, OK, thank you.'

I smiled weakly, nervously patting the tin through cloth, and slouched back to the Hyatt Hotel.

That night we played the first of a three-night stand at the Roxy on Sunset Boulevard. The shows were all sold out, and there was an excitement in the air. We delivered a storming set, and afterward we sauntered over to the notorious Rainbow Bar & Grill, scene of much rock'n'roll excess and revelry over the years. It was a favourite haunt of all the trashy hair-metal bands of the time, and on that night they were all on self-conscious parade with their disturbing spray-on spandex pants, rat's-nest hair, and chunky spiked jewellery. We sat in a large dark booth and took the piss over tequila and tortilla chips.

All of a sudden a very pretty little Mexican girl slid in beside me. Close. We said hello and I ordered her a drink. This Latino coquette was dressed appealingly in satin, lace, and black leather, with a short ruffle skirt over her fishnet tights and five-inch stilettos. When I got up to leave she slipped her arm through mine and we strolled back to the hotel. The night was soft and balmy, and as we walked we chatted about Tex-Mex music, Hollywood, and herpes. (There was a big scare about the disease at the time, which in retrospect, and in the shadow of AIDS, now seems almost quaint.) She also told me that she was from a very poor neighbourhood in East LA, and that she wanted to get a machine gun to protect herself in the ghetto. Quite a gal!

When we reached the hotel, we sat by the swimming pool, its dreamy underwater lighting throwing mercurial shapes amid the ripples of blue. The party that night was in the roadies' room, and we made it upstairs for a nightcap. I poured two large glasses of tequila as she sashayed onto my knee and into my lap, and suddenly I had a dilemma on my hands.

By now, I had been living with Annie for five years, and I was still head over heels in love. At night I would lie awake in bed, opening and closing my eyes, alternating from left to right to take snapshots of her beauty from different angles. She was also whip smart and funny with it. It was a relationship that was deeply satisfying on every level, and Eros was out of arrows. In a few days' time I would be back in England for Christmas, and Annie would be waiting for me. Did I really want to jeopardise it all with a groupie?

On the other hand, God, this girl was gorgeous! I poured myself another stiff one, stupidly trying to drink the problem away. The girl rubbed her slim thighs together, rustling with electric sex. She stuck her tongue deep into my ear and started to whisper: 'I'll let you into a secret. I'm shaved down there, like the Indian women. I think you'll like it.'

Steeling myself, I took a quick mental cold shower and told her that I would book her a cab so that she could get home.

'No!' she cried. 'Don't send me back there, please let me stay with you. Please!'

I told her to wait for me for a moment, as I needed to go down to reception for something. They had one room left. I booked it for the girl. When I returned to the party room, she walked over to me and threw her arms around my neck. I led her to the door and we walked out into the corridor. I took her to her room and explained what I had done. She gave me the saddest puppy-dog look as I put the key in the lock. I held the door open for her but she grabbed a hold of my arm and held on tight. I attempted to manoeuvre her over the threshold and leave her inside but she had me gripped like one those Chinese trick puzzle tubes.

'Let me be a bad girl,' she said. 'I want to be bad!'

She pulled my arm and we stumbled and landed on the mattress. I was on my back, she on top. There was a still beat and then we kissed. She unbuckled my belt as I slid my hand down her panties, to the promised smooth glide. Then came more pillow talk whispers, this time in Spanish. I had no idea what she was saying, but the words sounded beautiful as they rolled off her hot little darting tongue. Images of Annie crashed into my mind. *What if this chica has herpes—or worse?* I thought. Five days and I would be home. Five fuckin' days!

'I'm sorry,' I said, 'but I can't do this.'

'*What?!*'

'I can't do this, sorry.'

'Why? Am I ugly? Do you find my body ugly?'

I looked down at her oh-so-pretty face and pert little breasts and shook my head.

'No! Not at all. I think that you are very beautiful, but I just can't do this. I have a girl back home. I'm sorry.'

I hauled myself up and off the bed and hurried back to my own room, buckling my belt as I went. I was turning the key in the lock when the dishevelled girl suddenly appeared at the end of the corridor and started to run toward me. I slipped inside the room just in time, only for her to start pounding on the door with her little fists.

'*Bastardo! Cabron! Let me in, you bastard!*'

I buried my head in the pillow. The pounding continued, accompanied by kicks and cursing in Spanish. Then the phone rang. I snatched it from the cradle and snapped.

'*Yes? Who is it?*'

It was Annie. She asked me if everything was OK, and I told her that I had a situation that I was dealing with. Of course, this worried her.

'What's wrong? Is everything OK? What's going on?'

I said that I would explain later, told her that I missed her very much, that I loved her, that I was really looking forward to seeing her in a few days' time. She was not quite placated, but we said our soft goodbyes and I put down the receiver. The banging had abated. I looked through the fisheye and my little lady of the night had gone.

The next day, I heard from the roadies that she had returned to their room, stripped naked, and was wandering up and down in the half-light, driving them all crazy. Eventually, she lay down next to one of the crew and his lady friend. He said that she kept them awake all night by talking to herself in Spanish, and that he noticed that she had track marks up her left arm.

She turned up again backstage the following night. She had her hair tied back, which made her ears stick out in the most alluring way. (Hold on, Haskins! Not again!) She came up to me with that same sad puppy dog look in her huge brown eyes.

'I'm so sorry about last night,' she said. 'I misbehaved. I told my girlfriend what happened, and she couldn't believe that there were still men like you. You were a gentleman, and I'm sorry.'

I held her gently and kissed her softly on the lips. She smelled of cigarettes and jasmine. She smiled sadly as I turned and left for the street. I never saw her again.

The tour concluded with two dates in San Francisco, the first at the Old Waldorf Theatre, the second an 'evening with' type affair at Berkley Square. Jonathan Richman was in town to play an early solo show that same night. I managed to catch his set just before dashing back across town for my own. His performance had a profound effect on me. He was singing off the mic for much of it, and he had his old semi-acoustic turned down low. It was so minimal and pure. It all added up to a most engaging, intimate, and poignant experience, and it seemed a million miles away from the bombast and high-volume aggression of Bauhaus. I was knocked somewhat off my guard by this, and have to admit that my heart was not in it when it came to my own gig.

I had some serious thinking to do. Was *quiet* the new black?

* * *

The last thing we did in 1982 was sign a deal with A&M Records in America. The first single we released on our new stateside label was 'Lagartija Nick'—a colloquial Spanish name for the Devil—and we had a devil of a time getting it right. In fact, we were going through something of a dry spell (a situation that was not helped by my Bay Area epiphany), and this track was the result of cobbling together the music from one of our earliest songs, 'Bite My Hip', with a new lyric that vaguely addressed sadomasochistic sex. It was all pretty weak and hardly the barnstormer that we needed to follow up on the success of 'Ziggy'. We were asked to appear on *Top Of The Pops* again, though, and before the show, the producer nervously approached us to request that we not repeat the antics of our last performance.

'Sure,' we said. 'No problem.'

We'd lied, of course, and at the end of the song once again dived into the audience. This time Peter, resplendent in a very camp black-and-white sequined toreador outfit, was in on the stunt and came out unscathed, although I did bash some poor chap on the head with the end of my bass. The producer was enraged and threw a hissy fit. 'This band will never appear on the BBC again! That's the last time they'll ever be on this show!'

Three months later, however, we would be back, this time to perform 'She's In Parties'. This was more like it! It was one of our best songs. I had recently had a new bass custom made in the shape of a coffin. (How could I not?) The best thing about it was a unique pickup that made for a lovely deeper-than-deep dub-bass sound, which I employed on the song's extended coda.

'She's In Parties' would appear on our next album, *Burning From The Inside*. We had booked Rockfield Studios again, and were all set to record when Peter fell ill with viral pneumonia. Daniel, Kevin, and I visited him in hospital, and although he was deathly pale, he seemed to be in pretty good spirits. We asked him what he wanted to do about the sessions, and he enthusiastically encouraged us to go in and start without him.

In retrospect, however, I can now see that this rather over-the-top enthusiasm was probably a mask for his real feelings, which were quite the opposite. I have seen this many times, sometimes while working with him in the studio, and so, with hindsight, it does give one pause. At the time, however, we took him at face value, and made the long trip to south Wales.

For this, our forth studio album, Derek Tompkins was once again at the controls, and we would take great delight in his stimulating 'outside the box' philosophising and decidedly politically incorrect conversation.

116 • David J. Haskins

This kind of talk would rub Peter up the wrong way, though, so it was a lot easier to engage with Derek when Peter wasn't around.

Daniel and I were smoking copious amounts of cannabis at this time, and on one occasion we were sitting in Derek's car, skinning up and listening to The Beatles at their most psychedelic (always a favourite activity). So lost in our stoned reverie were we that we managed to set fire to the carpet in the front of the vehicle, an incident that inspired the title 'Derek's Car (Burning From The Inside)'. The 'Derek's Car' bit was eventually dropped but the rest remained.

These early sessions were a joy. In Peter's absence we felt a new freedom, a different kind of chemistry at work. Daniel and I hit our writing stride and the ideas flowed. Sadly, by now Peter had become so paranoid that a dark pall would be cast every time he was around. Having said that, we still respected him as the great singer that he was, and in that capacity we were looking forward to having him back. We started to record several instrumental tracks, with the aim that Peter would add his vocals on his return, although in the case of two new songs, 'Slice Of Life' and 'Who Killed Mister Moonlight', the lead vocals are Daniel's and mine, respectively.

'Mister Moonlight' was a surrealistic ballad inspired in part by the murder of John Lennon. Later on, the enigmatic character of Mister Moonlight took on a symbolic meaning and was seen (by the band) as being representative of the dreamy, poetic aspect of Bauhaus. My vocal was originally intended as a guide, the idea being that Peter would come in and sing the finished thing later on, but everyone liked it, and it was suggested that it should be the final vocal take. I didn't argue.

When the recovering singer finally showed up, the atmosphere was very strained. He was not pleased that Daniel and I had recorded lead vocals on two of the tracks. 'What am I going to do if we play these live,' he asked, 'bash away on a bloody tambourine?' The old paranoia was still very much intact. Sometimes he would be outside the mixing room while the rest of us were having a laugh about something or other, entirely unconnected with Peter Murphy. He would open the door just as we were cracking up and then immediately slam it shut before leaving for the rest of the day, having erroneously assumed that he was the butt of the joke.

Peter's paranoia and ill health did not affect his performance, however. He sounded in better voice than ever. 'Antonin Artaud' finally made it onto tape along with the sinister-sounding 'King Volcano', a Daniel-led number that conjured up visions of a torch-lit pagan cortege, like something out of *The Wicker Man*. 'Honeymoon Croon' was another excursion through the underbelly of London life, and 'Kingdom's Coming' a kind of existential blues. So too the title track, 'Burning From The Inside', which featured Daniel's repetitive monster-funk riff.

Peter added some great backing vocals to 'Mister Moonlight', but they were mixed too low. We were going for an ethereal effect, but in retrospect it is too subtle. The final track on the album, 'Hope', was the last thing we recorded, and as the two-inch tape rolled and we all played together at the same time—with Peter on electric guitar—I can remember thinking, *This is it. This is the end of the band.* Given the title and mood of the track, it was a very poignant five minutes.

One of the strongest cuts we recorded never made it onto the album. 'Sanity Assassin' was a blistering rocker, which at the time was the problem. We were always keen not to be a traditional 'rock' band, and we would go to great pains to avoid that well-trodden road. 'Assassin' had 'rock' written all the way through it, like the name of a seaside resort through that other kind of edible rock, and consequently stayed in the can.

When Beggars boss Martin Mills came to listen to the final playback of the album, 'Assassin' was still on the end of the tape. 'Well that's the next single!' he beamed. 'That's great! It should be the first track on the album as well!'

When we broke the news that we had decided to scrap it, Martin thought that we were joking. Eventually, he could tell from our unsmiling faces that we were serious, and he resumed his laughter, but this time out of nervous incomprehension, as opposed to joy with dollar signs on top. Hearing the song again, many years later, it struck me as ironic that our own sanity had been assassinated. The fucker does indeed rock, and there's Nothing. Wrong. With. That. 'Assassin' was eventually released as

118 • David J. Haskins

one side of a free seven-inch disc, backed with an impromptu cover of Norman Greenbaum's 'Spirit In The Sky' and limited to 325 copies, that was given away to members of our fan club. It was also included on the *Bauhaus 1979–1983* compilation. (Years later, the original vinyl edition would sell for big yen in Japan.)

Our final video was shot by the acclaimed British commercial filmmaker Howard Guard. He had directed the TV ad for Maxell tape that featured an elegantly attired Murphy being blasted by the superior sound quality of Maxell while seated in a leather armchair. Guard's award-winning productions were noted for their slick, high-end glamour and sophisticated wit. The video for 'She's In Parties' followed along these lines and was a beautifully photographed little promo. There was a disturbing tension apparent on the set, however, which was exacerbated by the presence of Peter's choreographer girlfriend and future wife Beyhan Foulkes, who insisted on coaching him through various modern dance moves, which the rest of us regarded as a bit silly and pretentious. Beyhan is a lovely lady but this really did go against the grain. ('Be a cat, Peter! Be a cat!') Peter and I were also besotted with Guard's beautiful personal assistant, Maxine, and our competition for her haughty attention added more fuel to the fire.

In spite of all the friction, we embarked on a promotional tour of Europe and the Far East, which kicked off in Paris and wound through Athens, Tel Aviv, Hong Kong, Tokyo, and Osaka. We had also booked dates in Delhi and Bangkok, but both were cancelled due to lack of organisation on the local promoter's end. The club in Bangkok lost its license while we were en route, so we still ended up going and spent three days in a beautiful old colonial style hotel as well as visiting several Buddhist temples.

Annie was riding shotgun on this tour, which was a rarity, but we all knew that the band was essentially over, and that we might never get another chance to visit these exotic locales. One day, she, Kevin, Plug, and I entered one of these sacred sites through the wrong entrance, and we suddenly found ourselves tramping across a raised platform full of seated chanting monks. Later on, Annie and I ventured out into the muggy night in search of local cuisine. I dined adventurously on curry laced with silver. As we were leaving the restaurant, we were approached by two sleazy-looking individuals who wanted to cart me off to the red light district. A tug of war ensued, despite my protestations, with these two characters pulling on my left arm while Annie held on to my right with every ounce of strength she could muster.

It was a good thing we didn't have a gig to play, as my exotic curry proved to be poisonous, and I was reduced to a trembling physical wreck, crawling around on the bathroom floor for the rest of the night and the following morning. I felt like I was going to die. When I was finally able to stand, I went down to the local pharmacy to find a cure, and after miming my malady, much to the confusion of the staff, I was eventually presented with a huge bag of random mixed drugs. God knows what was in this 'lucky dip'—everything from steroids, barbiturates, antibiotics, and crack, I shouldn't wonder. I passed on this drastic measure in favour of soldiering on. By the third day, I was feeling sufficiently recovered to make it down to the beautiful shaded pool area, where I found Murphy informing all and sundry how 'someone—must have been a fan—actually climbed up the side of the building, let themselves into my room, and sprinkled rose petals all over my bed out of adoration!' When he was informed that the 'fan' was the maid, and that all of us had been exalted in similar fashion, he was a little crestfallen.

In Athens, we had a full-scale riot on our hands when the Sporting Stadium was invaded by a mob of vicious skinheads. They were down the front, heckling us and making the old razor-throat gesture, and as ever Daniel and Peter responded with sarcastic blown kisses, which of course drove the thugs wild. At one point, Annie was standing by the mixing desk when a hail of missiles came raining down. Then some poor unfortunate was clubbed to the ground in front of her, and the crowd surged forward. Plug strongly advised her to lie on the floor. She dutifully obeyed and remained there for the rest of the gig.

Afterward, we were driven to a restaurant in the hills. This took forever, despite the location being only a couple of miles from the hotel. When we enquired as to why it had taken so long, we were informed that the driver had decided to take the 'scenic route'. The fact that it was the middle of the night and pitch black outside did not seem to figure. We then sat at an outside table in the freezing cold and endured another long wait until the nosh arrived. At the end of this protracted meal we were all pretty much shattered but the promoters insisted that we make one more stop-off on our way back to the hotel. Reluctantly, we conceded, and were taken to a nightclub, where a recording of fanfares blared from the PA as we were led through the parted crowd. We just wanted a quiet drink, but instead were led up onto a stage with a long desk and four seats. It soon transpired that they wanted us to judge a wet T-shirt contest.

'Fuck it!' we thought, as we decided to go along with the whole bizarre circus. As the pride of sodden local womanhood was paraded before us, we took the piss something rotten, marking the contestants with scores of minus 1,000 and the like. This apparently enraged the girls' proud boyfriends, and once the debacle was over, they tried to pick a fight with us, swearing in Greek and spitting as we left the stage. Annie, Kevin, Peter, and I decided to split straight away but Daniel and Graham stayed on. The inevitable brawl ensued, the slighted boyfriends intent on revenge. Our cohorts managed to slide out from underneath a large mound of grappling bodies and away into the night, only slightly scathed.

Tel Aviv felt like a war zone, with soldiers armed with machine guns patrolling the streets. National service was compulsory there, and I will never forget the image of the beach at midday break time, strewn as it was with female soldiers sun-bathing in bikinis, each one lying beside a neat pile of camouflage and khaki, their machine guns stuck barrel-end down in the sand. On our second night there, we all went down to the shore, and Annie and I skinny-dipped in the ocean under the stars. (The incident seemed to cause Peter some unusually prudish concern: 'But Ann, you're not wearing any clothes!')

The flight into Hong Kong was thrilling—verging on terrifying—as we dipped between tower blocks so close that you could see the occupants and even their TV screens. The city put me in mind of *Blade Runner*, a frantic, steaming megatropolis lit by hot garish neon, hissing in the clammy heat. On our first night there, the promoter took us out to dinner. The menu was in Cantonese, so we had no idea what we were ordering. We all sat around a huge round table, and when the lid on a vast silver platter was lifted, we gasped in horror as a large bird's head bobbed up and down in a simmering lake of broth, its beady black eyes starring accusingly at us all.

Arriving in Japan felt like going fifteen years into the future and a thousand years into the past at the same time. The technology evident on the streets of Tokyo was wildly futuristic, and everything was faster and smaller, while the people seemed to display an odd collision of individuality and drone mentality. When we appeared at Shibuya Kokaido Kabuki Theatre, the conservatively attired audience was so respectful that it was downright disconcerting. In this country where honour and protocol are everything, it is considered extremely bad manners for somebody (an audience member) to make a sound while another is having his say (or playing a song), so a stony silence falls like a thrown blanket as soon as the first note is played. Once the song is over, there is a flurry of polite applause, which stops on a dime and is immediately followed by that same awful, air-sucking silence.

We were booked to play a matinee performance as well as an evening show and after completing the initial set, we were told that the authorities had apparently announced over the PA that it was forbidden for anyone to dance. Well, we would just have to see about that! The first thing that we did upon taking the stage for the second show was to make a counter-announcement that we would be actively encouraging dancing. The poor kids were obviously very nervous about this: they desperately wanted to comply with our wishes for their own liberation, but they were shit-scared of the uniformed fascists patrolling the aisles. Very gradually, they braved the retribution of the guards, and more and more of them stood up in defiance and danced. It was a beautiful thing, and it forever endeared those sweet Japanese fans to me.

Back at the hotel, we would discover many of them hiding in the neatly trimmed bushes that were dotted here and there throughout the lobby. It was hilarious to see their little heads peer up over the topiary.

They would giggle, cover their mouths with their hands, and sink back down and out of sight. They looked like moving targets at a fairground rifle range. The concierge would be constantly shooing them away and out of the front doors, only to have them sneak back in, stifling their mirth as they went. Before we drove to the show for the soundcheck, our singer, in an outrageous display of egotism, decided that instead of joining the rest of us in the bus, he would stroll to the theatre while Graham filmed the event. 'What a fuckin' prat!' Daniel remarked, and there was no one on board who could disagree as Murphy, dressed to kill in a powder-blue suit and white shirt, strutted and preened through the adoring, incredulous throng.

Later, on an excursion to the ancient city of Kyoto, we four band members along with tour manager Harry Isles nearly ended up stranded on a mountain. We had gone to visit a renowned beauty spot that was only accessible by sky cart. On one of the high peaks there was a bizarre museum of gaming machines housed in a circular lighthouse-like building. On the rotating top floor, one could sit on a wooden bench and gaze out at the revolving view while munching on tentacular dried seafood and sipping delicious cold Japanese beer. Muzak versions of mountain-themed songs played continually through a tinny speaker system. So lost in all this were we that we missed the last call for the sky car and had to run like the clappers once we realised the time. We just made it.

Our international trek ended at the impressive Mainichi Hall in Osaka. We then had a few days off before we embarked on a twenty-date jaunt around the UK. Peter wanted to do something different on this tour. He had been getting into modern dance under the guidance of his partner, Beyhan, and his idea was to do an interpretive dance with a female dancer as we performed the song 'Hollow Hills'. He showed us some of the moves, which were greeted with horrified silence. We had to be honest and tell him that it looked really pretentious and that he would be laughed off the stage. He took great umbrage at this, accusing us of being philistines, and a blazing row ensued.

This was just one of many issues pulling the band apart, and as usual the old ego came into play. Daniel and I were both keen to perform the two album tracks that we had sung lead vocals on.

'I might as well stay at home then!' Peter remarked.

'Come on, Pete!' Daniel reasoned. 'You can just take a break, and then it will be really potent when you come back on.'

The look that Peter shot him in response would best be described as withering. He had a point, though, and to break up the set like that would have been counterproductive, as it would deny him his natural ability to build the momentum of a theatrical performance. We conceded defeat on that one, but still, the damage had been done, and the tour was very hard graft.

Halfway through the trip we lost our reluctant roadie, Glenn Campling. Following a show at the De Montfort Hall in Leicester, the road crew wanted to make a speedy load-out, as they had a long drive to Liverpool for the next gig, but this desire was impeded by the procrastinating Glenn. His attitude was that being a roadie was beneath him. We had put up with this behaviour for long enough, and when Harry chastised him for not pulling his weight, Glenn reacted in anger.

'Don't talk to me like I'm an arsehole!' he said.

'You *are* an arsehole, Glenn,' Harry replied.

The little fellow reacted by punching Harry square on the jaw, and it was a measure of our manager's self-control that he did not retaliate in kind. Needless to say, marching orders were duly issued.

There were also many altercations between the band, both onstage and off, and by the time we reached London, for the final two dates at the Hammersmith Palais, it was all-out war. The general mood was one of spiralling into a black pit of depression. After the first night's gig we decided to have a serious discussion about the future of the band. This took place back at our hotel, and it ended with flung crimping irons and slammed doors. The writing was well and truly on the wall.

Immediately following the last date, on July 5, we were scheduled to feature on a high-profile TV show called *The Switch*, and we also had an interview booked with BBC radio DJ David 'Kid' Jensen, but much to the chagrin of our record label, we decided to cancel both. The day before the last gig, it was obvious that it would indeed be the final show. We tipped the wink to Millie, and the hard-core fans were out in force. Also evident were some faces that we hadn't seen in many years, including our original wide-boy would-be manager, Michael Mason, who crawled out of the woodwork with the intention of staking his claim in the future of the band. (Ironic, that one!)

By the time we took the stage, the atmosphere was really fired up. We played our hearts out and did an extended encore, pulling out every old hit from the hat. Before leaving the stage for the last time, I uttered 'R.I.P.' into the mic, and that was that.

At the end of the night I stood on a shady balcony and watched sadly as the audience filed out. There is something about a gig after everyone has gone. A palpable atmospheric charge that hangs in the thick air above all the detritus on the floor. The roadies start to haul out the cases, and that energy slowly dissipates as the real hard work begins. That night it stayed a little longer, and was tinged with blue.

CHAPTER SIX
Sigil

I have always been a bookworm, and while ensconced in the country for the *Burning* sessions, I had my nose stuck in many a book, several of which were by or about William S. Burroughs. Among those in the pile was a copy of V. Vale's *ReSearch #4/5*, which featured interesting articles and interviews with Burroughs, Brion Gysin, and Genesis P. Orridge. One subject that was germane to all three was magick (Aleister Crowley's spelling, to distinguish the serious stuff from that which deals with cards up sleeves and rabbits pulled from hats.) In one of the articles, Genesis talks about sigils—an occult technique whereby one writes down a desire in very simple direct language. Any letters that are repeated are used to form a symbol that represents the desire. The sigil is then 'charged' by concentrating on it and visualising it as glowing brighter and brighter while focusing one's will on the intention and sending it out into the universe. The original is then burnt, and it is then necessary to forget all about it. I decided to give it a shot.

My desire was to meet William Burroughs. Six months later, much to my delight, I received an invitation from the young promoter Elliott Lefko to appear as part of the bill at an event to celebrate Mr Burroughs's seventieth birthday, to be held at the Danforth Music Hall in Toronto, Canada on October 11 1983.[1] Also on the bill were poets Jim Carrol and John Giorno. I decided to take along with me my old friend, saxophonist Alex Green, who was also a Wild Bill aficionado.

The day before the big event, we were invited to join Burroughs and the rest of the bill at the grand Hotel Victoria for drinks in his suite.

Before heading over, Alex and I decided to light up a couple of joints. We had acquired a bag of extremely potent grass, and by the time we arrived at the Victoria we were higher than NASA. John Giorno came to the door and warmly welcomed us inside. Burroughs was holding court as John ushered us to our chairs. Everyone sat in a big circle, and a bottle of Johnny Walker was being passed around—this having been purloined by young Lefko from his mother's cocktail cabinet, due to the fact that there was no room service or mini-bar.

Alex and I were almost catatonic with nerves, and when Burroughs addressed me personally, the ice in my drink was chinking from the shakes. He asked me what I did, and trying to be clever (but failing), I came out with a line Bob Dylan had once used in an interview: 'I'm a song and dance man!'

'Really?' Burroughs enquired.

'No, I'm just being daft. Uh, music … words and music. I sing, play a bit of guitar, and this is Alex, who's the real musician, on sax.'

Burroughs's face creased up in that forced, tight smile. 'Well, welcome aboard gentlemen. Now, where's the vodka?'

On show day, the writer Terry Southern turned up backstage. He linked arms with Burroughs and me and tried to get us to do a high-kicking chorus line routine. Bill whined his protests while half-heartedly swinging his cane. Before he went onstage to read, Burroughs wandered into my dressing room with a joint, which we then shared. Magick: the shit works, as they say!

* * *

As soon as the Toronto event had been confirmed, I set up two other gigs to help pay the way, one in Philadelphia and another at our old stomping ground, Danceteria in New York City. Alex and I took the Greyhound bus south, and the long night ride was made more interesting when I foolishly decided to enter into a game of three-card Monte with some travelling mountebank. Of course, the trickster let me win the first couple of times, but then our show fee started to dwindle as I failed repeatedly to spot 'the lady'. Alex was horrified. He covered his eyes and sank down low in his seat.

We took a break from the game at a pit stop, and I entered into conversation with the holder of our cash. I told him of our adventure so far, cracked a few self-deprecating one-liners and shared my hip flask. He said that he was a professional gambler, a 'rounder', travelling the country in search of high-stakes games. Great! He then asked if I would like to continue with the game. When I declined, he insisted that to carry on would be a 'Very. Good. Idea.' Alex was practically in tears at this point, but there was something in the old card-shark's tone—almost like a conspiratorial wink that pulled me in. This time I kept on calling it right and very soon had practically all of the Canadian moola back. It was obvious that he had let me win. Maybe there was a soft heart under his hard shell, maybe it was the hip flask, but I was certainly very glad to get out of it with greenbacks back in the bank.

Arriving in Manhattan, we grabbed a cab and headed over to the East Village, where we would be staying with friends of Alex's Swedish girlfriend. It was around 3am, and the terrain grew increasingly more sketchy as we drove into Alphabet City. Dope-peddling gangs huddled and hustled on street corners amid slow-cruising cars and vehicles on fire. When we arrived at our destination, the driver refused to accept Canadian money, so we had to borrow the fare from our sleepy hosts. It was an inauspicious introduction, but the girls proved to be most gracious, and we spent the next few days sharing their neat vodka and hamburger meat, dropped off by a friend who worked in a meatpacking place on Hudson. In a respectfully chaste arrangement, Alex and I also shared the lower cot of a bunk-bed setup, with the two gals doing likewise up top. Every morning, I would be woken by the flash of Alex's zippo as he lit up the first of the day and then smoked it in bed. We had both caught the flu, and we shared a terrible hacking cough as well. It was very romantic.

There was a good-sized crowd at Danceteria, but it was obvious after the first couple of songs that they had come expecting something in the vein of Bauhaus, not minimalist guitar and smoky sax. Predictable really. We soldiered on amid the rising chatter. Philly followed: we played in a cowboy bar and stayed in a punk-rock house, and that's about the gist of it. The old black guy who drove us back to the airport was intrigued by my apparel.

'You gots ta be an artist, man!'

'Why do you say that?'

'Well, it's very unusual to have a black tie and a black shirt all together like that! Yeah, you gots ta be an artist! Ha ha!'

Back in New York City, I ventured down to the Pyramid Club, a great little dive on Avenue A. It was part of a very vibrant scene populated by outré performance artists, drag queens, gays, beautiful Bohemian girls, and general misfits. The DJ was slamming down proto-electronic dance music, which sounded very fresh and exciting. I enquired after one record that had really made an impression on me. It was a pre-release cut of George Krantz' 'Trommeltanz (Din Da Da)'. I asked the girl running the show if she would be into having me play an impromptu gig there the next night. She was a Bauhaus fan and was enthusiastic about the idea. It was on!

Alex was late. I was waiting for him at the apartment after he had gone out on the town with Ruth Polsky, the personable booker for Danceteria. It was our last night in New York. I decided to give it ten more minutes, and if he didn't show, fuck it! I would do it solo. I was on my way out of the door when the AWOL saxophonist appeared, pissed to the gills. Despite this, he played a blinder—in fact, we were both totally 'on', and the crowd was much more receptive this time.

By the end of the night I was as drunk as my partner. After the set, I was packing up the cables when my left hand suddenly became wet. Very wet. Blood! A sliver of broken glass had sliced deep through my palm.

'Jesus!' exclaimed Alex. I was so drunk that I hadn't felt a thing.

On the flight back to London, I took out the roach that Burroughs had left with me. It was my only souvenir. (I had not wanted to bother him with a photo—something I have kicked myself over ever since!)

Turning the flaking marijuana stub over in my hand, I wondered about the effectiveness of magick. Not that I realised it at the time, but I was standing at the threshold of Chapel Perilous,[2] and about to plunge head first into the abyss of the Black Lodge. Things were about to get very strange indeed.

PART TWO
Alchemy
1984–2004

Through the darkness of future past
The magician longs to see
One chants out between two worlds
Fire walk with me
David Lynch and Mark Frost, *Twin Peaks*

Magick is the science and art of causing
change in conformity with Will.
Aleister Crowley, *Magick, Liber ABA (Book 4)*

Once more you hover near me, forms and faces
Seen long ago with troubled youthful gaze
And shall I this time hold you, draw the traces,
Fugitive still, of those enchanted days?
You closer press then take your chosen places
Command me, rising from the murk and haze,
Deep stirs my heart, awakened, touched to song,
As from a spell that flashes from your throng
Wolfgang von Goethe, *Faust*

CHAPTER SEVEN
New Directions

Once the dust had settled, following the band's last stand at the Hammersmith Palais, we split into three factions. Daniel, Kevin, and the former reluctant roadie Glenn Campling went off to pursue the spliffed-up otherworldly dub-pop of Tones On Tail, Peter joined up with Mick Karn from the band Japan in an interesting but beleaguered project called Dali's Car, and I finished my solo debut, *Etiquette Of Violence*.[1]

I had been slipping away to work on this album since early 1983. It was recorded back at Beck Studios, with Uncle Derek engineering. It was my secret garden hidden away behind the perimeter wall, full of exotic night-blooming flowers, crumbling statuary, mossy follies, and thorns among the roses. I played most of it myself but was helped out with beautiful contributions from Alex Green on sax, my brother Kevin on drums, and Annie on backing vocals.

I followed *Etiquette* with an album called *Crocodile Tears And The Velvet Cosh*, released on Glass Records in 1985. Glass was also the home to The Jazz Butcher, aka Pat Fish, a brilliantly witty songwriter in the classic Ray Davis mould, but more off-kilter. I had gone to check out this local talent when he was playing with the gifted guitarist Max Eider in the back room of a pub in Northampton and was sufficiently impressed that I offered my humble services as a producer. They accepted, and I also ended up joining them as full-time bassist, alongside Owen Jones on drums, in The Jazz Butcher Group. Together, we recorded two albums and travelled across Europe in a rickety transit van, during which time one's tolerance for alcohol increased significantly.

After that, I was once again reunited with Daniel and Kevin. Daniel had become increasingly frustrated with the attitude of roadie-turned-bandmate Glenn Campling, especially after their first tour of the USA, during which, as he put it, 'Glenn went fuckin' superstar!' Shortly after that, Daniel called me up and asked if I would be interested in forming a new band with him and Kevin. We all met up over at Dan's place, and Love And Rockets were born.[2]

The first Love And Rockets album was called *Seventh Dream Of Teenage Heaven* and was saturated in psychedelia—something that Peter was never really into, hence our love of it being somewhat tempered in Bauhaus. Now, with our new band, the genie was itching to escape the bottle.

Also contained in that vial was a large dose of LSD. My first trip happened on July 4 1985, at Castle Ashby in Northamptonshire. It was the perfect location: a beautiful 10,000-acre country estate with verdant rambling grounds that rolled down to a vast tranquil lake with overhanging weeping willows, oaks, and elms. I drove over with Kevin in my old 1959 Rover 90, but I wouldn't be driving back! Daniel then showed up on his Harley, followed by Natacha Atlas.

I dropped the tab and was starting to feel the effects as I lay by the lake's edge, grooving on the reflections of the water that were at play on the tree trunks all around me. I gazed out at the centre of the lake and was surprised to see a figure suddenly surface. There was a great spray of water that appeared to contain millions of glittering rainbow droplets. It was as if all of this was happening in slow motion. The figure—a lithe, athletic man with a blonde Mohican—swam toward the shore and eventually got out. The water fell from his body in a shimmering cascade. He was covered in tribal tattoos. The man's eyes met mine. Exton! I had not seen him in some seven years.

'Dave?'

'David?' He padded over and sat down beside me. 'God, I haven't seen you in …'

'Yeah, I know!'

Funnily enough, Exton asked if I had any acid, and I told him that I had just necked my only tab. He asked what kind it was and I told him.

'Oh, that's the real stuff!' he replied. 'I wish I had some of that. Oh, well.'

He smiled. I touched the tattoos on his arm and then traced the curling shapes over his shoulder and chest, lost in this journey of fingertip and eye.

'Is this OK?' I asked.

'Sure!' he replied with a smile.

'How long have you had these?'

'A few years.' He smiled again. 'Yeah, I would love to score some of what you're on right now.'

We laughed together and hugged. This was going to be a good day!

My old friend said that he was going back in for a swim. 'Really great to see you, Dave!'

'Yeah, and you. Have fun!'

With that, he dived in and disappeared under the water. I dragged myself up and wandered over to the car. I wanted to hear some music. I had my little Walkman with me, and had given this choice of music a lot of thought over the previous week. I had decided to play Steve Reich, as I thought that the trance-inducing mandala-like intricacies of his compositions would be most appropriate. I had loads of cassettes all over the floor of my car, but in my seriously altered state I simply could not find the tape. I started to fall into a mild panic, but then, laughing at myself, I decided to just dig in at random and pull something out of the pile.

The Velvet Underground's third album turned out to be the perfect accompaniment. At one point, I was looking up at the bright blue sky as 'Pale Blue Eyes' came on. Suddenly, the whole sky was made up of thousands and thousands of eyes. They resembled embossed watermark designs—subtle, transparent, blue-on-blue. Then I realised that they were multiples of my own eye, and when I blinked, all the eyes in the sky blinked back. I saw rays coming down from the eyes—cosmic rays. They were going into my heart, and it was very joyous. As I received, so I gave back, and that built the intensity. It was as if a kind of feedback was building up, like a generator, and what was at the heart of it was love. As the eyes faded away, I felt very connected to the great spiritual source. (Thank you, Lou Reed!)

'Pale Blue Eyes' became the trigger, the catalyst, that led me into that experience. Then 'I'm Set Free' came on, and it was all over.

I'm set free to find a new illusion
I've been blinded but now I can see

I was rolling around on my back in the tall grass, laughing my head off. 'I see my head laughing, rolling on the ground.' Then, as the epic 'The Murder Mystery' played, I noticed all the insect life below the wavering grass stems, and I went deep into that which could have been something of a dark heavy trip but wasn't, as I was in the right mind set to go with the flow. Instead, the insects seemed beautiful, like incandescent living jewels.

When the album finished, I crawled over to a dried-out riverbed by a bank of tall trees. Lying on my back, looking up at the shadows of leaves upon leaves, I had the strongest insight into the interdependency and perfect balance of nature and the universe. Everything made complete sense, and I was indeed set free … to find a new illusion.

At the end of the day, we all went back to Daniel's little terraced house to finish off the psychedelic collage that would feature on the inner gatefold sleeve of our new album. At one point, I was sitting on the floor, looking at Daniel's antique furniture, thinking about how sexy the curved legs of the chairs were! I remarked on this to Dan who smiled, shook his head, and glued another mushroom on the board.

* * *

Love And Rockets found immediate success in the USA and Canada, where our first single, a cover of The Temptations' psychedelic socio-political soul classic 'Ball Of Confusion', went gold. For the rest of the 80s we would never look back, with each successive album outselling the last. In 1989, we had a no. 3 hit in the USA with 'So Alive' and embarked on a long tour. While we were on the road, our booking agency kept adding extra tour dates to meet demand, one of which was in Kansas.

134 • David J. Haskins

This was interesting, as following my previous success with the sigil, I had decided to try the same thing again just prior to the tour. The desire was identical: to meet up with William S. Burroughs.

By now, Burroughs had moved to Lawrence, a rural spot outside of Kansas City. When this new date was added, I knew that the spell was working. I made contact with Burroughs's personal assistant, James Grauerholz, whom I had met during the Toronto event back in 1983. James said that if I could make it over to Bill's place the day after the Love And Rockets show, the great man would be pleased to see me. Still, I was a bit torn, as it would mean that I would not be able to travel with the band to the next gig, and would have to fly out on my own instead. Time would be tight. I left the decision right until the last moment, when I told Matt Murphy, our tour manager, that I would be staying put.

I had not booked a hotel, and I had no idea where I was going to stay or how I was going to get out to Lawrence, but my intuition told me that something would turn up. At the end of the night, with everyone gone except for the janitor, who was still sweeping up, I sat in the desolate dressing room and waited for a sign. This duly appeared in the form of a young Asian girl who ventured into the room with the news that she was working on a painting for the band. She wanted to know where to send it. I gave her an address and then asked where she was from. She told me that her name was Mia, and that she was an art student studying at the college in Lawrence. I asked her if she knew where Burroughs lived, and she said, yes—she was very familiar with his place, and would often see him in town, shopping at the local market.

After I explained my situation, the girl kindly offered to give me a lift to Bill's place the next day. She also told me that I could stay overnight at her place if I wished. Back in her small apartment, she insisted that she sleep on the floor and I in the bed. Despite my strong protestations, she won out. (I have to confess that I considered asking her if she would like to join me between the sheets, but propriety overruled.)

The next morning, she drove me out to Burroughs's rural retreat. I arrived with a two-litre bottle of Stolichnaya vodka as a gift. Wild Bill appeared at his front gate dressed in flack jacket and jeans, brandishing a huge, parasol-like mushroom.

'What do ya think to this?' he croaked.

I told him that it was impressive and asked if it were psychoactive. He said it wasn't, and that he intended to use it as a paintbrush. Turning it over, he displayed the texture of the gills. At this time he was doing more painting than writing, and he took me out to his little shed, where he had fired off rounds of ammo, blasting cans of spray-paint set up in front of wooden sheets, to create his 'shotgun paintings'. The place had clearly seen many explosions of mainly red and green paint. Lying amid the detritus on the floor was an old kabuki mask that had been spray-painted in this same colour scheme, and which I would take away as a gift that night.

In contrast to the shed, Burroughs's little bungalow was very clean and orderly. A large wooden desk occupied one corner, with a couch opposite. He had a collection of canes in a cylindrical holder, many scorpions in resin, and various bookshelves, mostly containing books on martial arts and cats. He shoved the vodka in the freezer and told me to make myself at home. He then sat at the desk and started to write in a small notebook while puffing away on a joint. I sat on the couch and breathed in the surreality of the situation (as well as the second-hand marijuana smoke).

Every now and again, the old writer would pause and lift his head from the book and put down his pen. Although I was very conscious of not wanting to interfere with his creative flow, I would use these breaks to throw out the odd question, most of them concerning the Beats. His responses were always quite terse, and he would soon return to his notepad. He would glance at his wristwatch on occasion before resuming writing.

I was nervous and dying for a drink. At the stroke of four, Burroughs rose from his seat, padded over to the fridge, and extracted the Stoli. At last! He poured himself a big drink over ice and then returned to the desk, relit the joint, and resumed his penmanship. I was pretty flabbergasted. *Where are those famous old-world manners now, then, Mr*

Burroughs? I wondered. I had half a mind to get up and fix myself a shot, but decorum prevailed.

My frustration—and thirst—was finally assuaged when one of the old man's young helpers, Toby, stopped by and asked if everything was OK, and would I like a drink?

'Yes,' I replied, 'that would be great!'

I had the sense that Burroughs was preoccupied with the world in his head, and that my presence was a very small blip on his radar, although he would occasionally break off from writing, retreat into a back room, and then reappear to show me something or other—a large diagram depicting the nervous system of the feline, for example. He had many cats, and they would be all over him, softly pawing at his legs and climbing onto his bony shoulders as he sat at the desk. He would dote on them, kissing them on the lips and making little 'meow' noises.

Bill seemed to warm up considerably after a couple of drinks and suggested that the two of us undertake a snake hunt. He led me out into the back yard brandishing his 'snake-stick', a long wooden staff with a fork at the end, which he used to ensnare the reptiles before dropping them into a cage at the back of the house. He would keep the snakes for a couple of days, admiring them before releasing them in the woods. There were several poisonous species indigenous to the area, and the main reason for their capture, he said, was to protect those beloved cats. 'I would never kill a snake,' he told me. 'No! No! No! *Beauuuuuutiful* creatures.'

As we stalked the circular spread, large tumblers of vodka and coke in hand (the old buzzard having now topped me up generously, following that initial neglect), I had to mentally pinch myself and once again wonder at the efficacy of magick. Back in the little bungalow, Burroughs sauntered over to the front door to pick up the local news rag, which had just been delivered. He flexed the paper with a rustle and snap and read the headline aloud in his dust-dry, rasping drawl.

'*ANTI-DRUGS CRUSADER GUNNED DOWN.* Mmmm, peel me an onion and I'll crrrrrrrrryyyyyyyy ...'

James appeared and more drinks were poured. Burroughs then gave me a couple of limited edition books featuring his new paintings, which he signed at James's suggestion. He also signed the painted kabuki mask, as well as my copy of *The Western Lands*, in which he wrote, 'For David, May he reach the Western Lands.'

Some years later, in 1996, Annie and I moved with our seven-year-old son Joseph to Pepperell, Massachusetts. For the next year the mask, along with most of our possessions, remained in storage, in an outbuilding on our new land. One day, I felt the strongest compulsion to find it and hang it up. It took a couple of hours of sorting through boxes, but eventually it turned up. As I was about to hammer the nail in place, Annie's father, Roy, appeared and asked me if I'd heard that William Burroughs had just died. When I later told John Giorno about this moment of synchronicity, he said that it meant that I had been with Burroughs in the Bardo—the Tibetan Buddhist term meaning the intermediate stage between lives.

* * *

Back in 1988, Love And Rockets were also between lives, as the world of guitar-orientated rock music suddenly seemed far less enticing than that of nascent electronica. The first evidence of this new influence on our music was the track 'Bike Dance', an acid house-type makeover of our song 'Motorcycle'.

That year, we had made the synergistic discovery of acid house and Ecstasy, and things were never quite the same again. We were recording our forth album at Blackwing Studios in London, and would listen to the pirate radio stations that were springing up all over town like so many 'shrooms and playing this strange hypnotic, repetitive music. Occasionally, we would slip out of the studio and head for a rave. The first one that we attended was Trip at the Astoria Theatre on the Charing Cross Road. It was all very basic, with kids in baggy cloths trance-dancing on tables amid smoke and strobes. Every now and again, someone would shout out 'Aceeeed', at which point they would all start to blow tin whistles. Daniel nearly got himself thrown out when he grabbed some poor raver and demanded he 'give me some fuckin' Ecstasy!' He found himself instantly on the wrong end of a headlock as a 300lb security guard leapt into action. Daniel apologised profusely, and it did the trick. We stayed.

Our American record label, RCA, would certainly have preferred it had we all been told never to return. They did not get our new direction at all. They saw us as the next big guitar-driven arena-rock band, and were all set to give us the big push into the world of stadia, so when we delivered our next album, *Hot Trip To Heaven*—an oddball experimental electronica excursion, notably devoid of electric guitars—they were perplexed to say the least. They were so confused by it all that they gave us the option of leaving the label—which, when it came down to it, was no option at all. We moved over to Rick Rubin's American Recordings, and made plans to transfer operations to the USA.

CHAPTER EIGHT
Enter Hecate

I was standing in the hall of a large Victorian house, intuitively aware of the presence of a pregnant woman in one of the upstairs rooms. There was another woman with me in the hall. Her features were vague. I could hear barking dogs. There was someone outside: a strong presence. I told my female companion not to open the door on any account. The dogs barked wildly, and there was the sound of a violent wind.

The woman seemed to be spellbound. She walked toward the door as if in a trance. I looked through the window to see who was outside. It was an old crone with a fierce countenance. The woman inside the house reached the door and was about to open it. I rushed over to stop her but it was too late. The door was open, and amid a twisting swirl of wind-strewn leaves, the crone entered.

She was fearsome. I grabbed her by the shoulders and tried to force her back outside. There was an awesome power emanating from her. I put both of my hands on her head and pushed with all my strength. I wanted to smash in her skull, but I held back, as instinctively I felt that to do so would have resulted in dire consequences.

Finally, with great effort, I managed to get her out of the house, pushed her away, ran back inside and slammed the door shut. The wind howled like a demon. The crone was staring through the window by the sink. I looked into the basin. There were long black hairs in it. She then levitated about two feet in the air and shouted through the glass, 'So, you think that this is impossible do you? Well, this is "impossible" too!'

As the crone peered into the sink, the hairs slid up the sides of the basin, then out and over the windowpane. From out of the plughole came thick tendrils of black hair, writhing, twisting, and growing. Alive! Unabated it came, lashing the walls and windows. Then, from the ceiling, more hair, thicker still. Dripping oily coils filled up the room.

I struggled through to the door, but the hair appeared to have a will of its own. It was trying to prevent me from leaving. The feel of it on my skin was sickening. I managed to beat it back and force the door open as the hair clung to it like a voracious jungle vine. I squeezed through, and finally was outside.

I ran away from the house in terror. A ball of hair had entangled itself about my head. It covered my face. I was enveloped.

* * *

I awoke from this dream in a cold sweat, weeping. I relayed the dream the following night at my old friend Alan Moore's house, and he immediately identified the crone as Hecate, the Greek goddess of the underworld, Queen of ghosts, Mistress of magic, the keeper of the keys of Hades and divinity of crossroads. Alan told me how, traditionally, she stands before the doors of the houses of pregnant women, whom she protects, and her appearance is heralded by the barking of ghost dogs and a wild swirling wind. A lunar deity, she presides over witchcraft and the magic arts.

This last detail was significant, as I was at Alan's at his invitation, to participate in an evening of ritual magick. For many years, Alan had been regarded as the most brilliantly gifted graphic novelist in the world. He had deconstructed and then reinvented the form, raising it to the level of literature. In the early 90s, he had an epiphany, centred on a vision of the ancient serpent god Glycon, and became a magician.

On an overcast night in his Northampton loft, looking every inch the wizard with his long flowing greying mane and beard and intense stare, Alan raised his wand and ushered in a night of transformative necromancy. Following the banishing (written by Alan in florid poetic form) we formulated our intention:

'To work magick in the name of Glycon. It being our Will to be given increase in experience and understanding of the magickal realm, that we likewise receive of inspiration for those arts which do themselves inspire great thoughts in others.'

We then partook of the sacrament. From a large round glass jar, we each took a scoop of viscid honeyed psilocybin mushrooms and placed them in our bowls. I poured two glasses of wine, and we raised a toast to our magickal endeavour. Alan put on Brian Eno's *The Shutov Assembly* as the soundtrack to our meditation. After about twenty minutes, the psychedelic mushrooms began to take effect. A pleasurable warm glow infused my body. I looked up at the attic ceiling to see delightful arabesques moving over its surface—delicate and elaborate patterns, undulating and constantly changing shape in a beautiful evolution of form.

Alan suggested that it was time to invoke the spirit of Glycon, and in his resonant baritone he intoned:

> *Sweet Glycon,*
> *sacred snake of light and wisdom,*
> *we entreat thee, come amongst us in thy glorious body if it be thy will.*
> *Come from the bright land without time,*
> *that we might know the touch of honeyed scales, thy splendour now*
> *uncoiling in our consciousness.*
> *Accept us into thine embrace,*
> *the blissful windings of thy perfect being,*
> *that our spirits are grown incandescent in thy golden radiance sublime.*
> *Immortal Glycon,*
> *luminous intelligence,*
> *immaculate and serpentine, anoint our eyes with thy delicious venom.*
> *That our sight may be as thine eternal sight.*
> *Let us now bask in the serene compassion of thy lidless gaze, all*
> *knowing, all encircling, exalted in thy grace and protection. In thy*
> *gleaming brow the sun is as a jewel,*
> *it's billion facets scintillant with joy and reason, flooding over existences*
> *with brilliance.*

O Glycon,
most profound embodiment of great Aesclepius, kin to the Moon and
disincarnate phallus of Osiris, rise within us now each one.
O dazzling worm of dream and vision, self-devouring, self-creating,
grant us thy flickering kiss, thy love divine, thy piercing revelation.
Father of the Garden,
let us taste the fruit of knowledge
and slough off the world's skin,
sweet magnificence, o, blessed Glycon, come!

I closed my eyes as Alan spoke, and a numinous serpentine image appeared: a ghostly grey shape-shifting icon reminiscent of the work of H.R. Giger, surrounded by scintillant buds of multi-coloured light, golden white in the centre with a nimbus of red, green, and blue. There was a deep sense of ancient wisdom and benignity—an awesome power withheld. It was a breathtaking vision.

We both regarded Alan's recent depiction of Glycon, which appeared to be textured like silk, the green snake body glistening and sparkling. Then the picture, which was propped up against the wall, started to slip. I went to catch it but realised it had not moved. It seemed to slip and fall repeatedly—again without actually moving.

Taking recourse to the great British standby, I proposed that a cup of tea would be in order. Alan applauded the idea before suggesting that on my way downstairs, I pay a visit to 'Our Lady of the S-bend', adding that it would be 'an experience which you should not deny yourself'. Alan had mentioned this curious phenomenon, before: once, while under the influence of psilocybin, he had dropped a sheet of toilet tissue into the lavatory bowl and watched, enchanted, as it danced under the black light.

'Welcome To Wars' read the legend on the bathroom mat as I entered the eerily lit room. I caught a glimpse of myself in a large gilt-framed wall mirror. I had turned into a black man! The effect was stunning and highly amusing. As I smiled, the illusion was exaggerated even more. I started to play with it, striking various cartoon pimp poses and chuckling to myself when all of a sudden, something sombre possessed me, and a deep, chastising voice boomed inside my head: 'That ain't it, that's just jive and shit! No, that ain't it! *This* ... is ... *it!*'

With that, I felt myself being transported along a kind of astral corridor. Back, back, back through time, through the ages and aeons, back to primordial Africa. Africa before it had a name. Then a sound: The First Sound. The First Music. Deep, deep, deep. A low, sustained guttural hum, resonant and sonorous. A sound full of wisdom. Primal!

I gazed into my eyes—not exclusively *mine* but merged with *it*. From far away I heard a yawning noise and was rushed back to where I started. Shaken to the core, I turned away from the mirror. I tore off a piece of white paper tissue and dropped it into the toilet. It sank under the water, where, illuminated by the ultraviolet light, it was transformed into an angel. The softly billowing form displayed two indescribably beautiful silver-white gossamer wings, which undulated in the porcelain grotto.

Mesmerised, I knelt down and peered into the bowl. A face! A tiny, perfect, pale angel face looking back at me. Peering down the loo, I was struck by the delightfully whimsical irony of the situation. As the angel danced, so I was charmed, seduced by this vision. She was talking to me. Angel words in whispers. Calling to me, this siren of the water closet. Our Lady of the S-bend!

It was then that I remembered that I had originally intended to make some tea, so with great reluctance I tore myself away from the magical communion and headed for the kitchen. As I passed through the lounge, my attention was drawn to something on the floor: a rectangular piece of paper, about 1x2 inches, containing one of the small panels that made up Alan's illustration for the cover of Peter Whitehead's novel *The Risen*. It depicted Osiris lying with Isis and Horus in the form of a hawk, hovering above them. In the background was a pyramid divided into seven coloured panels, each covered with hieroglyphs.

I held the paper up to the light. It resembled a tiny stained-glass window, the colours radiant, vibrant. I put it into my pocket. When I returned with the brew, I asked Alan if he could produce the postcard of Jean Cocteau that I had sent him while on tour in the States. This he

144 • David J. Haskins

did, and in turn he requested that I play the new track that I had just recorded, 'YSL', which describes how the French fashion designer Yves Saint Laurent was mercilessly bullied at school, and how this became a source of rebellious inspiration.

'You're a clever cunt!' Alan proclaimed when the track was over. He asked me if we should play it again but then decided that it would be better not to. 'It's tempting, very tempting, but it's too big. No, save it … perhaps later. Is that the best thing you've ever done? No, I know that's a silly question but, God, that's really something!'

I sucked up my blushes and played him a new remix by Locust of the Love And Rockets track 'This Heaven', a radical deconstruction of the original, with the vocals mixed way down and ethereal as they ghost-whisper under a thick wall of fuzzy machine noise.

'You've invented a completely new type of music!' Alan exclaimed.

We dipped into the honey jar to partake of some more of the mushrooms. As I scooped out a large glob, I noticed that it contained a long golden hair. I stretched out the glistening strand and then coiled it around my finger. I then removed the circle of hair and stuck it to the back of a piece of card on which I had written down an I Ching reading pertaining to the current working. The reading had been auspicious and interesting. In response to my question, 'Is the time right to undertake a magickal ritual with Alan?' the oracle advised the following: 'One should undertake something great. Good fortune comes from selflessness. When divergence emerges, act quickly. When one finds oneself alienated, be objective, moderate, and just.' All of which was to prove pertinent.

Spotting the head of a mushroom on the floor next to the card, I picked it up and placed it within the circle of hair.

'This is it.' I said to Alan. 'This is the start of the magick.'

We focussed our attention on the seminal fetish. I tried to pull a hair from my head but this proved impossible, as it was cut very close, so I asked Alan if he had something I could use to cut it. He told me that he had a knife.

'A knife would be good.'

As I said these words, they seemed to hang in the air, pregnant with loaded significance. Time seemed to slow down. Very strange. Something was happening. Alan handed me a craft knife with three detachable blades. I cut off some hair and placed it within the circle. In silence, I passed the knife back to Alan. I stopped him from putting it away and asked that he cut off some of his own hair. He complied. Then I requested that he snip off some of his beard. This he did. Next, I told him that there is one more contribution to make, but the knife should not be used, as there should be an element of pain involved. He shot me a quizzical look and then twigged what I meant. He slipped a hand inside his pants and yanked out a pubic sprig. I did likewise.

'A splendid effort, sir!' the magus proclaimed, and we mixed the bristles in the circle.

I poured some more wine, and we chinked our glasses in a silent solemn toast. I placed the fetish between us on the bed, took another sip of wine, and then spat it out into the centre of the now messy circle. Alan followed suit. The atmosphere had become thick, heavy and intoxicating. Alan suddenly fell back onto the bed and started to writhe and twist, like a big, heavy snake. Between his fingers was a half-smoked spliff. I took it from him and took a deep drag as he continued to slither. The joint went out, so I struck a match and relit it. I passed the spent match to Alan and asked him to break it. He did so with the fingers of one hand, which I then took in my own. We clasped firmly and stared deeply into each other's eyes. We wrestled in slow motion, never breaking the eye-lock. Eventually, with thumb over thumb, we executed the classic brotherhood handshake.

Following a slow, intense release, the broken matchstick was transferred into my own hand. I dropped the charged pieces into the fetish. Alan returned to his shape-shifting. His long hair fell in front of his face, exposing a rarely seen ear. In this instant, he became the very living image of Glycon, as represented in his own portrait of the deity. He pulled himself up and started to yawn in an exaggerated manner.

I was sitting on the floor. The knife was between us, and my attention was drawn to it. I did not want to focus on it, but I felt compelled to do so. It had a terrible latent power. I knew that if I were to continue to think about the knife, Alan would pick up on it, telepathically, and do likewise. The blade was suggestive of one thing and one thing only: bloodletting.

I felt the presence of something in the room, something heavy and brooding, and whatever it was, it wanted a sacrifice. A ritual commitment. The room had taken on an oppressive, cloying atmosphere. I had to get out. I told Alan that I needed to get some air and climbed down the narrow stairs to the landing. When I reached the ground floor, I tried the door to the lounge, but it would not open. It appeared to be locked. Moreover, it was sealed.

My heart started to pound. From upstairs, I could hear the sounds of moaning and groaning, then violent crashing and banging. It sounded like a brawl between man and beast. What the fuck was going on up there? I tried the door again. I attempted to slide it into the wall, imagining a recess, but seeing the little window adjacent to the door, I realised that this theory was sunk.

My mind was spinning in a maelstrom of paranoia and panic. I considered leaving by the front door, but there was a part of me that did not want to abandon ship, although another part was yelling, 'Flee!' in a very loud voice. I had the distinct notion that all of this was Alan's doing, that he had devised a trap. I was the fly to his spider. I remembered the I Ching reading: 'When divergence emerges, act quickly. When one finds oneself alienated, be objective, moderate and just.'

I tried to push the door, as opposed to just sliding and pulling it. It opened with ease. *Forgive me, Alan!* I thought. I had to smile at myself for being such a paranoid fool. I stumbled into the garden and lit a cigarette. Standing under the night sky, I became intensely aware of a great challenge, and my immersion into something that was very serious and full of danger. 'Chapel Perilous' indeed. It was inextricably bound up with the knife, the letting of our blood and its mixing. I had elected to enter into this magickal realm, and I was now teetering on the abyss as this challenge from a powerful and demonic entity had been laid at my feet. The issue was one of courage and commitment, but I also intuited a trick. I needed to be very careful here. An honourable solution needed to be sought.

When I returned to the attic, Alan told me that he felt that he was not involved in the magick in the usual way, whereby he had always felt himself to be the centre of attention. He said that this time, the energy was very much focussed on me.

'It is interested in *you*,' he said. He suggested that we should think again about the lyrics to my new song, 'YSL'. 'What do you really mean?'

The coda at the end of the song revolves around the repetition of the taunting jibe: 'Sissy, sissy, sissy!' I glanced down at the knife. Alan remarked that the fetish we had made was very strange; that it had a beauty—an awful beauty—but needed something more. He said he wasn't sure what that something was, but I knew: blood. It was crying out for blood.

I did not speak my mind, as I knew that to do so would inevitably lead to a ritualistic bloodletting, and the mixing thereof. I was most apprehensive about this, as it crossed my mind that my old friend might have some blood-transmissible disease—fuck, he might have AIDS for all I knew. This was only part of my concern, however. There was something else, something even more dangerous, but it was something that I could not put a finger on.

Alan handed me an issue of the epic serialised graphic novel *Cerebus*. It was issue 31, 'Mothers and Daughters'. I opened the book at random onto an extremely bloody battle scene between the hero, Cerebus—a sword wielding hermaphrodite aardvark warrior—and his foe, a white-robbed and masked matriarchal fascist called Cirin. They were depicted struggling over the blade, each cutting the other to shreds as they engaged in mortal combat. Page after page of blade and blood. The synchronicity was unnerving.

Alan then picked up another copy of *Cerebus* and started to read from the text at the back. It was about Alan himself and his correspondence with the author, Dave Sim. Each paragraph was punctuated by the lines 'Tell me what you're thinking' or 'What are you thinking about?'

Each time Alan read these words he would look up at me and, as it is written in another part of the same text, 'his eyes widened as they seemed to bore twin holes into my own, as he drove his thoughts deep into the recesses of my own awareness'. *What are you thinking?*

Breaking away from the terrible glamour of this situation, I went downstairs to select some music. I returned with R.E.M.'s *Automatic For The People* and a Cockney Rebel compilation. I decided to play 'Nightswimming' from the former. Before I put on the disc, Alan sighed deeply.

'Yes,' he said, 'we're swimming in deep waters now.'

I had not told him what I was going to play.

After that, I played 'Sebastian' by Cockney Rebel and told Alan about the first time I had heard it. I was fifteen, sitting alone in my Dad's parked car, when it came on the radio, and I was transported by this strange baroque yet modern music, delivered to another place.

'Where did you go?' Alan asked.

'Here!' I replied.

'Although I hate to say it,' Alan concluded, 'in a way, I think that you are a better magician than me. You have a real gift for it.'

* * *

Asmodeus is a fearful, wrathful entity that feeds on the terror it induces. It is the king of the nine Hells, the demon of lust, and a thoroughly nasty piece of work. Alan, having had a few run-ins with this beast, had created a beautiful rendering of it in coloured pencil, and now he wanted to destroy it in an act of dedicated sacrifice.

We went downstairs and into the garden. In Alan's work, the demon was represented as part spider, part peacock, in an intricate, repetitive mandala-like image. It was probably the most exquisite graphic work that he had ever done.

Looking up at the night sky, Alan intoned, 'I'm not asking you to pull any strings here, but please just let him off the hook.' I felt that he was directly addressing my predicament, which had by now—in my head, at least—become a matter of life and death. I felt that the continuation of my very existence was bound up in this fiery ritual.

Alan lit the edge of the paper. A little gust of wind picked up and the flames flickered into life. Soon it was ablaze.

'Come on, come on,' Alan exclaimed. 'Wow! Look at it! These are the most beautiful colours I've ever seen! Oh!'

He held up the flaming paper until his fingers started to burn then gently dropped it to the ground. We crouched over the crumpled, crackling black and watched as the orange-red embers traced a series of intricate insect-like glyphs over the surface of the shrinking sheet. In these shapes I clearly discerned the awful face of the demon. It was like an Austin Osman Spare rendering in flame. The demon lasciviously licked its lips and slowly disappeared.

I placed my hands over the dying heat emanating from the brittle wafers. Alan followed suit.

'Thank you,' he said, looking up at the stars.

I thanked Alan, too. I felt extreme gratitude toward him for initiating this powerful act of catharsis. An exorcism! We embraced, there in the garden, in the thick of that deep night.

As we went back inside, a fierce gust of wind blew some of the blackened paper back into the house.

'The demon,' I said, as I scooped up the burnt shards. 'It's trying to get back in.'

'Right!' Alan exclaimed. 'I know exactly what to do in that case.' He proceeded to lick the ash from my hands. 'Excuse me!' he said, ever the gent. He swallowed the ashes. Now we were safe. The air had cleared. A discharge had taken place. Negative ions filled the house, and the smell was just like that following an electrical storm. The relief!

We returned to the womblike cave haven of the attic. By now it was 9am. At various points during the night, I had been collecting an assortment of items with the vague intention of making some sort of collage: the Osiris panel from the *Risen* cover, the Cocteau postcard, a picture of James Dean, an empty packet of Camel cigarettes, and the top of a box of Randy Candy chocolates, which depicted the bejewelled navel of a woman, with an oval inset of another scantily clad temptress sitting on a sand dune in the desert, eating a sweet. The chocolates had names like Carissima, Submission, Buck's Fizz Jazz, Strawberry Sonata, and Turkish Delight, all conjuring up a flood of exotic connotations.

Using the copy of the I Ching as a base, I started to glue the pieces together. The original hair/matchstick fetish resembled a human body, so

I made a 'head' from an illustration of one of the chocolates, which was in the shape of a metallic blue fan. I cut a square hole from the book's pages to create one of those secret hide-away cavities and placed some of the mushrooms inside, along with two dead honeybees I had found in the bathroom, some earth from Alan's basement, a pinch of frankincense, and a dead spider. The three blades from the craft knife were stuck down the spine. There was also an illustration torn from an incense packet, a blue multi-armed Hindu goddess playing a flute surrounded by arabesque patterns that reminded me of the intricate latticework of shapes I had seen earlier, under the influence of the mushrooms.

Alan made some erotic drawings on the opening inner page: a man engaged in sexual intercourse with a woman who is going down on another female. In elaborate symbolic lettering, he added a title: *The Book Of Copulations*. Beneath the postcard of Cocteau, I added his line, 'Every orgasm is the death of a king.'

Exhausted, we repaired to the kitchen to make another pot of tea. During my initial tea-making session, I had felt the compulsion to paint on Alan's walls. I could not find any paint so I concocted a solution made of cough medicine, tea, and sugar. In a kind of trance, I watched as my hand painted the letters 'PSI' on the wall. As the sun blazed in through the kitchen door, we added the same words to the book and poured the remainder of the 'paint' into the hollowed out crevice.

'It has a sticky heart,' Alan said.

We went out into the garden amid a cacophony of birdsong.

* * *

I walked home across the old racecourse. A violent storm whipped up out of nowhere. The tree branches groaned and swayed as a wild swirling wind tore between them. I could not help but see the hand of Hecate in all of this, and hear her ancient voice in the howling.

In retrospect, I believe that had Alan and I cut our palms and mixed our blood, the demon Asmodeus would have gained access to our beings. It had been goading us all the while, hoping to achieve this, but mercifully its efforts were thwarted.

My suspicions would later be confirmed when I consulted with my friend, the renowned demonologist Adam Blai. Adam told me that blood could potentially act as a conduit through which demonic entities can gain access to humans, with that possibility heightened if the sigil of the demon is present during the working. (He added that, in some cases, semen could also act in a similar way.) He also strongly recommended that I should have banishing prayers said over me, in order to rid myself of any entities that could still be around. 'Once that door is opened,' he said, 'it can let in any number of things, and they do not leave of their own volition.'

Soon after our first consultation, I visited Adam in Windber, Pennsylvania. He lit some rare and sacred incense in an antique burner used for exorcisms that had been given to him by a Benedictine priest, and then sprinkled holy water around the small, sepulchral room. 'There is something here,' he said. The energy in the room intensified. 'It's reacting to the holy water. The water doesn't do that on its own. Can you feel it? It's snarling because it knows what is to come.'

Adam flicked some of the water over my body and took up his small wood and metal Benedictine Crucifix. Incantations and prayer followed. At one point, he asked the Lord to allow his angels to come among us, and I had the strongest impression of several shimmering beings of white light entering the room through the black walls. He was then inspired to call upon the guardian angels, and I perceived the powerful holy presence of strong white wings, marbled with rivulets of light blue. The wings moved toward my chest and enveloped me. I felt a surge of positive energy. Later, Adam told me that he had felt this energy run down his arms, out of his finger tips, and into me, and at that point I had apparently jerked violently, although I could not recall doing so. At this same moment, I was also aware of the presence of malevolent entities like ectoplasmic tumbleweeds, which shrivelled into black twisted balls before scuttling away into the darkened corners of the room, leaving through the walls.

Toward the culmination of the prayer session, Adam asked if I was having any impressions that I felt might be significant. I told him that

I was seeing a mental image of chainmail. He asked God to help me to understand the meaning of this, and I gleaned that it was a symbol for the burden of sensuality. The image was then supplanted by that of an ascending ball of white light, which I recognised as a representation of spirituality. Adam placed the cross on my hands, which were held together in prayer. He remarked that there was an awful lot of energy in the room. More prayers; Adam's voice was tender, and he seemed to be on the brink of tears. I was feeling lighter by the second, as if a great dark cloud had dissipated and been transformed into refreshing clean rain.

Finally, Adam concluded the session. 'That which needed to be removed is now gone,' he said. 'That which needed to be moved from one place to another has been moved, and there is now a sense of things being in their right place.'

A large man with a shaven head and dark, soulful eyes, Adam smiled and closed the book of prayer. I told him that I felt that I should kiss the cross. He nodded his approval, and my lips met the tiny silver body of Christ. Adam told me that he had taken this cross to many of the most holy places of the world. While in deep prayer, he had held it against the wailing wall of the temple of Jerusalem, dipped it in the sea of Galilee, placed it in the room where Mary was impregnated with Jesus, the cave where Jesus was born, the rock in the garden of Gethsemane upon which Jesus sweated blood, the dungeon cell in which Jesus spent the night before his crucifixion, the hole the cross was placed in, the tomb of Jesus Christ (the actual stone sarcophagus his body was in), the stone upon which Jesus's body was anointed, the stone on which the resurrected Jesus prepared food for the apostles, and the stone where Jesus stood and ascended into Heaven. In that kiss, I believe that I travelled to all of those holy places simultaneously, in an instant.

Adam advised me to go away and meditate on what had happened, and to pray. Before I left, he gave me some holy sacramental wine from Cana, the site of Jesus's first miracle, where he turned the water into wine, and some incense, which Adam had obtained from the same Benedictine monk who had blessed his cross.

At the same time that I first made contact with Adam regarding my concerns over bloodletting and ritual magick, I started to suffer extreme chest pains, which continued and intensified right up until our meeting in Windber. They stopped completely following the conclusion of the prayer session. In later correspondence, Adam indicated that this discomfort was probably a physical manifestation of the anger of the attached spirits and their fear of failure, its cessation an indication of their loss of power and confirmation of deliverance.

Amen.

* * *

On July 16 1994, Alan and I staged a ritualistic live performance as part of the event called Subversion In The Streets Of Shame at the Bridewell Theatre near Fleet Street, London. This fascinating gathering was hosted by the novelist Iain Sinclair and included a performance by the shamanistic poet Aaron Williamson.[1] Also present were Peter Whitehead, James Havoc, and an unscheduled, out of the blue Kathy Acker, who gave a riveting impromptu reading which also, sadly, turned out to be her last.

Our piece, 'The Moon And Serpent Grand Egyptian Theatre Of Marvels', was directly inspired by that extraordinary night of magick at Alan's. It consisted of pre-recorded atmospheric soundscapes (made by Tim Perkins and myself) in support of Alan's reading of a brilliant and extremely dense text that addressed the macro of the magickal universe via the micro of the subterranean history of London. During the reading, I wore a white mask and set about creating a magickally charged space through various symbolic physical acts. At one point, I was laying spread-eagled on the floor inside a pentagram of candles when I felt an intense visitation. An urgent spectral presence. There were definitely three of us on the stage at that point.[2]

Many more miracles and wonders were to follow as I embarked on the creation of a series of animal fetish objects. I would sit and meditate, clearing my mind of static and eventually the particular animal power/theme would become intuitively apparent. The first of these was a horned skull. Following this directive, I trained my will on the object's manifestation. Every day, I would concentrate intensely, drawing it to me.

I was working in a studio in Chipping Norton at the time on what would become Love And Rockets' *Sweet F.A.* album. When we arrived at the studio, I decided to make a pentacle out of a black candle, but as I was kneading the molten wax I felt that I was being directed to make something else manifest, and in that moment I experienced a definite shift in consciousness. My perception became acute, and I had the strange sensation of falling into a kind of psychic slipstream. A sweet delirium. What was it that was taking shape in my hands? A figure, female. A goddess. Venus Aphrodite! The wax had become silvery grey. I stuck seven feathers to the head and mounted her on a small block of quartz crystal.

The night before, I had spoken to Alan on the phone. He wanted to try an experiment in telepathy, whereby I would attempt to transmit an image to him back in Northampton. When the time came, I decided to send him Venus. As I had to be present in the studio, and did not want to take the actual figure in with me, I sat down and drew it instead. The next day, I called Alan for his report. He said he saw a grid of green lights, and that it had something to do with cyberspace—although I was not concentrating on it at the time, I had been sitting directly in front of the studio computer, and on the screen was a grid of green LED lights. He said that he saw me sitting down with a white tablet—my drawing book—and the shape of a letter *T*—the feathers, which were arranged in such a fashion that the outline of the figure did indeed resemble this letter. He also perceived something 'Indian, celestial, and divine', as well as 'serpentine lines'—the body of the little effigy, which was curved in such a way that it could certainly be described as serpentine. All in all, a pretty successful transmission.

During my quest for the skull, I had started to collect feathers found along the way, hence the seven feathers used to make Venus's headdress. These would also be employed in my next creation. During a break in recording, I went to my room to smoke a joint and play some music—a mix-tape that a DJ friend had made, consisting in the main of incessant electronic beats. As the music built in intensity, I was suddenly seized by the compulsion to make another figure. I grabbed a bunch of the feathers and started to stroke them over and over. I broke two of the black candles, pulled out the wicks, and used them to tie the pieces together. I melted the wax and poured it into a bowl, flicking into the mixture some ash from the reefer, a dash of Hermes cologne (to represent the messenger of the gods), a drop of beer for Bacchus, and a sprinkling of earth taken from the nearby ancient sacred site of the Rollright Stones, which I had visited earlier.

The music was building to a wild, sexually charged climax. I scooped up the wax and moulded it around the sprig of black feathers, my senses reeling. In my hands, the wax felt like the warm body of a small, wild bird. The drums were frenzied. A god was dancing, and that god was Pan. I added more feathers to make twenty-six—Pan's number. The quills stuck out of the top of the head. Multiple horns—a satyr's grinning face!

At this point, someone came into the room. I thought that it was Daniel, but I did not look up, as I needed to concentrate on the matter at hand. When I raised my eyes a few seconds later, no one was there. There was a sense of discharged energy. I felt exhausted but elated, delighted with this spontaneous creation—Pan made manifest. Curiously, although I had employed the same candles used to make the Venus figure, Pan remained black, whereas Venus inexplicably turned light grey.

The phone rang.

'Dave, it's Daniel. We're ready to get on with the mix now. We were going to get you earlier, but I told Kev not to disturb you. I told him, *No. Don't knock on Aleister Crowley's door cos he's probably summoning up Pan!* Ha ha! … Hello, David, are you there?'

'Yes, Daniel,' I eventually replied. 'I'm here.'

'Are you OK?' he asked, having picked up on the astonishment in my voice.

'I'm fine—it's just that you shocked me a bit as that is exactly what I have been doing, as it turns out.'

'What do you mean? You're joking me, right?

'No, Dan, I'm not.'

'Christ! Do you know what you're doing? I mean, that's serious stuff, man!'

I really did not know what I was doing, but I assured him otherwise, and we both hung up. Then I heard him go into his room, which was next door to mine. I knocked on his door, as I felt that the mad magician owed him an explanation. I told him what I had been up to, and he said that he had stood outside my door and was about to knock but felt very strongly that he should not disturb me, so instead he left and went back into his room, where he picked up a book, Robert A. Johnson's *She: Understanding Feminine Psychology*, and opened it at random. (Knowing of Daniel's ongoing tribulations with women, it figured that he would be reading that!) The passage he alighted upon was all about Pan.

I asked Daniel if he would like to see what I had made, and he responded with some enthusiasm. He was very respectful, and asked if he could pick it up.

'Yes, certainly,' I said. I asked him what time he had come to my room, and it was the exact time I thought I had felt him come in.

* * *

Two days later, immediately following my daily meditation on the manifestation of the skull, I went for a walk in the village. I headed to the old graveyard, and as I passed the Gothic mansion that neighboured it, I saw something in the driveway that stopped me dead in my tracks. There, set up on a long wooden table, stark white against the dark verdant foliage that surrounded it, was the horned skull of a ram.

My heart started to pound. Collecting my thoughts, I decided to enquire within. The large oak door had an old-fashioned bell-pull, a long vertical rope like something out of *The Addams Family*. I gave it a good yank and a sonorous chime rang out. No response. I gave it another tug, and after a several minutes I could hear slow, deliberate footsteps coming down the hall. The door creaked open to reveal a diminutive old lady. I apologised for disturbing her and told her that I was interested in the skull. Would it be possible to purchase it, I wondered?

She told me that it belonged to her daughter, who was an artist, and had been using it in her work. She was sure that her daughter would not want to let it go. She then told me that she was only at the house because her husband had just died. I told her that I was sorry, thanked her for her time, and was about to go when she told me to come back in a couple of hours, when her daughter would be back, and to ask her about the skull. If she was really sure, I said, then I would. Yes,' she replied, 'do come back.'

I spent the next two hours visualising the skull sitting atop the table in my room. At the appointed hour, I returned to the gothic pile. This time, a young man answered the door. 'If this is about the skull,' he said, 'then, yes, my sister said you can take it. She said that she would like you to have it.'

I gave him a copy of Love And Rockets' most recent album, *Hot Trip To Heaven*, to pass on to his benevolent sibling, and left with the marvellous prize.

CHAPTER NINE
Juju Shit

It started out as a spontaneous, surrealistic art project. I was throwing random images together using a new video camera. I did this very quickly, trying not to think about what I was doing, so that the subconscious would come into play. Snatching pictures, scenes from TV, stop-motion dinosaurs, Mexican Day of the Dead figures, an antique skeleton puppet, pornography, images of Pan, and so on. As I was doing this, it started to feel powerful, in a magickal sense. *Something was happening!*

A few days before, I had woken from my sleep with the words 'Magick gets what magick wants' going through my head. I scribbled this down on a scrap of paper, and then continued to write out permutations: 'Magick wants what magick gets', 'What gets magick wants magick', and so on. Later on, I heard a song on the radio, and grabbing the nearest sheet of paper I wrote down the name of the band: Spell. Turning it over, I discovered that it was the same sheet on which I had written the 'Magick gets …' transcript. I decided to overdub the transcript onto the film that I had made.

Watching this back, I was struck by the realisation that it was about resurrection: specifically that of Bauhaus. It ignited a fire in me, and I decided to contact Peter, Daniel, and Kevin about the possibility of reforming the band. The general consensus was hesitant and noncommittal. Further action would be called for.

* * *

The ram's skull was placed on the altar. It was studded with various semiprecious stones, pearls, and a RAM chip. Painted feathers were tied to the horns, and inscriptions in the 'witches' alphabet' were etched into the crown.[1] It was to be the centrepiece for a magickal working to bring about the reformation of Bauhaus. The presiding warrior gods were Mars and Athena.

I lit the candles and meditated on this intention, before pressing *play* on my tape machine: *Mystic Sufi Music*, a tape that Peter had given to me. I lit a cigarette, and as the music built in intensity, I brought the glowing end of it up to my eyes. I suddenly realised that I was looking at a face: the face of a god. Two glowing sulphuric eyes and a cruel, sardonic mouth. Mars![2]

The more I looked, the more this strange perception grew in intensity. I took a deep drag and inhaled the god. It felt extraordinary. Communion! Once again, I stared at the face, and it stared back, glowing with renewed ferocity. I took another drag and felt the tendrils of smoke uncoiling and entering my lungs. I inserted the lit end into my mouth, held it there; took it out and reinserted it, deeper this time; held it, took it out; in, further still, and held … and out.

The face of Mars was burning crimson as I flicked ash into a pearlised shell. I started to rock back and forth, entering into a semi-trance-like state. The cigarette was still burning in my fingers. I pushed the burning end into the palm of my left hand and gave out a low delirious groan as the flesh sizzled. It smelt like bacon. I poured sanctified salted water over my burnt hand. There was hardly a mark. Then I dripped candle wax over my hands, placed them over a grimoire (a book of spells), and pressed down.

I lowered my head, resting it on the back of my hands, and began a spontaneous chant of 'Resurrection Hex', over and over, and then 'Red Hex'. The music rose to a climax and stopped. I raised my hands from the book, continuing to chant 'Red Hex, Red Hex, Red Hex, Red Hex, Red Hex', faster and faster.[3]

I suddenly felt a great urge to piss, which brought me back down to earth with some rapidity. The last thing I wanted to do was to leave the circle, so instead I picked up an empty wine decanter from the altar and used that. Struck by a sudden inspiration, I knew what I had to do next. It tasted wonderful. I poured a libation onto the grimoire and meditated deeply on the meaning of Athena, the protective virgin goddess of war and wisdom, patroness of the arts.

I meditated on Peter, on Daniel, on Kevin. I meditated on myself. I appointed a cardinal location for each of us: Peter in the East (Turkey), Daniel in the South (Brighton), Kevin in the West (Los Angeles), and me in the North (Northampton).

I poured a final libation of red wine onto the book and inscribed the RAM chip with a pentagram. The final banishing was made in the name of Athena, and the working concluded. Three years later, Bauhaus would take the stage for the first time in fifteen years. It would be called the Resurrection Tour.

* * *

It was a cold, stormy night in January 1995. Standing in Alan's grotto-like cellar, I placed the ram's skull in the centre of the five white candles that formed a pentagram on the dug-up floor. This craggy basement would represent the Underworld during the working that was to ensue.

After a while we repaired to Alan's loft. We were joined by Tim Perkins, who was somewhat apprehensive about this, his first formerly structured ritual. Alan reassured him that all would be well. It had been three months since Alan and I had conducted our previous working, and in that time I had become immersed in the study of the occult arts. Although obviously still a neophyte, I felt confident enough to take on more of a lead role in the proceedings. To this end, I constructed a makeshift altar and suggested that we enter into a group meditation. During this session, we all experienced strong feelings of fraternal empathy. A coin was spun to determine which of us would read the banishing. I was pleased that it was Alan. His deep voice, strong and authoritative, set the right tone. I then purified the water with salt, crossed my forehead, inscribed a pentagram over my chest, and completed a circuit of the surrounding circle, scattering the water as I went.

'The sacred circle is about us. We are here of our own free will, in peace and in love. We now invite the gods to witness this rite which we hold in their honour.' With this, I pointed my index finger high in salutation. 'Hail to the goddess and god! Two poles yet one, the Source. Guard us and guide us within this circle and without it, in all things. So mote it be.'

'So mote it be,' the others repeated.

I picked up the wooden chalice, made a libation before my handmade god and goddess effigies that sat atop the altar, and raised a toast to 'The Source!' I drank and passed the cup to Tim, and he in turn passed it to Alan, who then returned it to me.

Setting the cup down on the altar, I concluded with the words, 'Now is the temple erected. We shall not leave it but with good reason. So be it.'

'So be it,' my brothers repeated, and so we began. We meditated further on the reason for this coming together and then partook of the sacramental 'shrooms. I suggested that we formulate our intentions, write them down, and then read them out loud. Alan had asked for knowledge and inspiration; I had requested experience in the realm of the Underworld; Tim said that he preferred to voice his Will internally in silence. He then raised his hand like a sheepish schoolboy and sweetly requested that he be able to leave to go to the toilet. I showed him how to open and close the circle using Alan's magickal sword.

While Tim was away, I remarked to Alan about the fine line between high magick and high farce. He proposed a toast to the god of farce, and I suggested that this was probably Groucho Marx. More appropriately, Alan ventured the name of Brian Rix and told me that he had once met this great old stalwart of the stage. I asked if he had been coming out of a closet without his trousers at the time. 'You were there, too!' he laughed.

Upon Tim's return, Alan, in his wonderfully resonant manner, read the beautiful 'Invocation to Glycon'. Church bells chimed eleven o'clock in the distance, and the night closed in. Music was played: Pachelbel's Canon. The effects of the mushrooms had just started to come on, and the music sounded divine, glowing with warmth; elegant, refined, and spiritually uplifting. Perfect!

I remarked that there was a fractal quality to the music.

'That's strange that you should say that,' Alan replied, 'as I was just looking at this cigarette smoke, the way it unfurls, and thinking that it was extremely fractal.'

We all watched the serpentine smoke, which seemed to dance to the inspired music. Alan started to talk, and would continue to do so for some nine hours. The three aspects of the goddess of the Underworld were invoked through an excavation of childhood memories, which would emerge as the underlying theme of the session. The archetype of the maiden appeared in the form of fondly remembered but unobtainable childhood sweethearts. Three evocative names were recalled and written down, enclosed in an arrow-pierced heart. For Alan, the name of the object of my adoration, Vivian West, conjured 'silver screen images of a Hollywood siren from the golden age'. Tim's Angela Bass was 'she of the profound marine heart,' and Alan's lost girl, Janet Bentley, brought to mind 'a silvered bonnet mascot signalling the English form'. The mother appeared in Oedipal recollections of sharing our mother's beds when we were infants and being sexually excited by touch, smell, and proximity.[4] The crone was most evident in memories of old, witchy teachers, eccentric aunts, ancient grannies, and doddering shopkeepers retrieving rancid dust-covered sweets from jam jars in dingy village shops. I recounted my fever dream of Hecate, mainly for Tim's edification.

We talked of the magic 'nights' that took place in the cinema on Saturday mornings, the faded gilt and velvet theatre of dreams. We talked of the battlefield that was the playground, its terrors and ecstasies. 'The child is the father of the man,' Alan said. 'Everything that we are comes down to that primordial playground.' We spoke of tree-house fraternities, gang initiations in attic dens, the mysterious dark world of the public park spinney, and the secret hordes of semi-burnt pornography found there, which led us onto the fascination of 'dad's drawer'. (The more lurid pages of the Henry Miller novels in my dad's bedside treasure trove would fall open with ease, as they had been fingered so often.)

We spoke of those moments when the light gets through the cracks; the fissures in everyday humdrum 'reality'; those moments of awe-inspiring, 'kick in the eye' revelation. Poetic insight spilled from Alan's mind, and I handed him a notebook and pen, telling him to write. He scrawled down a few words, and then his hand started to move with a very different rhythm.

'Oh!' he exclaimed. 'Did you see that? That's the first time that I've done that. Did you see?'

I answered in the affirmative. Automatic writing. I looked at the words on the page, where he had written

The secret holy animal heart of our pubic hair, radiant and angelic

Another hand had then completed the verse:

Burning like an iron storm in the heart of universal flame.

After this, it was as if an extra-bright light had been lit within Alan. He ascended to new peaks of poetic inspiration, holding Tim and I in thrall to his brilliance. Most of these utterances would form the text of *The Birth Caul*, the recording of which the three of us would complete later in the year.

Before retiring for the evening, Tim told us that his father had died two weeks earlier, and the Underworld moved in a little closer. We hugged him and bid him sweet dreams. After he had gone, Alan turned to me and posed a question.

'What are we?' he asked, and then answered it himself. 'We are monsters! You, me, Tim, and others like us—we're monsters. We're what happens when working-class children are given a certain amount of good education, which we then take and use to turn the tables on those who gave it to us in the first place. Those authorities and lawmakers. We're monsters!'

Addressing me, now, he went on, 'You! You're not like everybody else. You know that, don't you? You share with the rest of us a kind of glorious madness. There's something very birdlike about you. That description of you as Ariel is pretty spot on.[5] Mel agrees. You make beautiful elegant shapes in the air. It's the energy of birds. The mad eyes of gulls! Yeah, you obey a different law and everyone who knows you or knows of you, they respect it, because … what you do is powerful! Then there's Tim. Tim is like a great mad Victorian steam-driven machine of an infinitely elaborate construction. An engine that blows out jets of steam all over the place. Yes, definitely mad!'

'And what about you, Alan?' I asked. 'Or perhaps I should try to say?'

'Yes, perhaps that would be better. It's harder to see what you are when you're so close to it.'

'Well,' I began, thinking, *where does one start?* 'You have great depth. It's like layers upon layers upon layers. Your mind whirs. It's hard to put into words really!'

'You're highly intuitive, more so than me, and that's saying something.'

'But you are a great articulator,' I replied.

'Yes,' he said, 'I can name things, define them, and that's what I have to do here. I have some magic words to find, but that's what we are: monsters. Old genes, an old stain. Tough genetic lines. Different, powerful, and there was a moment when your dad recognised that power—didn't understand it, but grew to respect it. Your mother, your mother knew it all along. From the first kick. She knew you were special. Yes, the mothers of monsters.'

It was 6:30am and we decided to go down to the Underworld in the cellar. We crouched down before the ram's skull, and Alan spoke of the 'original ancestor', and of the correctness of the talismanic skull. Smiling, he kissed his elaborately ringed fingers and placed them on its crown.

Returning to the attic, Alan described the events of the evening as being similar to coming across a cave painting; to holding our flaming torches up to discover something wonderful. It was, he said, 'One of those times of discovery where we'll look back and say: *we were there.*'

* * *

Shortly after this long, spellbound night, I either a) entered into a prolonged ecstatic communion with the gods, or b) went completely mad. It's a fine line.

A burst of white light inside my head, a tingling flash of intuition, and

I would be off. It was as if my entire nervous system had become a finely tuned psychic antenna. The ordinary everyday world would recede, and I would zone in close to the etheric field, there to retrieve treasures.

Sometimes, these seizures would strike while I was driving, and my intended route would be abandoned in favour of a magickal mystery tour. I would motor on until I felt the pull of a kind of electromagnetic force. There would be no ambiguity in this: it was as striking as a slap in the face. *Here! Stop here! Get out and find it!*

Quite what 'it' was would not always be apparent, but gradually, as I surveyed the foreign environment, so it would dawn on me. On one occasion, having pulled over by a long, narrow ditch in the middle of god knows where, I had the distinct directive that I was to find some kind of skull. 'Where are you?' I started to say to myself as I foraged about in the undergrowth. 'Where's my skull?' I began to perceive a strobing red light behind my eyes—a sign that the object of my search was close. It built to a climax, and as I sank my hands into a thick pile of damp leaves and bracken, I clasped something small, rounded, and hard. The leaves exploded in a cascade as my clenched hands re-emerged, and there, cupped in my palms, was a fanged skull. Intoxicated and thrilled, I held it up to the stark white sky. A cat!

BLAAAAAAAAAAAAAH!

I was rudely shaken from my reverie by a loud car horn. I had parked in front of a farm gate, blocking another car's exit. Pulling myself back together, and with prize in hand, I rushed over to my old Rover and moved it forward a couple of yards. Apologetically, I waved the other car past, but instead of driving on, the driver turned off the ignition and got out. It was a tweedy, country-set woman in her middle years. She strode over to my door and nervously peered in.

'Can I help you?' she asked.

'No, thanks, I don't think so.'

'Are you sure? Are you looking for something?'

'I just found something,' I said.

'You … found something?'

'Yes.'

The woman shot me the most suspicious look. I was in an altered state of high excitation, and I am sure that my wild disposition must have been alarming.

'It's just that some horses have been stolen from that field,' she continued, 'and it's just as well to be cautious.'

I told her that I had found a skull, which I am sure did nothing to assuage her suspicions of my lunacy. I held it up to show her, and it seemed to induce a nervous tick in her eye. She was obviously dealing with a complete madman.

'Oh!' she exclaimed. 'It looks like a cat!'

I vociferously agreed and told her that I was not looking for horses. Nervously, she apologised for acting as she had and beat a hasty retreat back to her car. The accelerator was quickly engaged, and she sped off in a cloud of exhaust fumes and a huge spray of mud.

The next day, I received another mental directive that I should find a dead blackbird to go with the cat's skull. This thought occurred to me just as I was driving off on a short errand, and when I returned home, there was a dead blackbird lying in the road where my car had been parked. Excitedly, I scooped it up. The body was still warm, and there was no sign of a predatory skirmish. It must have dropped from the sky, dead on the wing.

I took the bird down to the cellar and cut off its wings, tail feathers, and legs using pinking shears. These I then nailed to a wooden cross, setting the feline skull above it and completing the assemblage with quartz, topaz, and aquamarine. Over the coming six months, I would create many similar fetish objects. Years later, these objects would be displayed alongside drawings from the same period in an exhibition entitled Ju Ju Shit. The following is my introductory statement from the catalogue:

All of the work exhibited here (with the exception of 'Blue Jay Fetish', 1997, and 'Warrior' and 'Hecate', 1998) was created during a highly intense six-month period in 1995.

Prior to making a piece, I would often become seized by a sort of precognitive intuition as to its nature and constituent parts.

I would then see portents of this form in the simulacrum read into various phenomena such as discarded detritus (the shape of a skull in a wind-blown paper bag, a snake in a length of hose, a dead bird in a small pile of leaves.) Very soon after these visionary 'misreadings', the imagined article would manifest; a condition of shamanic arrest would then be experienced, in which I would become totally absorbed in the assembly of the piece. Finally, I would emerge from this altered state of consciousness to consider the strange and marvellous object presented before me, the wax still hot and pungent to my reeling senses. Often, I would incorporate intuited references to Gematria and obscure arcane correspondences that would later be borne out as accurate by referring to various occult writings (in particular Crowley's *777*).

On occasion, objects would appear as a result of conjuration. I would consciously visualise a required material and its subsequent acquisition. An immediate result would follow. This all served to magically charge the pieces, as they became both containers and conduits of power. Collectively, they form a pantheon of personal gods and daemons, each possessed of a particular identity/energy. Each, a shamanic loadstone of impacted force. By definition, the pieces could be described as fetishes, power objects used as focusing agents to bring about magickal change, mediators between the material and spiritual realms. They remain alchemical totems, talismans rendered from dream.

My good friend Alan Moore, being witness to the seminal product of this mysterious process, proclaimed, 'You're really onto something with this juju shit, man!' Hence the title.

With the creation of each object would come a lesson. One of the final pieces was 'Hecate'. A curved tree root was used for the main section; three cowrie shells and a glass eye were affixed to the front, and a series of interconnecting wishbones formed a kind of spine down the back. Wax was employed as a binding agent. Three other 'eyes' were formed using wax and small stones, and set atop the yearning upper branches.

I wanted to mount the whole thing onto a beautiful piece of spiked purple amethyst crystal, but the surface was too sleek and would not bind. This was a problem, and I felt that its solution was of great import, beyond that of the merely practical. After much contemplation it dawned on me. I simply turned the subterranean stone over, so that the flat dull underside was on top. The tree root stood solid as the wax seeped into the porous dull grey surface. The exquisite gleaming purple was now unseen. Underneath … under … Underworld! Of course! Hecate had taught me another lesson: hidden beauty is sometimes more potent than that which is exposed.

With this, I suddenly realised that I was famished. There was an apple in the fruit bowl, and I sank my teeth into it. With this bite, I was seized by the notion that to fully honour the goddess, it might perhaps be appropriate to destroy this thing of great beauty that I had just created with her help. I took another bite. The idea was agonising. This was the most sublime piece thus far, and the thought of destroying it was painful. But no! It would have to be done. The act should be simply like that of biting into an apple—*like this!* I chomped down for the third time. Then came another revelation. Echoing around in my head, I distinctly heard an ancient female voice, 'No, not like that, but rather like the first bite. Pure, and without attachment.'

This was the art of letting go—ultimately at the time of one's death—another invaluable teaching from the goddess of the dark hours. A lesson to live and to die by, and one that would find urgent application in the weeks to come, as juju was inexorably followed by voodoo, amid a powder keg of unexploded sorcery. The fuse had been lit.

CHAPTER TEN
Voodoo

The incessant rat-a-tat-tat of rainfall hammered down on the London taxi's roof. The sky was dark steel grey, as usual. It would be good to get some Californian sun. It was the winter of 1995, and I was on my way to Heathrow airport to catch a flight to LA, to continue work on the new Love And Rockets album. We had a meeting booked with Rick Rubin, head of American Recordings, and Marc Geiger, our old friend, agent, and confidante, now the label's head of A&R.

'Do you guys have enough room back there?' Rick asked, as we scrambled into his huge black Bentley.

'Are you kidding?' Marc replied. 'You could get ten of these guys in this thing!'

The car rolled through the night lights of Hollywood and headed west on our way to Jones's restaurant, which was part-owned by the man at the wheel. Rick phoned ahead to order his 'special bread'. When we arrived, we were ushered through to one of several big booths (in the one next to us were Madonna and her fawning entourage).

The bread arrived, piping hot from the oven, just after we sat down. Rick, it seemed, wanted to be involved in the making of our own special bread. What direction did we have planned for the new album, he wondered? Did we have a sound in mind? Were there any musical reference points? We chatted up a storm, and then came the question of where would Daniel and I stay while we worked on the album. (Kevin was already living in LA at this point.)

'Why don't you stay at my place in the hills?' Rick suggested.

The following day, Daniel and I relocated to the old Steinway Mansion at 2451 Laurel Canyon, a sprawling, all-white Spanish-style residence that had been built in the 1920s for the Prince of Wales, who had been planning a visit to California. Apparently, he bypassed the great house completely, carrying on down south instead for an illicit tryst with Wallace Simpson. The imposing stone lions that flank the driveway still await the gaze of royalty that will never come. The impressive building then fell into the hands of an early Hollywood mogul, who used it to stage wild parties for the glittering stars of the nascent celluloid firmament. Louis Brooks danced cheek-to-cheek with Charlie Chaplin, the reluctant recipient of a 'gentleman's excuse-me' from Rudolf Valentino, who would become the next owner, followed by Rita Hayworth, and then the Steinways.

Four decades later, the house would be the location for more Bacchanalia, when the resident Beatles would kick off their Cuban heels and host trip parties, the booze and cocaine of days gone by replaced with LSD and pot. Jimi Hendrix also lived there during that turbulent decade, while in the 70s it was a temporary home to Led Zeppelin, David Bowie, and Mick Jagger. Toward the end of the decade, the building became vacant and fell into disrepair. It was taken over by a marauding horde of druggy, troglodyte squatters who lived in the basement, venturing forth only at night to feed on smack and moonlight amid the crumbling Grecian pillars that lined the grounds. The mansion is situated directly across the road from what is reputed to be Harry Houdini's old gaff, and rumour has it there are a series of tunnels connecting the two buildings. Wooed by the association with the Fab Four, Rick purchased the place in the nineties, and produced the Red Hot Chili Peppers' album *Blood Sugar Sex Magik* there.

Daniel was in the kitchen when I stumbled in to make some tea at 5am. We were both still feeling the effects of jet lag—this was not our usual wake-up time—when we were suddenly shaken by a resounding crash coming from the entrance hall and rushed out to investigate.

The huge iron double doors were still vibrating from the slam. I tried the heavy handle, and it took some considerable pressure for the door to open. I had walked through the hall a few minutes before we had heard the sound, and at that time the doors had been closed. There was no one else in the house. My eyes locked with Daniel's. We furrowed our brows, shrugged, and drank some strong, hot tea.

* * *

Our gear arrived on a Monday. Everything—all of our musical equipment had been shipped over from the UK: our old and trusted backline, which could be traced back to the early days of Bauhaus; Daniel's H&H amp tops and Marshall amps; my vintage Ampeg bass rig: the 1974 fretless Fender Precision Bass that I had been playing ever since the 'Bela' session; Daniel's silver Fender Strat and his 1956 Selmer sax; my 1967 Gibson J-45 acoustic, and the rest of the classic guitar arsenal.

We had also arranged to borrow Steve Perkins's Keith Moon-style drum kit, and that too turned up on the same day. Back in 1987, we had taken the fledgling Jane's Addiction on a tour of America with us. We became fast friends, and had stayed in touch over the years that followed. The day before our meeting with Rick, former Jane's Addiction frontman Perry Farrell had contacted Daniel to ask him to play on a record by his new band, Porno For Pyros, who were working at the famous old Shangri La Studio in Malibu. Kevin and I were invited to hang out, too, and we all ended up playing on a track called 'Porpoise Head', which detailed one of Perry's extreme paranoid wig-out episodes—and which were occurring with alarming frequency at that time.

Perry was convinced that the studio was haunted, and indeed a strange thing happened when I was about to shoot some pool with him there. He had just finished playing a game with someone else, and all of the balls were in the pockets. We started to set up for the new game but discovered that two of the balls had inexplicably gone missing.

I stretched out my arms and leaned over the table. 'Oh great spirit of the pool hall, please may we have our balls back?'

At this, Perry looked down, and saw that the two errant balls were sitting in one of the pockets. We thanked the mischievous spooks and got on with the game.

Back in Laurel Canyon, we started to work on our own songs. We were very much in the flow, and ideas were coming thick and fast. It was a wonderful environment to work in and the resident muses seemed to egg us on. It was inspiring and heady to think that The Beatles, Hendrix, Bowie, and Led Zeppelin had all made music within those walls. One of the most powerful pieces that we produced was called 'Ritual Radio'. It was one of those rare, magical tracks that spontaneously rise to the surface, when you as a musician appear to be acting as some sort of a conduit for an outside energy. The subject matter was concerned with that very notion (aligned with a strong sexual undertone). The words came to me like gifts:

> *Sending, receiving, sending receiving*
> *You're wide open, wide open and I'm sending, sending … receiving*

The night we produced this seventeen-minute epic, we had simply picked up our instruments and started to play. The music happened instantly. It was slow, deep, and heavy—relentless crashing waves of spacey sound. I found myself singing in a new voice, and it was very odd: I felt somehow removed from what was coming out of my mouth, and yet at the same time completely immersed in it. It felt mediumistic. This 'channelled' voice was deeper than my usual voice, and had elements of Ian Curtis and Jim Morrison about it; indeed, the feel of the song was very Doors-like. We caught the whole thing on tape; you can hear Daniel calling out the chord changes and myself also giving instructions. Magic in the can!

Of course, there was also another kind of magic being conducted at this time—the kind that is spelled with a *k*. Upon my arrival at the mansion, I had a strong intuition that the next fetish object I should make would be all about The Snake. Fire energy. Rejuvenation. Primal instinct.

On the day we arrived, I decided to seek out a power spot, and after scouring the grounds, I found it: an elliptical flat stone laid into the earth a couple of yards from the south wing. I circled its circumference with my right index finger and sat there in meditation for an hour. I started to visualise snakes. They were in the bushes all around me, and I began to mentally draw them in. I hauled at the air with both hands and tuned into the centre of ancient reptilian repose.

I thought of a dream I had in which I had been surrounded by thousands of snakes. I had felt great fear but then calmed down as I tuned into their strange slow, slow frequency, and ultimately experienced an ecstatic communion, acceptance, recognition, and response, my fear abating as I made the great psychic leap into that alien dimension. Lizard time! Into the bush and the long grass flew my thoughts. I heard the sinewy slither and swish and felt the intense laser-beam focus of predatory instinct.

Crouching, I turned in the circle, all the time concentrating on drawing in The Snake. In my mind's eye I saw sloughed off skins. I pulled in these flaky sleeves as I completed the clockwise circuit. Over the next few days, I repeated this ritual at three other cardinal points around the house, ending at the eastern spot. Here, I shot a Polaroid of the house, which I took back to my room to conduct the final part of the rite: a splat of gold wax on the right of the picture, red at the bottom, blue on the left, and green at the top, these colours representing the four points of the compass. With each extinguishing of the candles, I traced a circle in the smoke, and then, using a Magic Marker (which made me smile), I drew a pentagram enclosed in a circle over the entire area of the house.

I held a lighter under the picture and watched as the chemicals reacted with the heat and the image buckled and cracked. I peeled off the upper layer to reveal a startling image underneath: a bubbling cauldron of snakes entwined around the two ghostly lions, those spectral guardians of the northern gate, and between them a charred hole where the rehearsal room was located. Within three weeks, I would have my snakeskin, and within four, that room would be gutted by fire, everything in it reduced to ash and molten metal.

* * *

The previous year, while recording in San Francisco, Daniel had become quite friendly with Genesis P. Orridge, who had relocated to a place just north of the city. Daniel and I made a couple trips over the Golden Gate

Bridge on his Harley to visit the former enfant terrible of the avant-garde. With his gold teeth and purple dreads, he looked very different to how I remembered him, but he was as charming and eccentric as ever.

Now, with this reconnection having been established, we received a request from Genesis while we were working at Rubin's mansion. Psychic TV had a gig booked at a club called Cinematic in LA, and he was looking for a place to stay and rehearse. Could we help? I told him that we would have to check with Rick. The request was approved, and on April 6 1995, Gen drove down from the Bay Area in his sky-blue gas-guzzler. The rest of the band turned up the next day.

Gen asked if I would be interested in playing with them on a cover of Pink Floyd's 'Set The Controls For The Heart Of The Sun'. The previous day, I had shown him a new experimental setup with which I was producing some pretty extraordinary sounds by rolling a Chinese metal meditation ball along the open tuned strings of my fretless bass, which sat horizontal in its case, plugged into various effects units, including pitch-shifter, fuzz, and delay. Gen loved it and wanted me to use it on the track. The rehearsal went well, and I was looking forward to playing it the following night at the gig.

Gen's personal assistant, Lisa Lupa, arrived on the day of the show. She introduced herself and handed me a large plastic bag full of silvery white snakeskin, apparently obtained from an albino python that had been reared by a high priestess in the Bay Area. A few days earlier, I had asked Gen if he still had the large snake I remembered from his days in Brighton, but he told me it had been confiscated, along with everything else in his home, when the police had swooped during the time of the witch-hunt that ultimately brought him to America. He had made inquiries, however, and I was holding the results in my hands.

* * *

Gen and I were sharing a large room at the back of the house. At one point, he was in the tub in the bathroom, which was adjacent to our shared quarters. Lisa was bathing him, and as I was lying on my bed a few feet away, I could not help but overhear their conversation. Gen was submerged not just in soapy water but also in a morass of self-loathing.

'Am I just a really fucked up person?' he asked. 'Sometimes I really hate myself.'

'Oh, Gen, please,' Lisa replied. 'You're a great person. A really great person! You inspire people.'

'Maybe, but I'm still fucked up.'

I felt uncomfortable being privy to this, so I went downstairs to make some tea. When I returned, Gen was trying on the outfit he intended to wear for the performance: Doc Martens sprayed silver, red tights, a silver corset drawn in wasp-waist tight, and the old snake's nest of dreads decorated with multi-coloured ribbons, beads, and bows. He flashed his gold teeth in an Artful Dodger smile.

'What do ya think?' he asked.

'Lovely!' I replied. 'Give us a twirl, then!'

Dead camp, he granted my request, and then asked if I could pull the corset strings tighter.

'Are you sure?' I asked. 'You're not going to faint, are you?'

'No, of course not. Come on!'

As I complied with his wishes, a bizarre thought crossed my mind: *what would my dad think if he walked in now?* Later that night, I would be amused by the chinking sound produced by the little man's many piercings as he walked across the room to the bathroom, naked in the dark. It sounded like a team of Morris dancers in full flight round the Maypole.

* * *

Cinematic was a dimly lit, dungeon-like S&M club in the heart of Hollywood. I entered to the audio face-slap of 'Open Up', Leftfield's killer collaboration with John Lydon, and its incendiary hook of 'Burn Hollywood burn!' As I squeezed through the sweaty leather, pleather, and latex, I suddenly came face to face with the former Sex Pistol himself.

'Nice one, John!' I exclaimed, only to be met with that infamous blood-curdling, twisted stare. I smiled, shrugged, and moved on, eventually finding my way to the secret back room, where I whispered the password ('Nipple Clamps'). Inside, I found Howard Hallis—Timothy

Leary's personable personal assistant, whom I had met when he had accompanied Gen to Rick's place—resplendent in a powder-blue suit with matching derby hat, bent over a table and receiving six of the best from a leggy dominatrix. Seated to his left and egging the girl on was Dr Leary himself. Howard shrieked out in mock agony. I removed his hat and placed it on the head of the whip-cracker. Tim, dressed in red dickey bow and striped suspenders, raised his glass in a salute. Howard stood up, brushed off his pants, and introduced me to the gentleman whom Richard Nixon had once described as 'the most dangerous man in the America'. The night was off to a good start.

I decided to go back into the main room to get another drink. Gen suddenly appeared and leaned in close to my ear. 'There's someone I want to introduce you to,' he explained. He led the way back to the bar, where Lydon was still holding beery court.

'John, this is David J., from Bauhaus.'

'Hello John,' I said. 'We meet again!'

'Oh, 'ello,' he replied. 'Sorry, if I had known who you were I wouldn't have been such a cunt earlier on!'

'That's all right. I meant what I said about that track. It's bloody marvellous.'

'Cheers! All right, let's get some drinks in.'

A fan picked up on this suggestion and offered to buy John a drink.

'Thanks, mate. I'll 'ave two beers, and my brother will 'ave two 'n' all.'

Another poor unfortunate sycophant appeared soon after.

'John! John! I don't mean to bug you but I'm your greatest fan!'

''Ello, greatest fan,' Lydon replied, 'goodbye, greatest fan, fuck off!'

With that, the poor fellow slumped off into the throng. The beers arrived, and we all clinked bottles with gusto, spilling the foaming brew all over the place.

I tugged at Lydon's sodden lapel. 'John,' I began. 'I'm not your greatest fan but'—again with that pop-eyed screw—'I have to tell you, and I know you must get this all the time, but it's fuckin' true: you changed my life when I saw the Pistols at the 100 Club back in '76. Without that, I wouldn't be in a band right now. So, cheers!'

The former Johnny Rotten crooked his index finger, beckoning me to come close. With a degree of apprehension, I complied. He then planted a big wet smacker on my cheek. I grinned and repaid in kind. *Mmmmmmmwah!* Lydon shook up his bottle, spraying a torrent of beer over me, himself, and the crowd.

The night roared on. At one point, Tim Leary popped up like a little leprechaun. Gen started to introduce us, but the doctor interjected. 'We already know each other,' he grinned. 'We're old pals!'

Soon it was time for Gen to get ready to go onstage and he slipped away though the packed house.

"E's a chap, in' 'e!' John's brother, Martin Lydon, remarked. 'I thought 'e'd be a right poncey cunt, but 'e's alright! Yeah, 'e's a chap!'

Lydon and I moved closer to the stage. The band were already up there. The music started to swell, a thick, churning psychedelic stew. Gen joined them and launched into a rap about the significance of this event and the fact that there were three generations of rebels in the audience: Timothy Leary, Wayne Kramer from the MC5 (whom I did not meet that night, but who later became a friend and collaborator), and Johnny Rotten. He started to ramble and riff in a somewhat garbled fashion. It went on and on. People in the crowd were handing gifts to him. Gen stuck out his tongue to show off what looked like a large white horse pill nestled in the furrow of his tongue. (I have no idea if he swallowed it or not.) Howard was down the front filming everything.

At one point, a striking, raven-haired woman climbed onto the stage and started to grapple with Gen, wrestling him to the floor. They rolled around for several minutes before the security guys pulled her off. Gen stood up, raised his arms high above his head, and then collapsed. He stayed down and appeared to be out cold. The band shot nervous glances at each other but continued to play. After several uncomfortable minutes, the security men once again took the stage, this time to check on the supine singer. The big guard shook his head and frantically gesticulated to someone at the rear of the club. He looked to the band and shook his head, drawing a line across his throat with the back of his hand. Something was seriously wrong.

I looked at Lydon, who shrugged and grimaced as Gen was carried off and taken outside into the street. I pushed my way through the bewildered crowd. Gen was sitting, slumped over on a chair on Hollywood Boulevard, his long dreadlocks and silver boots splattered with puke.

'Water!' somebody shouted. 'Give him some water!'

'Someone should stick an ice cube up his ass!' another voice added. 'That's the way to bring him round.'

This sage advice came from Z'EV. It was the first time that I had seen him since 1982.

'Ice cube up the ass!' the voice of experience continued. 'Does it every time!' No one was stepping up to the plate, though.

After that, the paramedics turned up and asked Gen the usual questions.

'Are you CIA?' he cheekily asked, before satisfying them that he was sufficiently recovered and *compos mentis* enough not to require their services.

Back at the mansion a caffeine-fuelled vigil ensued. The night watch consisted of Daniel, Lisa, Larry Thrasher from PTV, and myself. We wanted to keep Gen awake long enough to be sure that he was out of danger—and no longer in need of the anal insertion of frozen water. Eventually, once we were satisfied that this was the case, we left him to sleep it off on the couch in the great hall.

I woke around noon and went down to check on the occupant of the black leather couch. He wasn't there, but propped up against the pillow was a startling little figure: a black-faced voodoo doll of extremely sinister aspect.

I looked closer. The head was covered in real skin of some sort. It had what appeared to be grey human hair, which was tied with a red ribbon at the back. The doll was wearing a fine antique lace dress and a necklace of tiny shells and coloured beads, and its little beady eyes gave the impression that they were actually seeing out. It looked ancient and malevolent.

Gen suddenly appeared in the hall. I asked him how he was feeling, and he said that he was fine.

'What's this?' I asked, pointing to the doll.

'That was the strangest thing. This morning, when I woke up, I felt something stuffed down the front of my pants. It was that thing! It's very disturbing isn't it?'

'Yes, it certainly is! How the fuck …?'

'I've no idea!'

I suggested that he'd be wise to leave it outside.

* * *

That night, Gen took the strange doll out into the grounds. He said he wanted to 'talk' to it. He and Lisa searched until they found the right spot. Once located, Gen made a protective circle of salt and stepped inside. Lisa stood outside the circle, holding the doll.

'I just want to know why you're here,' Gen asked, staring into the tiny black eyes. 'Where did you come from? Why did you come?' He would receive his answer later that night, while he slept.

The following day, Gen told me about his dream. He was standing in the dark, surrounded by smoke. There was something moving though this thick grey morass. It was the doll. Staring blankly into his eyes, it spoke, telling him, 'I've come to make you love yourself.' With that, the weird apparition walked backward through the smoke until it was gone.

After Gen told me this, I immediately went out onto the balcony and looked down. The circle of salt was in exactly the same place I had located my own power spot.

* * *

Flames leapt from the charred top of the speaker cabinet, licking at the walls, as the small room filled with choking, acrid smoke. Fortunately, Lisa was on hand, and had the presence of mind to throw a dampened towel over the blaze.

'It was a good thing you got to that when you did, Lisa!' said Billy 'Pink' Goodrum, the keyboard player with Psychic TV, as he surveyed the semi-renovated, wood-panelled walls of the old house. 'This whole place could go up like a tinder box!'

That night, Daniel, Kevin, and I resumed our writing session. Gen asked if he could jam with us, and we were soon locked into a thunderous riff. Gen was using his old 'Gristleizer' eight-string bass, which he had been playing since the 70s with Throbbing Gristle. The instrument was fed through a unique custom-built distortion device, and it sounded incredible. We definitely had something cooking, and we rolled tape to capture the magic.

The music was a great grinding beast, a leviathan over which Daniel started to shriek, 'Hey you! You owe me money!' over and over, like some crazed black mantra. At the same time, words were also coming out of my mouth: 'Mojo here, mojo there, mojo working everywhere.' There were other lines about 'drawing down the power', 'shinning through the grave', and 'the hot wire'.

Daniel broke into a new refrain:

You'll take to drink in the morning again, beware of them blues
A heartache from hell, my friend, is on the cards for two

After that, he returned to his motif, with the addition of a philosophical and placatory 'but it's all right'. Toward the end, we joined together in a chant of 'Got my mojo working'—like the old Muddy Waters blues number—which mutated into 'Money is my mojo, blood money!'

The track was propulsive and massive, frightening in its vicious intensity. It went on for fifteen intense minutes, and then we quit for the night. Nothing could follow that!

One by one, we all slipped off to bed for a relatively early night, except for Daniel, who stayed up for hours, playing the same track over and over again: 'If 60's Were 90's' by Beautiful People, which sampled Jimi Hendrix's 'Voodoo Chile' and 'If 6 Was 9' to great effect. Lying in bed, hearing the track boom through the floorboards, it occurred to me that Hendrix's original songs might well have been written in the very room in which these deconstructed versions were now being played.

As I drifted off to sleep, I was aware of a weird floating presence that I had felt several times since moving into the Steinway house: a female spirit that hovered above my body. There was nothing negative about this; in fact, I perceived it to be a positive, warm, and encouraging entity. It seemed to feed off creativity. It was the archetypal muse, in fact.

This was in stark contrast to whatever it was that I had encountered in the vine-covered granny cottage adjacent to the house a week earlier. Instantly upon entering the building, I had felt the extremely unpleasant sensation of being heavily weighted and dragged down. It was like psychic quicksand. A mirror covered the entire north wall, and I felt that this dark energy was somehow emanating from it. I hauled myself upstairs, and the awful atmosphere grew even stronger. There was one room at the back that was just screaming with bad vibes. I knew I had to get out, fast, and I did.[1]

*   *   *

'FIRE!'

Somewhere, far off in the distance, a bell was ringing under water. My body leaden, I slowly emerged from dreaming into the sharp clear light of waking consciousness.

'FIRE! FIRE! DAVID, QUICK! GET UP! FIRE!'

I stumbled out of bed and opened the door. It was Keith Joiner from the band The The, who was also resident at the house.

'What?' I mumbled. 'Is it bad?'

Keith's eyes answered before his mouth. 'Yes, it's bad!'

I rushed over to wake Gen. He immediately ran next door to check on Lisa. Her bed was empty, as she had been the one to discover the fire, and it was she who had woken Keith. For the past three mornings, she had been waking up at 7:30 on the dot, which was curious, as she was usually a late riser.

Lisa had once again stirred at that relatively early hour this morning, but this time the alarm was ringing. When she ventured downstairs to investigate, she discovered that the rehearsal room was ablaze. By the time Gen returned, there was a thick column of lethal black smoke, barrelling down the hall and heading toward our room. I shut the door and laid towels along the space between floor and door. We threw duvets and pillows out to break our fall, plus a few precious items—my acoustic guitar, books, boots, and bags—and prepared to jump from the second story window.

Gen went first, climbing out onto the narrow ledge. Suddenly he slipped, twisted around, and fell backward, desperately grabbing at the thin branches of a tree before crashing down hard on his back. His head was an arm's length from the circle of salt that sparkled in the rising sun.

I jumped down and landed on my feet before rushing over to Gen. 'Are you OK?'

He told me, no, he was not OK, and that he had never felt such pain. An asthmatic, he was badly out of breath, and he wheezed out a request that I locate his inhaler. I ploughed through the piles of clothes and bags and eventually found it. I applied it to his mouth. He was in a very bad way. The heat being generated was incredible, and I feared that the large windows of the house would shatter at any moment. I gently stroked his hair and tried to reassure him that he would be OK. He did not seem convinced.

Lisa turned up and took over nursing duties from me, and I went to look for help. We had to get Gen away from those windows. Rounding the corner, I saw Daniel standing on a ridge. He was staring at the roaring flames, which had now completely consumed our rehearsal room. I stood by his side. Daniel said he was OK, although, like me, he was obviously very shaken. Despite this, we both shared the view that this terrible event was also beautiful in its own warped way.

The fire engines had arrived, and Rick's girlfriend had turned up, too, and was busy hauling clothes out of her design studio in the south wing. A freestanding circular clothes rail stood outside, and I was alarmed to see that its shadow had formed an inverted pentagram. I wanted to take a photo of this, so I ran down to Kevin's jeep, which was parked at the foot of the hill, knowing that he usually kept a camera in the glove compartment.

As I was looking for the camera, I was surprised to come across a bible. I clasped the holy book with both hands, held it to my forehead, and said a prayer. I could not find the camera, though, so I went back up to the house. When I got back there, Rick's assistant, Amy Lou, was taking a photograph of the shadow.

'This looks so ominous!' she exclaimed.

I nodded in agreement. 'I thought I was the only one who had noticed that.'

Amy asked if I wanted to take a photo of it. Looking at the simulacra through the camera lens, it occurred to me that the diameter of this black circle and the white circle of salt were the same. I took a picture, being very careful not to get my foot or those of anyone else in the frame, as I intuitively felt that this could be dangerous. Then I measured the two circles. They were exactly the same. I felt overwhelmed by it all, and I collapsed down onto a rock. I held my head in my hands and prayed again. I prayed for spiritual light and some positive energy to balance out the darkness, which, at that point, was symbolised by the black inverted star cast by the sun on the crazy paving.

I felt a hand on my shoulder.

'Are you all right?'

I looked up to see a beautiful young blonde woman, her hair haloed by the blazing sun. She had a multi-coloured pentagram tattooed on her upper left arm. This one was not inverted. It was the perfect balance to the other.

'I'm a friend of Rick's,' she said, 'and I was driving, and this report came on the radio about a fire at a house in Laurel Canyon, and somehow I thought that it might be Rick's place. I came straight over.'

I told her that I was fine and thanked her with an enthusiasm that must have seemed somewhat over the top. She smiled radiantly. I stood up and gave her a big hug. The firemen had moved Gen onto a wooden board and were now carrying him at shoulder height down through the tiered gardens. It resembled the courtly procession of an exotic demigod.

* * *

'Morphine! He needs more morphine!'

The nurse refused our plea, informing us that the maximum legal dose had already been administered, and that the next shot would be in two hours time. Gen stoically accepted the news and asked if someone could help with his drink. I held the straw to his lips. He took little sips, punctuated by gulps of oxygen from an inhaler. A saline drip was inserted into his right arm, since his left had suffered the brunt of the damage: eight breaks and a shattered elbow. He had also sustained four cracked ribs and suffered a pulmonary embolism.

The nurse applied an ice pack. Charming as ever, Gen thanked her for her care and spoke about the wonderful dinner of peas and mashed potatoes in gravy that she brought to him. 'My favourite meal,' he added, 'and there's good news about the arm: the doctor says that I'll be able to play the guitar.'

'That's funny, Gen,' I said, unable to resist the opening. 'You couldn't play it before the accident! It's a bloody miracle!'

'You bastard!' he replied. 'Only an English person would come out with something like that! Bastard!' He smiled ruefully, flashing gold.

Before we left his ward at Cedars-Sinai, Gen related some very interesting information about the voodoo doll. He had become obsessed with the notion that it had had something to do with the fire.[2] He and Lisa had made contact with some voodoo experts, who informed them that it was a traditional voodoo love doll, but that it had been specifically altered to generate fire. The red ribbon sewn into the hair was symbolic of this. They were also told how to negate the doll's power. For twenty-four hours, it would need to be submerged face down in a bath of water mixed with natron, a purifying salted clay from the Nile that was used as an embalming agent in ancient Egypt. After this, the face would be removed, and the hands should then be cut off. Finally, it was to be bound to a lump of iron, placed inside a hessian bag, concealed inside a wooden box, and drowned in water, its opposite element.

The following night, Lisa returned to the grounds of the Rubin place and retrieved the doll. All of our instruments had been completely destroyed in the fire. Daniel's vintage Selma saxophone and all the various metal microphone stands and cymbals had melted in the heat. But the doll, which had been left in the entrance hall next to our rehearsal room and was made of cotton, lace, hair, and dried skin and stuffed with straw, was completely intact. Lisa followed her instructions to the letter, and twenty-four hours later, in the early hours of the morning, made her way to the ocean.

En route, she decided to stop by the hospital to check in on Gen. Following a strong intuition, she decided not to leave the doll in her car, instead hiding it away in a roadside dumpster, with the intention of retrieving it following her visit. Gen was in stable condition, and was smiling when she left. As the glass doors of the hospital slid open, however, Lisa met with an alarming sight. An LA County waste disposal truck was in the process of scooping up the very dumpster wherein lay the doll. She ran toward the vehicle, shouting for it to stop, but she was too late. The contents of the bin were unceremoniously dumped into the reeking guts of the truck, which then drove off at speed. Utterly despondent, Lisa watched as the truck's tail lights shrank and merged with all the others as the traffic became one long scarlet snake, winding its way into the smog of breaking dawn.

* * *

After the fire, Daniel and I relocated to the seedy Saharan Motel on Sunset Boulevard. I had borrowed several books on all things esoteric from my friend Kerry Colonna's extensive library, and spent all of my spare time studying the way of the shaman. One day, I decided to try out an experiment, following an exercise in one of the books. The idea was to induce a trance state in which one would be able to travel on the astral plane.

Looking out from my motel room window, I could see the tops of distant hills. I was curious as to what lay beyond them, so, lying down on the floor on my back, I concentrated on the location that I wished to 'remote view'. As advised by the book, I started to drum a slow repetitive beat on the floor with my hand. I soon found myself floating through the ether, while still aware of my body on the ground. It was as if I had been split into two, each component part being equally present in the moment. Focusing on the ethereal, I could see a winding path leading up to a high hill. Despite the lofty location, I sensed that this area had something to do with the Underworld. It exerted an intense pull, and I resolved to go to this place and investigate further. With this thought, I was immediately back in my body. I got up and headed for the hills.

Runyon Canyon Park is located to the north of Hollywood Boulevard, and is easily accessible from the street. There is a large metal gate at the entrance. Once inside, I followed my intuition, which led me to a winding path that appeared to be the one that I had seen in astral form. At the top was a hill with a solitary bare tree. It was calling to me. I knew that this was the spot.

When I reached the apex, I was somewhat taken aback by the sight of the charred body of a dead dog. It stank to high heaven. On closer inspection, I noticed that its head had been placed in a hole. It looked like someone had intended to bury the animal but had given up the dig. The tree had also been set alight, its gnarled silver branches blackened, twisted, and dead.

I sat at the foot of the tree and contemplated this scene. It suddenly struck me that this was the entrance to the Underworld, which in Greek mythology is guarded by the three-headed dog Cerberus. I pulled one of the animal's hairs from its rotting body and made my way back to the motel.

The next day, I tried the same astral exercise as before. I was back at the top of the hill in an instant. As I descended to the ground, my astral form shrank, so that I was about six inches tall. I stood gazing into the hideous maw of the dog. I entered its blackness and traversed through the canine's decaying corpse, going deeper and deeper through the repellent guts and bone, which gradually turned into stone and stalactite. I was in the Underworld! Then, as if waking from an especially vivid dream, I was back in the motel, lying on my back.

That was interesting, I thought.

I decided to go back to the Canyon on foot. The dog was gone. I sat with my back against the tree and meditated. After about twenty minutes, I opened my eyes and spotted a small, yellowed bone where the dog's body had been. In an impulsive act of wilful transgression, I picked it up and put it in my mouth. It tasted extremely sour and disgusting. I wanted to spit it out, but recognising this act as a rite of passage I did not. Instead, I rolled it around with the tip of my tongue. It felt pliable, and I had the impression that it was a small bone from the dog's ear. I had the distinct sense that I was in direct communion with Hecate, goddess of the Underworld. Some of the putrid flesh that was still on the bone slid off and I swallowed it down. It made me want to wretch, but instead I continued to sit, cross-legged in contemplation of Hecate's realm. Finally, I took the bone from my mouth. It would become part of a fetish object dedicated to the goddess of the dead.

This place on the hill was now a potent power spot for me, and I would return many times over the coming weeks. The last time I went thee, I decided to cut off a branch of the tree, from which I would fashion a wand. I climbed up to the highest point and made good with my knife. I felt a euphoric intoxication as a brisk wind blew through the silver branches and birds soared below.

As the blade sank into the flesh of the tree, I became aware of the sound of a distant drum. A simple Indian beat. I would find its source. Carrying the severed two-foot branch, full of gnarled knots, I made my way down the winding hillside. I thought about the gang—kids, no doubt—that had set fire to the tree from whence my wand in the making had come. *Maybe they had also set fire to the dog.* What did this act of arson mean to them? I felt that it was magickal on some buried level, not consciously but recognised as such in the subconscious. Although wantonly destructive, it must have been a very powerful event, especially considering its location, high above the city, the lights spread out like a panorama of neon jewels glinting in the poison fog of LA. Might it have been transcendental? Something primal and ritualistic, beyond the usual shits and giggles? Something outside of time?

The beat was getting louder. At the foot of the valley was a large abandoned amphitheatre. I ventured inside to find a group of about twenty young people painting large canvas flags in preparation for a rave that was to be held there that night. The drummer was sitting at the far end of the lichen-covered space, a tall, dark-skinned, dreadlocked man, his arms festooned with coloured bands and metal bracelets, a large

African djembe drum nestled between his legs. He smiled as I stood off to one side, nodding to the beat. I asked one of the kids if I could help them paint a flag.

'Sure, man,' he replied. 'You should come to the rave tonight!'

I dipped the end of the nascent wand into some silver paint and daubed a design: a large open eye, with the sign for infinity in the centre of the pupil.

* * *

We played our first show following the fire in late December 1995, at the Hollywood Grand. It was a great gig, played out with gusto in front of a very lively audience. In the wings, I had found a life-size cardboard cut-out of a white-suited John Travolta from *Saturday Night Fever*, which I grabbed for the encore, concealing myself behind it as we came back out. I promptly handed it over to the crowd, and 'Tony Manero' crowd surfed to the back of the room.

There was a large crowd of people backstage after the show, from which two individuals made their presence felt strongly but in very different ways. Back in 1989, I had recorded a version of the eden ahbez classic 'Nature Boy' for my album *Songs From Another Season*. It was recorded late one night at Woodbine Studios in Leamington Spa, as something of a casual afterthought, with Max Eider on guitar, Owen Jones on drums, and Alex Green on sax. I had earlier suggested we might explore the song if we had time, and now, as we were wrapping up a long session, Max started to play those lovely jazz chords. Everyone joined in, and the voice of John Rivers the engineer suddenly crackled excitedly over the intercom.

'Guys! This sounds amazing! I'm going to roll tape!'

We captured a little bit of magic that night. Later, I sent a copy of the recording to the composer's publishing company. It was a real long shot, and I was not counting on a response, but that night in Hollywood I received one. Amid the after-show throng, one gentleman stood out, as he was wearing a smart suit and tie rather than the *de rigueur* leather and black denim. We made eye contact across the room and he tentatively approached me. He told me that he had been eden ahbez's personal assistant and care-giver (ahbez having died in March that year) and that he had come to the show in order to convey his employer's words. He went on to tell me that my recording had been well received, and that eden had wished to impart the following message, which he now read aloud from a piece of paper:

It pleases me greatly that someone working in the modern idiom should interpret my song so effectively.

I was flabbergasted! Immediately after that came a tap on my shoulder, at which point I was introduced to some record execs. I had no interest whatever in schmoozing—as all I wanted to do was to re-engage with the mysterious ahbez envoy, but by the time I managed to break free the man was nowhere to be seen. He had completed his mission and left.

I pushed my way through the thick crowd of noisy liggers, desperate to find the man. My trajectory was suddenly blocked by a wiry young man of the most evil countenance. He had long, unkempt raven hair and looked like Hollywood Central Casting's ideal of a Satanic warlock, and I believe that that is quite possibly what he was, for when he held out his paw for a handshake, I instinctively responded, but was shocked to feel the sharp edge of a metal talon scratch into my palm.

'What the fuck?!' I exclaimed as I searched the man's gleaming black eyes with my own. In return, my assailant shot me a look of twisted glee and fled the scene. I looked down at the bloody gash, confounded and perplexed. Black magick? A hex? Motherfucker!

* * *

The following year proved to be a challenging one. My family had moved with me to the States, but we had not yet sold our old house in England, which was creating a serious drain on our finances. Love And Rockets toured extensively in support of our *Sweet F.A.* album, of which we were very proud, but it was poorly promoted and failed to sell. Attendance of our live shows dropped off drastically, even as the band was playing better than ever. It was all very disheartening, and I couldn't help but cast my mind back that strange encounter with the suspected black magician in Hollywood. I felt that I needed to counter this curse with some good strong mojo.

On the September 9 1996, I was back home in Pepperell, Massachusetts, when I awoke with an intense compulsion to go out into the grounds and dig. I found a spot near to a copse of tall pine trees. I dug feverishly with my hands, not knowing if I was looking for buried treasure or about to bury something myself. I intuited that it was the latter, and once the hole was about a foot deep, I set about finding the right thing. This proved futile, and I gave up the search. *The 'right thing' will become apparent*, I reasoned. *Let it go.*

Come the early evening I strolled over to see my neighbour, Gary Cook. A brilliant software engineer and expert on the Mayan calendar, Gary had invited me over to meet his friend Magdalena Garcia Soriano, or Malena for short, a shaman of Mayan descent who was visiting from Mexico City. When I arrived, Malena and her translator, Denise, were sitting on Gary's porch, two middle-aged women in jeans and T-shirts, chatting away and smoking cigarettes, at ease in the balmy Massachusetts Indian summer night.

At Malena's suggestion, a psychic reading ensued. For this, we adjourned to the attic. Malena had once been a highly respected doctor with a thriving practice in the city, but after receiving her calling to work as a shaman, she gave it all up and moved to an impoverished Southside ghetto to work with the poor people who resided there. She became renowned as a very powerful 'brujo', and would often work with the element of fire, making it appear spontaneously and then dance around the room in flaming spirals.

In the cloistered confines of the wooden attic, however, a less dangerous medium was employed. Two small glass vials of flower essence were unceremoniously set atop one of Gary's kids' books. Malena picked up one of the little bottles and held it to my nose. I recoiled at its pungency, although it was not unpleasant. She poured some of the liquid onto her hands and rubbed it in. Then she took my hands, placing the palms face down on top her own. She closed her eyes tight and spoke softly in Spanish while her friend interpreted.

She said that I had a very noble heart but that I might have a problem with my kidneys, adding that I should take care of this area, as the energy there was blocked. (As it transpired, I would later develop several kidney stones, and would undergo an operation for a hyperthyroid tumour in my throat—a condition that affects the kidneys, taking calcium from the bones and releasing it into the bloodstream.) She also said that I had experienced a lot of cash problems over the last three years, and that I had found it hard to make my money go very far. (Correct, alas!). She predicted that this situation would soon change, and that I would acquire wealth through music. She said that I had often been in this situation in the past where great progress is made but that each time it is stopped just at the point of becoming very successful. (Also true.) She said that there is someone who I work with, someone who is very important to that success, but that it is as if he slams a brick into the engine of a moving car. (I thought of Daniel, who for years had exhibited just such a self-destructive streak.) She said that this person would come around, and that the success that had eluded us would finely be achieved.

Malena went on to tell me that I had great energy, but that it tended to build up and explode. She said I must learn to contain and control this energy in order for it to work for me and not against me. She said that I needed to learn how to become balanced. She then said that she would unblock the energy. She asked the four of us to sit in a circle and requested that we close our eyes. She made a great exhalation of air. I then experienced a series of physical sensations, all of which Malena would describe immediately after the sensation was felt. I felt light-headed, dizzy, hot. When she asked where this heat was most concentrated, I told her it was in my forehead. Concentrating on this spot, I perceived a spiral, and without my saying anything about it, she described exactly what I was experiencing. She told me to go with it, as it would guide me.

By now, I was feeling extremely spaced-out. Malena told me that I would feel very full, and that there would be gases, and if it felt like they needed to come out then to let them do so. (Look out everybody!)

I immediately felt an intense, gaseous pressure in my stomach. She said that I would feel very light—I did—and that the goddess was with me. She named her as Xochitl, adding that if I were simply to say her name out loud, she would remain with me forever.[3] This I did, and I immediately felt an infusion of warm enveloping light coursing through my body. Then, evidently channelling this divine entity, Malena spoke:

> Thank you for being with me and visiting my lands. I have been dormant for centuries but now I have been awakened. From now on I shall be watching over you.

Then in a different tone of voice, she added, 'The energy is unblocked now.' With that, Malena and I each emitted a loud, barfly belch. Everyone laughed.

'You see?' she said, smiling. She then gave a sudden shudder, turned serious, and added, in a surprised voice, 'Who was that?'

Malena listened intensely as the interpreter went over everything that she had been saying in her trance state. The shaman then told me about Xochitl: that she is a solar deity, like a radiant light emitting positive energy, the light expanding ever outward, without end; that she is of the Universe, the cosmos, all embracing and powerful; an Aztec goddess connected to the Maya. She said that I would work with flower essences in the future, and that Xochitl would be the goddess presiding over this work.

I asked if there was a connection between Xochitl and Hecate. She said that there was, but only in as much as Xochitl is the balance, the solar to Hecate's lunar. She told me that Xochitl is more powerful than Hecate; that Hecate is very powerful, but Xochitl more so; that they were now both with me, working together. She explained how Hecate is a part of the triple goddess: Artemis is the half moon, Diana is the half moon, Hecate is the full moon, and when they are together, they are very, very powerful. She told me that I was with Hecate in the ancient past, and that I had served her. She said that I had been out of balance for a long time, occupying the lunar only, but now the solar had entered and was living inside me, and that balance had been restored. She smiled and said that no one could use magick to harm me; that if they tried, it would come back on them with great severity.

All of this prompted me to tell Malena about Genesis P. Orridge. I told her that he was something of a magician who, in my perception, had followed the left-hand path. I explained how I had known him for seventeen years, and that, although he had remained on the peripheral of my life, I had always felt a strong link with him. I told her that I dreamt of him a lot, and that I was somewhat wary of him.

I was about to show Malena a picture of Gen in the book that I had brought along when she sprang up and said, 'He is outside now, let's go!' We all followed her downstairs and outside onto the front porch. She requested that we all sit down, close our eyes, and place our hands in a prayer position.

'You will see him three times,' she said, 'then you will start the voyage.'

Three images flashed into my head: one of Gen when I first met him outside the town hall in Northampton; one of him with his dreadlocks piled high, standing in the kitchen in Rick Rubin's house in LA; and a third of him lying on his back, having just fallen from the bedroom window during the fire. Then another image roared into my mind's eye: an older man, partially bald, his remaining hair pulled back in leonine strands that fell down his back. He had an intense stare and was dressed in ceremonial robes.

Malena asked if we had all seen 'him', to which Denise and I answered in the affirmative. Gary said that he had felt him. Malena told us that his name was Erius, and that he was an alchemist. Denise said that she had had a vision of him coming to her and handing her a large book of wisdom. Malena said that, in a former life, Denise had been a student of his. She then said that Gen and I were this man reincarnated, but split; that we were like twins, and that Gen is the alchemist's essence, and that he is aware of this. She said that soon there would be a fusion.

I showed Malena a picture of Aleister Crowley and told her of Gen's affinity with him. She was unfamiliar with Crowley, but said that he and the alchemist were one. I suddenly felt winded by this revelation and clasped Malena's shoulder. Unfazed, she continued, saying that Gen and I were both priests of Hecate, and that we had been together in different incarnations through history—one of them being Aleister Crowley. I told her that I thought that you could only be reincarnated as one being. She said that sometimes, when a person dies, the soul is fragmented and then reincarnated in different bodies. This is what had happened with Crowley. She said that I still had something of his spirit, but that Gen had most of it.

I asked her if I should be wary of Gen. She gave a light shrug and smiled warmly. 'No,' she said. 'You will be fine.'

I thanked her and we went inside. Malena repaired to the attic to do a reading for Gary's oldest son, Jeff. My head was reeling, and I needed to absorb the events that had just taken place. I decided to take a walk. I told Gary that I would be back later to say goodbye to the ladies and strode back down the hill. I wanted to give Malena a gift—something meaningful and appropriate—and soon realised I had the very thing. A couple of years earlier, when Love And Rockets played a gig in Mexico City, I had visited the ancient pyramids of Teotihuacan. I was very sick with food poisoning, but I was determined to climb to the top of the pyramid of the moon. Once there, I collected some tiny stones from the four corners of the construction. I planned to give one of these to Malene and one to Denise. By the time I made it back to Gary's, however, they had gone.

* * *

As I made my way back home, it suddenly occurred to me just what that hole in the ground was for: the stones! There was no light pollution out there in the sticks, and as usual the night sky was emblazoned with countless stars. I knelt down by the hole and placed the first of the stones in the cavity while making a dedication to Denise. As I pushed it into the moist sod, I was overcome by a wave of emotion, and suddenly I was on the brink of tears.

'And this is for Malena,' I said, holding up the other stone so that it was haloed by the moon. I pressed it deep into the earth. As I started to fill in the hole, something extraordinary happened. Emanating from the earth was a tiny, dazzlingly bright green light. It was like the energy of a star compressed into a pinhead—a scintillating electric green.

I scooped up the clod of earth and held it close to my eyes, trying to rationalise what I was seeing. A firefly? It was the wrong season, though, and there was no insect there, only light. It remained aglow as I got up and carried it over to the porch. I wanted to put it in a jar, so I lay the clump down on the table but as soon as I did this, it simply disappeared.

The next day, I called Gary to tell him about these strange events. He contacted Malena. She was not at all surprised by my experience, and she had a message for me: 'Yes, that is Xochitl, that is how she comes—as a green light. She is with you now.'

It was a good thing, too, as over the coming years I was going to need all the help that I could get.

* * *

My father was also in need of help. He and my mother had moved to Australia in the early 80s, and he was in hospital there with a staph infection he had contracted while undergoing an operation on his knee. I was back in England at the time, as we were still trying to sell our house. I decided to employ the shamanic trance and travel technique that I had learned in LA in the hope of helping him.

Lying on the floor of our old Edwardian home, I started to play a slow, repetitive beat on the floorboards with my fingertips. With my eyes closed, and concentrating on the spot between my eyebrows, I induced a hypnotic, trance-like state in myself. I stilled my hand and spontaneously shape-shifted into the form of a bird. I was on my way!

As I soared on the wing, I could see shifting landmasses below me. Over patchwork-quilt fields and lakes I flew, over rolling hills and oceans, too. All the time I was still quite aware of my solid human form, lying on the floor in Northampton. My consciousness seemed to be split. Something told me that I had reached my destination and that I should descend. Swooping through the clouds, I could see what I realised were cars, and then a few tiny people.

It was night. A white building came into view, long rectangular interconnected structures. I swooped down and entered the building through a set of glass doors, making my way down the corridors, unseen in my stealth. Finally, I came to a room with an open door and went in. Quite clearly I saw my father lying in the hospital bed. He was sweating profusely, feverishly tossing and turning under the sopping sheets. I alighted at the foot of the bed, perched for a moment on the metal frame, and then, spreading my wings wide, shifted into another form: a black panther.

With my head bowed low, I padded onto the bed. My father's knee was exposed, the wound raw and red. I leaned in closer and started to lick at the infected tissue. Once I had cleansed it, I transformed back into bird form and fluttered above my father's chest. There was something dark inside him that needed to be taken out. I entered his chest cavity and found another bird inside, black and malignant. I embraced it with my wings and then left his body, carrying the creature with me. The bird dissipated into nothing. I hovered one more time above my father and felt a sense of relief. In that instant, I found myself being pulled back to my human form. I flew backward at incredible speed and then—*slam*—I was back. Shaken by all of this, I went to bed and slept for many hours.

The next day, I called the hospital to see how the old man was doing. The nurse told me that she was glad that I had called, as during the night, my dad had become very ill and had developed a high fever. The doctors had thought he might die, but the fever had inexplicably broken, and he pulled through. She said that he was comfortable now, and that I could speak to him if I wished.

When he came on the line, my father reiterated what the nurse had just said, but then told me that he had seen me come into his room and stand at the foot of his bed, and that there were many deceased family members standing behind me. He was hardly a man prone to flights of fancy—on the contrary, he was extremely down-to-earth, and of a highly cynical disposition—so this revelation carried some heavy weight.

CHAPTER ELEVEN
Raising Old Ghosts

Eventually, the house sold—with a little assistance from some practical witchcraft—and I returned to Los Angeles to work on a new Love And Rockets album, *Lift*. We had enlisted the help of producer/engineer Doug DeAngelis, who suggested that we bring in some Bauhaus vinyl to sample as a starting point. We selected 'Stigmata Martyr' and lifted from it various guitar parts, around which we built a driving electronic rhythm. Then, in the mixing room, I started to quietly chant the words 'Resurrection Hex' over the top.

'What's that?' Doug asked.

'I don't know,' I replied. 'It just kind of bubbled up.'

Doug suggested I record a vocal immediately, which I did, adding the refrain, 'Whatever, whatever, whatever, whatever possessed you?' As I was singing, it occurred to me that the song was about Peter Murphy, and also a continuation of the magickal working aimed at bringing about the reformation of Bauhaus. At the exact same time, in Ankara, Turkey, Peter was firing off an extraordinary, obsessive fax, a mad rant concerning, as he saw it, his unheralded and injured position within the hierarchy of the band.

To: Dave
From: Peter
Ankara
Saturday, May 10 1997

Hello Dave,

Since coming across a few times recently where, for various reasons, the perception of my part in 'the band that Danny after all started', that dog that nobody will let lie, our collective goose that laid your golden egg, the band that meant more to me than sleep itself, that betrayed love, rainbows end, not so much dark but hard as in diamond hard, the struggling graphic x-designers with a 'solid gold' front, that passion, accession, deception, cold hearted, 'The Sweet Gone Moldy', majestic, ill treating/treated, ulteriorly motivated, damn hard to shake, completely and utterly extraordinary .... well ... has been that of a mere part time singer stooge and m/puppet, of the real heart of the band ... 'indeed, they not only wrote the music but Dave also contributed largely to the lyrics' ... I've decided to collate the enclosed clarifying lotion to be applied when clear memory overcomes my willingness to forgive and forget. You girls might want to apply it too when talking publicly. Don't get me wrong (again) Dave, there's nothing personal intended, but it is time that I stood my own ground, as opposed to my hitherto demurring from raising old ghosts.

    STILL LUV YA—ALWAYS WILL ...

    I simply want to pay you, and the others, if they're interested, the courtesy of knowing that in some form now or later I'll get these, what after all are plain facts, out and known, as a way of getting it off my chest. Much the same emotions involved in your very long campaign to gain what you all felt was your right in going about your lack of recognition in the bands reputation.

Love to the rest of the girls ...

This was followed by an extensive chronological list of every Bauhaus recording, obsessively detailing P.M.'s contribution, entitled 'The "Peter just sang vocals" myth-dispelling Peter Murphy/Bauhaus credit list', and including such data as 'Bela Lugosi's Dead: Vocal music composition, gen. co-optive arrangement' and 'Ziggy Stardust: Initiated, conceived & provided guts'. The document ended with a list of 'statistics', showing how 'over half the lyrics were written by Peter' and 'Peter plays instruments on over a third (36 percent) of the songs'. It was nuts. What had possessed him?

Still, going back to those old Bauhaus recordings provoked a conversation about the possibility of our getting back together again. We spoke to our manager, Charlie Hewitt, about it, and he agreed that the time could be right. 'Would you like me to contact Peter's manager about this?' he asked.

Despite the crazy fax, we answered in the affirmative. Peter had evidently been thinking along the same lines, and his fax could be taken as a cathartic broadside blast intended to clear the air prior to reconciliation. It was agreed by both camps that we would all meet up in LA and attempt to bury the bloody old hatchet.

The location for our meeting was a restaurant, El Coyote, in Laurel Canyon, just across from Jim Morrison's old pad. After the meal, we repaired to my old friend Kerry's cosy hilltop cabin for a nightcap. The mood was indeed very amicable, and the evening concluded with a champagne toast, proposed by Kerry, 'To the new Bauhaus!' The resurrection was on its way!

Soon after this little get-together, the four of us were ensconced in a Hollywood rehearsal studio. It was very much like the old days: we plugged in and started to jam, conjuring something out of nothing. Shards of noise exploded from Daniel's guitar, a Japanese Fernandez model that featured a wonderful 'infinite sustain' device that he would employ to maximum effect. Kevin started to lay down a light, almost jazzy beat, and I came in with a sneaky serpentine bassline, based around an Eastern-sounding scale. Peter started to intone in Arabic over the top. Later, he told us that these were sacred lines from the Koran, and that because of this they could not be recorded. It was a great track, but we let it go out of respect for Peter and his Muslim beliefs, a powerful initiatory invocation lost to the ether.

Next, we played 'Bela Lugosi's Dead' for the first time since that last show at the Hammersmith Palais back in 1983. We then revisited other selections from the old set, including 'A God In An Alcove', 'In The Flat Field', and a blistering 'Dark Entries'. Fifteen years fell away in an instant, and we were very much back in business. We shared a collective grin and decided to take a break. That's when the trouble began.

> DANIEL: Well, there's no problem with the music, but have you thought about what we're going to wear?
> PETER: I shall wear whatever I want to wear.
> DANIEL: Yeah, of course, I know, but what will that be? It's important to get that right. I mean, you're not going to go onstage in jeans, are you?
> PETER: Daniel, if I want to appear in jeans and carpet slippers, then I shall!
> DANIEL (*shooting a rueful look at Kevin and me*): Ah, come on, Pete. I mean, you wouldn't go on dressed like you are now, surely?[1]
> PETER: Well, rather like this than looking like you! You're forty and you dress like a fucking kid! Look at you! It's pathetic.

At this point, Kevin and I chimed in, trying to pull the focus back to how great the music was sounding, and how unnecessary all of this fashionistic mud-slinging was. All to no avail, alas.

'All right, OK,' Daniel continued, 'but look, Pete, I've gotta say something about your hair, man. I mean, you are going to do something about that, right?'

At this, Peter exploded.

> PETER: Fuck you! Look! If Peter Murphy wants to go onstage in fuckin' jeans, then he shall and if he wants to go on as bald, fat old Peter Murphy, then he shall and the fans will still think that he's marvellous because … *I am*!
> DANIEL: Yeah, sure, all right, but look … what if you were to shave your head? You'd look brilliant like that, Pete!

PETER: I'm not going to parade around like that! Like one of Satan's fuckin' sporn!
DANIEL: All right, fuck it then!
ME: Tour's off!
PETER: Yeah, fuckin' right! The tour's fuckin' off!
KEVIN: Guys! Guys!
PETER & DANIEL: Fuck off, Kevin!

Daniel turned off his amp and started to pack away his guitar. Peter lit a cigarette and stormed out of the room. We were booked into the studio for the entire day, but having been there an hour it looked like we would not be coming back.

We had a meeting scheduled later that day with our respective managers, Peter's guy, Chris Gilbert, having flown in from London. The plan was to discuss the prospect of a tour. Oh, dear, oh, dear, oh, dear!

* * *

We entered the Thai restaurant across the street and were shown to our table, where Charlie and Chris were already seated, celebratory cocktails on the go, broad smiles on their faces, dollar signs spinning in their eyes. Were they in for a shock!

Charlie stood up, spreading his arms wide in welcome. 'Gentlemen, this is Chris, Peter's manager. Chris, meet David, Daniel, and Kevin.'

'Hello chaps,' said Chris. 'So, we have some rather good news for you.'

'Yeah,' Daniel replied, 'and we've got some bad news for you.'

'Bad news? What?'

'No, Chris, you go ahead, first,' said Peter. 'What's the good news?'

'Well, we've been quietly putting the word out about the reunion and there's a *lot* of interest, to say the least!' he replied, glancing at Charlie with a smile. 'We're already getting some major offers coming in. So ... uh, what's the bad news?'

Charlie leaned in, eyebrows raised.

'We're not doing it,' said Daniel.

'Not. Doing. It?'

'We're not doing the tour,' Daniel replied.

'Tour's off,' I added.

'*What*?! Why?'

'Daniel doesn't like Pete's trousers,' I explained.

'Guys, is this a joke?' Charlie asked, growing increasingly perturbed. 'This is a joke, right?'

'I wish it were,' said Peter.

Chris mouthed a silent *what the fuck* to Peter, who rolled his eyes to the heavens, nostrils flared.

'There was a fight,' said Kevin. 'The music was sounding great and, um … we had a stupid fight.'

'About Pete's trousers?!'

'Yeah,' the four of us replied, en masse.

'Look, chaps, why don't we just order some drinks and calm down and have a proper chat about this?'

'Good idea!' Charlie added. '*Waiter!*'

The drinks came out, and then some more, and somehow, by the end of the meal, it was all back on.

'OK,' said Daniel, 'tell us more about the good news.'

'Well,' Charlie began, 'we know that you guys were only thinking of doing a couple of dates in LA, but since the word got out within the industry, there's major interest from all over the place. If you wanted to, you could easily do a big international tour and make a considerable amount of money.'

'Pete could buy some new trousers!' I said.

We agreed to do two nights at the Hollywood Palladium, as well as a secret warm-up show, and then, depending on how it all went, we would talk about extending the tour. Before we could embark on this new adventure, however, we had some pressing legal business to get out of the way.

* * *

Monday, May 18 1998. Los Angeles County Court.

'Call the plaintiff, Genesis P. Orridge.'

In his tight green suit, white shirt, and dark tie, his dreads newly shorn and nary a piercing in sight, it was a very different Genesis P. Orridge that stood up in court that day. He resembled a psychotic ventriloquist's dummy, or one of those trick boxes that springs open to jettison a shower of colourful snakes, such was the restrictive containment of his naturally outré persona. We had also been advised by our lawyer, Mr Anthony Kornarens, to tone it down, especially Daniel. ('No ear-rings or eyeliner,' came the sage advice.)

Following the fire at the Rubin house, and the subsequent treatment of his injuries at Cedars-Sinai, Genesis had been presented with an astronomical medical bill. Faced with this, he felt that he had no other viable option but to do as his lawyer suggested and sue Rick Rubin. Rubin was, after all, a multimillionaire, and Genesis had no health insurance. What the plaintiff did not count on, however, was that Daniel, Kevin, and I would be dragged into the proceedings as cross-defendants when Rubin's insurance company filed a counter-suit in our direction, claiming that the band had been responsible for starting the fire.

Two nerve-wracking weeks ensued, during which the insurance company lawyers pulled out all the stops and tried every dirty trick they could muster. Genesis played to the gallery throughout, hamming it up to the hilt, at one point even sniffling into a white hanky like some melodramatic Southern belle. In the end, the jury ruled in his favour, and he received $1,500,000 in damages. We were found to be innocent, but we still came out of the proceedings with an enormous legal bill. Fortunately, we had those dates at the Palladium coming up. The total profit from those shows would go toward our lawyer's bill, but we would still end up short to the tune of $17,000. (When Genesis was told of this, he dropped it into the hat.)

* * *

The court case was not the only obstacle to the Palladium gigs, which were almost cancelled when Daniel developed a case of eleventh-hour cold feet. One day that spring, he called me to say that he had thought the whole reunion thing over, and that he did not want to do it. Knowing

Daniel as I do, I did not rise to this. Instead, I played it cool, telling that if he was really sure then OK, no one was going to force him. The next day, I made a sigil to bring him back into the fold. I did this while standing on a high peak in the Hollywood Hills, setting fire to the paper and blowing the flaming embers into the wind.

Back home in Massachusetts, I made what would prove to be one of my last of the fetish objects. 'The Warrior' took the form of a kind of Samurai figure moulded from red wax, with six serrated knife blades sticking out of its body, and various power objects concealed inside its form. I made it while conducting a magickal working dedicated to Mars. This was on Saturday, April 11, the night of the full moon.

As soon as I had completed this session, with the wax still warm and congealing, the phone rang. It was Daniel. He told me that he had just had a moment of revelation.

'Dave, a big light bulb just went on in my head, and I realised what a fuckin' idiot I would be not to do the Bauhaus thing. So, count me in, man!'

It was three years to the day since the fire at Rubin's.

* * *

Rehearsals for the Bauhaus reunion gigs began in LA on June 15. The World Cup had just started, providing a perfect way to let of steam. The four of us would watch the games in Peter's hotel room. There was none of the bitching that had marred our original get-together, even if Daniel was still secretly perturbed by Peter's potential wardrobe. Weighing far more heavily on his mind was a death threat from a crazy ex-girlfriend, which he took seriously enough that he employed a bodyguard.

Despite this, by the time of our first warm up gig, at the Hollywood Athletic Club, we were feeling strong, focused, and bonded. And so, on Thursday, July 9 1998 (another full moon), we prepared to take the stage for the first time in fifteen years. The gig was beyond sold out, and there was an electric crackle in the air—that, and some projectiles.

'Fuck you, Daniel!'

'Yeah, and fuck you too, you cunt!'

'Guys, guys, come on. Fuckin' hell!'

Peter and Daniel were having a little pre-show 'chat', and, as usual, Kevin was endeavouring to calm things down—without success. A pool ball rocketed through the smoky air, smashing into a bottle of vodka. Then came a tentative knock on the dressing room door.

'Uh … fifteen minutes, gentlemen.'

'Don't they know the gig's off … again?' I said, semi-jokingly.

'It fuckin' well might as well be!' Daniel replied. (Ah, just like the old days!)

Bauhaus was always a highly volatile mixture of unstable elements. Chemistry being chemistry, it was never likely to mellow with age. It was clear right from our initial get-together that the test tube was still bubbling and spitting sulphurous flare. As another pool ball flew across the room, I joined Kevin in his attempts to break up the affray, and we were playfully roughed up by the brawlers for our efforts. This defused the situation, and we all ended up having a big sloppy group hug, the old hatchet buried once again. And with that, it was time to get out there.

To get to the stage, we had to walk along a first-floor balcony that circled the club. Courtney Love was sprinting in front of us, and when the word got out that we were on our way, the crowd started to go nuts. We climbed down the steps at the end of the hall and walked onto the stage.

Our first number would be 'Double Dare', which starts with a solo fuzz bassline, so it was down to me to kick it all off. Gathering in this magical, protean moment of suspense, I decided to wait. This was, after all, the bridge between the last note sounded in London, fifteen years before, and the announcement of the resurrection to come. The energy in the small room built to an almost unbearable climax. Catcalls, shrieks, and clapping of all speeds ensued. One more deep breath at the edge of the precipice and then—*GGNNNNNNNAAAA*—we were off. The crowd exploded. We were on fire that night, sounding epic, with a vicious edge.

The following night, we were at the famed Palladium—an enormous venue smack bang in the middle of Hollywood. We had placed one full-

206 • David J. Haskins

page ad (just our logo, the venue name, and the dates) in *LA Weekly* a couple of days earlier, and had been quite worried about selling enough tickets. But when we nervously asked Charlie Hewitt, who had been elected as manager for the run, how tickets sales were going, he informed us that both nights had sold out in fifteen minutes, setting a new record for the venue, and that the promoter wanted to add a third night. He had also been inundated with requests for more shows elsewhere.

As we drove by the venue on the afternoon of the first show, we were amused by the never-ending snake of steaming black leather and rubber that wound its way around the sun-seared streets. The majority of those in line appeared to be very young, too.

The shows were amazing—the band was so 'on'. We performed those old songs with more confidence and strength than we ever could muster back in the early days. In the years we had been away, it seemed, we had actually learned how to play! Plus, of course, the nucleus of the band had been playing together for thirteen years as Love And Rockets, while during that same period Peter had honed his voice to perfection. The audiences were ecstatic, and many old friends stopped by backstage after we were done. We were also paid well. This wasn't too bad at all!

We decided to commit to a full-on tour of the USA, Europe, and Japan. For these shows, we revived the old TV monitor opening that we had first used at the Rock Garden in London all those years ago, with Peter's blown-up face appearing on the screen for the duration of the opening 'Double Dare'. When he then made his 'second' grand entrance for 'In The Flat Field', it would raise the roof every time.

As a logo for the tour, I came up with the idea of featuring two Bauhaus faces, one white and one black, the latter positioned under the former and looking up, as in repose. It was projected above the stage each night. The black (dead/dormant) face appeared first, and then the white (alive/resurrected) face emerged from behind the black, ascending as the black faded away. Resurrection! This pivotal transition occurred during our version of the poignant Dead Can Dance song 'Severance', at the climax of an extended middle section of the show built around a repetitive primal beat. Peter would kneel in the middle of the stage while I paced around him in a circle; the music built and built and then came to a brief pause at its peak before it all crashed back into the soaring melody again. It was spine-tingling, and, on a good night, bloody shamanic!

In Boston, a gifted craftsman friend of mine, Ken Elwell, presented me with a beautiful ceremonial dagger (an athame) made to my specifications. It had an ebony handle inlaid with an image of a brass serpent snaking toward a silver moon made from melted-down heirlooms, the steel cross guard shaped like a crescent moon. I would carry this magickal weapon as part of my hand luggage for the rest of the tour (unthinkable, now, post-September 11.)

Also in my luggage during the tour was an exquisite black onyx crystal ball, given to me by Malena the shaman, whom I had first met back in Massachusetts. She had attended our show at the Opera House in Mexico City, and told me that she loved the song 'Spirit', and especially the moment when Peter implored the audience to 'Raise the roof!' The following day, I went to visit her in her home. I had been up for most of the night, suffering from food poisoning, and when Malena's relatives came to pick me up, I was doubled over with severe stomach cramps. The hour-long ride felt like hell. We rode in a beaten-up old car with a dilapidated sofa in place of a back seat, but I was determined to proceed with the visit.

As soon as I walked into Malena's study, the pain vanished. She did a psychic reading for me, during which she said that Bauhaus would not continue after the tour. She also told me that I would be doing a lot of writing in the future, and that it would have a degree of spiritual content; that I would be working with flower remedies, and that Mexico would become very important to me. She then told me of her plan to establish a spiritual community in the Mexican mountains. She gave me a diamond-shaped dousing crystal on a long silver chain and asked me to let it spin over a scale model of the proposed compound. She wanted to know what my perception was.

I held the crystal in the centre of the layout, directly above a large, domed structure. As the crystal picked up momentum—apparently of its own accord—I had the strongest impression of water.

'What are you feeling?' Malena asked.

'Water,' I told her.

With this, she lifted the dome to reveal a circular pool, which she explained was the central water source. She gave me a small pink egg-shaped crystal from the mountain area of which she had spoken and then passed over the large black crystal ball. She told me that this was to help me commune with Hecate and the spirits of the Underworld.[2]

As she said this, I could feel those spirits move in a little closer.

DENISE ELSMORE   TERESA ELMORE   SANDRA GILBERT

JEAN HUBBARD

SUSAN EVES   ZOE PHILLIPS   ANGELA ETHERIDGE   SHARON GREEN

DAVID HASKINS   ANDREW DOUGHTEY   SIAN LONGSTAFF   ROSEMARY LOOMES   ANGELA LAWRENCE

OPPOSITE PAGE, TOP Jack Plug & The Sockettes live at the Racehorse pub, Northampton, 1977. Left to right: Dave 'X' Exton, my brother Kevin Haskins, me, Daniel Ash. **LEFT** A flyer taken from the wall of the Hope & Anchor pub in Islington, London. The Sex Pistols were about to change everything!

ABOVE The Craze (formerly Jack Plug & The Sockettes), featuring all the usual suspects, 1978. **RIGHT** My Xeroxed flyer for the first gig by Northampton's seminal punk band The Submerged 10th. Left to right: Dave 'X' Exton, Kevin Haskins, Janis Zakis, and me.

ABOVE Bauhaus live at the Guildhall, Northampton, 1979.
OPPOSITE PAGE, TOP Derek Tompkins at Beck Studios,
Wellingborough, 1983. **BELOW** The first ever photograph
of Bauhaus, taken in the gents at Wellingborough Railway
Working Men's Club, 1979.

ABOVE With Annie at Eric's in Liverpool, 1980. **RIGHT** Live at the Rock Garden in London, 1980. Note fuzzbox and photograph of Oscar Wilde taped to bass, plus 'No Dinosaurs' sticker.

RIGHT AND BELOW
Backstage and onstage at Tier Three, New York City, 1981.

ABOVE *Champagne Supernova* by John Cornelius, which documents an unlikely meeting between Adrian Henri, George Melly, and Bauhaus at the State in Liverpool in 1981. **RIGHT** 'Oi! What you got in that bag?' Wax Trax! Records, Chicago, 1981. **BELOW** 'Show us those profiles, boys!' During the recording of *Mask* in London, 1981.

OPPOSITE PAGE With René Halkett at Paddington Station, London, 1981.

ABOVE The Hearse, aka the Bauhausmobile, with Annie striking a pose. **LEFT** A poster for William S. Burroughs's seventieth birthday event at Danforth Music Hall, Toronto, 1983. I was an eleventh-hour addition to the bill. **BELOW** With Nico at Fagin's, Manchester, 1981.

OPPOSITE PAGE Tim Perkins, Alan Moore, and me. 'Three very intense young men', as Alan remarked upon seeing this image of the cabal.

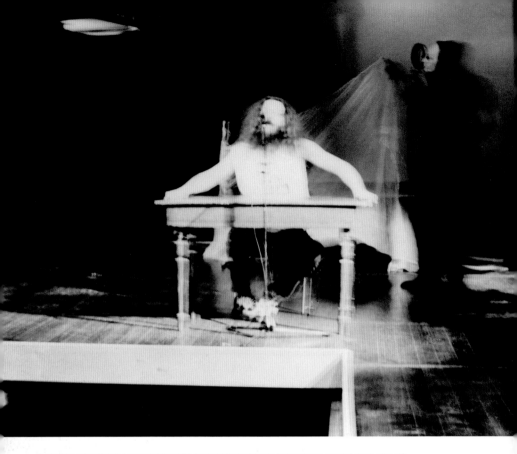

Kevin Haskins   Daniel Ash   David J

LOVE AND ROCKETS

TOP 'Here's to the new Bauhaus!' The mad magician grins a maniacal grin, Los Angeles, 1998. MIDDLE Bauhaus, happily resurrected, 1998. BOTTOM With Annie, backstage at the Palladium, Los Angeles, following the first of three shows, 1998.

OPPOSITE PAGE With Alan Moore, rehearsing for our performance at the Subversion In The Streets Of Shame event at the Bridewell Theatre, London, 1994. Note the strange ghostly figure behind me, a raised spectral hand behind my right shoulder that appears to be holding a gauze-like veil over the seated Mr Moore. (Both of my hands are clasping an oval mirror.) BELOW An American Recordings promotional photo of Love And Rockets, 1996.

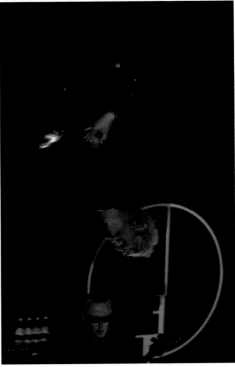

ABOVE With Billy Corgan backstage at the Riviera Theater, Chicago, 1998. **RIGHT** Performing 'Bela Lugosi's Dead' at Coachella, 2005. Note the water bottles atop my amp. Someone was obviously concerned about dehydration in the desert.

OPPOSITE PAGE, TOP Bonhomie in Berlin, 1998. **BELOW** With Genesis Breyer P. Orridge at the Knitting Factory in LA, 2004.

KAMERADSCHAFTL VEREINIGUNG
D LANDWEHR INSP BERLIN MCMIX

ABOVE Performing 'Bela' with a string trio during our Halloween show at the Fillmore West, San Francisco, 2005. **RIGHT** Live at Red Rocks in Denver, Colorado, 2006.

CHAPTER TWELVE
The Undertaker

One major difference between touring in the early 80s and the late 90s was the omnipresence of the internet. It was instructive to get instant feedback online, and it became something that we took quite seriously, modifying the details of the show based on the fans' response. It was apparent that there was an enormous community out there on the web: a vast network of followers who would arrange shared rides, sleepovers, and meet-up points. I named them The Undeadheads.

Utilising the web for the first time, I decided to have a bit of fun by writing an online journal under the pseudonym of The Undertaker, a fly-on-the-wall insider with a literary bent, prone to hyperbole and florid purple prose. It would appear in instalments on the band's website. Here are some selections:

September 10
The Cabinet of Byronic Splendour
The term coined with reference to the *LA Times* review of one of the already legendary Hollywood shows in which Mr Murphy was described as 'dressed in Byronic splendour' *(actually, it was 'Byron-esque splendour')*.

The legend is now embossed on the front of the mobile wardrobe, which conveys the collective sartorial accoutrements of Bauhaus from theatre to theatre across the globe. This black, crushed-velvet-lined box contains such elegant items as Mr Ash's blue/black ostrich feather boa, Lestat-esque regency frock coats and a menagerie of faux-leopard, snake, and tiger-skin ensembles, Mr Haskins's Nosferatu-style mid-calf-length opera coat and fishnet apparel, Mr J.'s custom-made mandarin style, nine-buttoned ebony suit and vintage Brooks Brothers midnight-blue velvet smoking jacket, and the aforementioned Mr Murphy's 'Eternal Fall' collection, featuring multifarious finery in velvet, silk, and brocade.

As evidenced by the above, there has been a certain rediscovery of the opulent dandyism present at the group's inception (although, back in the day, this predilection was catered for via thrift stores and the occasional raid of girlfriends' closets). Bauhaus was always much enamoured of the glorious style of Mr Oscar Wilde, and the spirit of this perennial hero still resides over today's reincarnation.

One of the highlights of the current set occurs during the opening of 'Boys', during which Mr Murphy executes an onstage costume change, assisted by two personal valets.

Suits you, sir!

September 16
The Inner Sanctum

Picture, if you will, the sepulchral interior of a Bedouin tent. Decorative silken drapes forming a canopy above a central seating area, in the middle of which, atop a large Moorish coffee table, is displayed a veritable cornucopia of fresh fruit, a smorgasbord of delicacies and an elaborate Egyptian hookah. The evocative aroma of frankincense and myrrh permeates the air, whilst a scattering of mirrored velvet cushions, peacock feathers and orchids complete the heady atmosphere of exotica. The fact that this opulent environment exists inside a mobile Nissen hut is a minor miracle to the credit of one Brian Lowe, provider of environs conducive to the appropriate collective mind set.

A little illusion goes a long way!

Tonight, the daily recreated decor provides the setting for yet

another audience with the popes of G***. The visitors to the Court
of the Undead on this occasion being the respected personages
of Mr William Corgan esquire and his charming escort, Miss
Yelena Yemchuk, 'dark angel', photographer and muse. The
result of this summit meeting, an impromptu cameo appearance
by the aforementioned Mr Corgan on a spirited rendition of 'the
bopping elf's' 'Telegram Sam' and, at Mr Corgan's request, a
poignant reading of 'All We Ever Wanted'.

'Chicago is a SMASHING town, you've been a SMASHING
audience, and now we have a SMASHING pumpkin for you!'
Thus spake Mr Murphy, to the delight of the ecstatic crowd,
and despite Mr J.'s bass guitar taking an unfortunate knock on
his approach to the stage, resulting in an interestingly dissonant
version of the Bolan hit, a smashing time was indeed had by all.
Helping matters along most splendidly was the highly talented Mr
Steven Perkins, providing a more than fair imitation of Bolan's
side-kick, Mr Mickey Finn, albeit considerably less hirsute.

Prior to these two sell-out shows at the Riviera Theatre, Mr
David Bowie had requested the usage of two live numbers to
feature on his new internet service. Pipping the divine Dame to
the post, however, was Rollingstone.com, who provided the world
with a live cybercast of the whole event.

You too can be there!

September 19
Sing On!
September 19th found the Byronic Four at home in the haunted
avenues of the New Orleans Garden District, perusing the
sumptuous environs of the estate of Mrs Anne Rice for a private
tour of the 'domain of dolls'. The night belonged to voodoo,
as three of the four cleaved through the miasmic air of the
French Quarter on an expedition to 'The Dream Palace' for an
impassioned preview of forthcoming songs from the diminutive
but mighty Mr James Hall. Mr Hall, the Beau Brummel of thrift-

store chic, would join the House of Bau the following night for some soulful trumpet stylings during an extended version of 'She's In Parties'. In attendance that same evening, Mr Trent Reznor, Mr Clint Mansell and his band Pop Will Eat Itself, White Zombie, and the rest of the James Hall Band.

The set was distinguished by a second helping of 'Ziggy Stardust' as the band succeeded in deconstructing the concept of the encore. Confusion and delight reigned in equal measure.[1]

Waiting for the celebrants in their dressing room, afterward, was a bottle of a limited edition Cuvee Lestat wine, courtesy of Mrs Rice, along with a signed photograph with the inscription, 'All Blessings, Sing On!' Indeed!

October 12
'El Pandemonium de Murphy!'

With a resounding metallic shudder, the enormous steel gate, the hitherto impenetrable portcullis of the Cine Opera, came crashing to the ground. Five hundred wildly impassioned renegade fans had illegally entered the arena. These impoverished anarchists, denizens of Mexico City's dirt-poor southern district, had accomplished their aim and were now fully and imperceptibly entrenched amongst the legal, paying entrants, absorbed in a deliriously swaying throng of black. Aficionados of the 'Dark Scene', Mexico City's thriving underground cult, the rebel crowd pushed the attendance figures beyond the 6,000 mark, the official capacity for El Opera. It was at this this point of forced entry that the police department decided to throw in the towel, it being the second of two full-on riots that evening. Inside the antiquated venue, the great glass chandelier swung precariously above the audience and a rain of gilded plaster anointed the faithful as the continual pounding of many feet upon concrete threatened to reduce the building to a pile of rubble, and all this before the band had taken the stage! The spontaneous roar that issued when they finally did could have put Mexico's national soccer stadium to shame. The performance that followed was one of the best, culminating in an astonishing 'Bela Lugosi's Dead', the Catholic-style candelabra (a fan's gift) set atop Mr J.'s speaker cabinet adding a suitably gothic touch to the proceedings.

Post-show, a decoy manoeuvre was employed as four security guards disguised as El Hombres de Bauhaus, their visages concealed beneath black towels resembling monks' cauls, made an intentionally conspicuous exit to mislead the be-fanged followers thronging the stage door. The headline of the *Reforma* newspaper the next morning was emblazoned with the headline: 'El Pandemonium de Murphy!'

Some events to which The Undertaker was privy never made it into the blogosphere, however.

The Crowne Plaza Hotel, Las Vegas, August 21 1998.

I was forty-one, and I had been faithful to my wife for twenty-two years —which, in rock'n'roll years, is more like ninety-two. I had also yet to be entertained by a lady of the night. Now, it seemed, it was high time to put this paucity of life experience to rights.

Never one to do things by half, I let my fingers take a stroll through the red-light district of the *Yellow Pages* and placed an order for two 'escorts': a blonde and a brunette (for contrast). When they arrived, they asked for the cash up front, of course, and when I produced my 500 bucks it was met with abject consternation.

'Eh, and the rest?' piped up the blonde.

'The rest?'

'Yes, sugar, one grand, total.'

'A grand? They quoted me 500 over the phone!'

'That's 500 each, honey.'

'Well, they certainly didn't make that clear.'

The girls raised their finely plucked eyebrows and exchanged a beleaguered look.

'Hey, look,' I said, 'that's all I've got, so if you ladies want to leave it then fine, and I'm sorry, but I'll give you a hundred each just for coming out.'

Again, they shared that look, this time coupled with a sharp cock of the head from the blonde.

'OK, bud, we need to discuss this situation. Why don't you go in the other room for a minute?'

Following these orders, I repaired to the bedroom and sat on the bed, straining to catch their whispered confab. Finally, another 'HONEY!?'— at which I rose and stood in the doorjamb.

'As you're not ugly, we've decided to give you a bargain. We're working with you here, honey.'

'Well, OK. Thanks.'

I handed over the five Benny Franklins, and the blonde asked if she could use the bathroom. While she was powdering her nose, her slender friend requested that I unzip her dress. It swished to the floor like the sloughed-off skin of a snake. She stepped out of the ring of black material and took off her bra. Her tits were small and stretch-marked, the nipples like battleship rivets, large with dark areolae.

Ouch!

'Hey, what's going on out there?' the blonde called from the bathroom. 'You all right, girl?'

'He bit me!' the brunette replied.

'Sorry,' I muttered sheepishly, this followed by an irrepressible wolfish grin.

'Hey, steady there, tiger!' the blonde admonished me, peeling off her pants as she re-entered the bedroom. 'Careful with the merchandise!' She flopped down onto the bed with legs akimbo. I sat in the chair opposite.

'How about I sit here and watch while you two girls get it on for a bit?'

'Oh, no,' the blonde replied. 'For that, you would have to lay down 2k.'

'Really?'

'Yeah, babe … really.' She pulled off her panties and started to touch herself. My attention, though, was drawn to the dirty soles of her white bobby socks.

'Take off your socks,' I said.

'My socks?'

'Yeah, they're putting me off. They're dirty.'

'Well, don't look at the socks, sugar. Look here instead,' she suggested. She was evidently not a natural blonde.

'No, please,' I replied. 'Take off the socks. The details are important.'

She rolled her eyes and shot me a look—*this guy!*—before pulling off the offending footwear, which she then disdainfully tossed across the room. Meanwhile, the ravishing brunette was gyrating in front of me. She turned her back to me, slowly bent down to touch her toes, and then ran her fingers up those long gleaming gams. She then clasped her derriere, took a firm grip, and spread the cheeks wide. I reached out my hand, but the blonde immediately lurched over and slapped my wrist.

'Don't touch her pussy!'

'*What?* Five hundred smackers and I can't touch it?'

'No, it's dirty!' she countered, and they shared a filthy little laugh. *Touché!*

The blonde then dressed me in a rather fetching French letter and the untouchable brunette fell to her knees. A lacklustre and perfunctory blow job ensued, alternated with a vigorous and professional hand job by her pal. Back and forth it went.

'Is this giving you any satisfaction whatsoever?' the beast with five fingers enquired, my ennui obviously evident.

'Eh, somewhat,' I replied, keen for it to be over with, and very soon it was.

After the girls had gone, I discovered that my Givenchy Gentleman eau de toilette was conspicuous by its absence. Oh well, all's fair in love and whore, I suppose.

* * *

Another memorable incident that The Undertaker failed to log occurred in St Petersburg, Florida, at the Mahaffey Theater. Toward the end of the set, Daniel suddenly jumped off the stage and made his way through the seated audience. He sat down in a vacated seat next to a young girl and asked her for a cigarette; she obliged and lit him up. Casual as you like, he chatted to her while still playing guitar. He stayed there for the rest of the gig.

When we questioned Daniel about this strange behaviour after the show, all he had to say was, 'I never get to meet people on tour! Also, I've never seen this band live so I thought I'd check it out!'

A true eccentric, Daniel Ash is also one of the most generous people I have ever met, gregarious with a big heart. He is also hypersensitive—to the point where that sensitivity lays him open to emotional torture—and rather than fall victim to it, he has become extremely well armoured over the years. There is a deeply poetic soul buried there under all those layers of biker bravura, like black leather on a ballerina. I love him to bits, but he can be crushingly frustrating to work with.

As our old mentor Derek Tompkins would always say, Daniel has tunnel vision, and he's so blinkered that he literally cannot hear you when you are trying to reason with him or make a conversational point. He is also highly commitment-phobic, as evidenced by all the on-off-on-off shenanigans that our band projects have experienced over the years. Having said that, once he does commit, his work ethic and determination are formidable, his focus intense. I suppose it's the flip side to that tunnel vision thing. He's a complicated individual, and it is something of a contradiction that he is, at once, one of the most enervating and draining people to be around—a true psychic vampire in that regard—and at the same time, one of the most exciting and inspiring—and fun, too! A skirt-chasing creature of the night, the boy certainly knows how to 'Party, big time!' (to borrow one of his many pet phrases).

I have spent countless crazy, boozed-up nights in Daniel's colourful, clown-like company. There was the time in San Francisco in 1994, while we were working on the *Sweet F.A.* album, that we attended the annual Betty Page Lookalike Contest. Following the sexy parade and party, Daniel persuaded the barman to sell him several crates of booze—at a greatly inflated price, which we transported back to our temporary digs in town along with several of the comely contestants. We were also joined by various members of the San Francisco chapter of The Hells Angels, who provided a motorcycle escort through the hilly streets of the city, countless residential lights flicking on as their Harleys rumbled toward our temporary gated-community digs. (There was the potential there for a living tableau straight out of an S. Clay Wilson cartoon.)

Once we'd arrived, I handed out beers to the Angels as they filed in through the front door. They were all very polite, each offering a sweet little thank-you as they received their booze. Later in the evening, however, the mood changed when one of the bikers became exceedingly ticked off that the girls were not showing him the same kind of attention as they were us. He was doing lines of crystal meth and tapping menacingly on the top of the glass coffee table with a small hammer. I was talking to one of the girls on the balcony when the table exploded, sending smithereens of glass shards and white powder across the room. Two of the girls immediately snapped into dominatrix mode, severely scolding the disgruntled biker before kicking him out.

Another time that comes to mind is when, in 1996, Love And Rockets played a gig as part of Perry Farrell's ill-fated ENIT tour. We were in the hospitality tent before the show, when Daniel, flying high on Ecstasy, was tried to persuade me to engage in a French kiss.

'Come on, Dave. How many years have we known each other? And we've never kissed! Come on, man! It's not a gay thing, it's a biker thing!'

I declined, despite the qualification, and the next thing I knew, Daniel was locked in an interminable passionate snog with our old friend and confidante, Kerry Colonna. Right at that moment, Kevin came into the tent with some friends, and stood aghast at the sight of his next-door neighbour and bandmate so engaged.

'God,' Daniel remarked, as he came up for air, 'guys taste really different to girls!' (Kerry seemed to enjoy it.)

Ten minutes later, there was an almighty upheaval when the long table on which everyone's drinks and food had been placed suddenly collapsed, splattering the now full tent with spilled liquor, fresh fruit, cold cuts, and hard candy. In the centre of the carnage was—surprise, surprise—Daniel Ash, and struggling beneath him, a pretty young girl, dress up around her armpits. His bi-curious phase was evidently to be shortlived. Or was it?

As Perry's band Porno For Pyros were about to take the stage, I made my way out into the crowd with Kevin and Scott, our lighting guy. We found a good spot from which to watch the show—and what a show it would be! The band were barely into their third number when a disruption occurred. Were we hallucinating, or was that Daniel running onto the stage, taking a flying leap to slam into Perry's back, knocking him to the floor, and then violently dry-humping him? Yes, indeed it was!

Years later, I mentioned this incident to Perry, and he told me that he ended up completely winded and in a lot of pain, as he had no time to prepare for the impact. He said that he was trying to work out what the hell was going on, and then how to contain his anger, as he felt beard bristle scrape against his face. He realised it was Daniel, and in that moment was thrown into a quandary as to how he should react. Fortunately, two security guards arrived to peel Daniel off and lead him gently to the side of the stage. They had also recognised the perpetrator, and were similarly conflicted. Had it been an audience member, he would have been hastily ejected from the venue, no doubt incurring a few bruises on the way. But Perry's respect for Daniel as a musician is such that he would never dream of doing him any harm, even in the face of such provocation. I can understand this. The man is genuinely innovative, capable of producing sounds from a guitar that are like wailing banshee spirits, bewitched and bound to do his bidding. Unique sounds, never obvious. His whole approach to the instrument is unconventional. Refreshingly, he has no interest whatsoever in scales or muso technique, instead relating to the guitar in a totally oblique and primitive way. His playing is intuitive, instinctual, and all-together brilliant. And highly underrated, too—especially by himself. They say that those who are hard on others are harder on themselves. One of the qualities that I value highly in Daniel is his honesty, which is brutal, and honed by a well-greased bullshit detector—something that's invaluable in a collaborator and a true friend.

Daniel Ash. Kids love him, girls love him, dogs love him, and I love the old, mad bastard, too![2]

* * *

For most of the '98 tour, the four of us would fly and the crew would travel by road. On one memorable occasion, however, everyone would be thrown together for a landlocked journey into the absurd.

It's 5am on August 31 1998, and thanks to a sudden termination of the nausea-inducing vibration that denotes the rolling of wheels, I am roused from a state of irritated semi-slumber. Minutes pass … and then many more … seemingly enough to usher in a count of hours. *Why aren't we moving?* I wonder. *Are we there? Impossible!*

We are not due to arrive at our destination—Rochester, New York—until nine in the morning, and even if we had got there earlier, we would have all been gently kicked off the bus by now if that were the case. No, something is evidently up, and an investigation is in order.

Dragging myself from my (previously mobile) coffin, I venture forth into the tobacco-smoke-clouded environs of the front cabin. Here, my olfactory sense is alerted to another top note, sharp, acid, and stinging. Realising I need to take a leak, I enter the loo, where I am greeted by copious chunky deposits of purple-green-black slime. Someone has been ill—very ill indeed. I cast my mind back to the sordid scene of some four hours previous.

A bottle of red wine, tilted at an angle of eighty degrees, the last of its contents trickling into the puckered mouth of a well-known guitarist, this now-dead soldier having been passed to him by our on-tour hairdresser, affectionately known as 'Vampire Boy' due to his nocturnal lifestyle and general darkly glamorous appearance.[3] They were gradually working their way through the liquor cabinet, plus a box of fat Cuban cigars. This was a two-man bacchanal on wheels, and it looked set to go on long into the night. I bid my farewells and retired to my rocking crib.

That was four hours ago. Now, I appear to be aboard a stationary, landlocked *Marie Celeste*. Abandoned drinks, half-

236 • David J. Haskins

eaten pizza, cigar blunts, empty (but still warm) seats, and not a soul in sight.

Suddenly, a frantic looking tour manager appears. 'Have you seen Ian or Daniel?' she splutters.

I answer in the negative. 'What's going on?'

'What's going on' is as follows. Having become inebriated to the point of near to life threatening toxicity, the one-who-could-still-walk (just about) decided that a pit stop would be very necessary in order that the one-who-could-not-walk-anymore could put head to porcelain and pray to the patron saint of the sozzled, seeking penitence for his sins and cure for his sorry condition. The bus had pulled into a scene out of a Wim Wenders road movie: a gas station in the middle of the middle of nowhere, with greasy spoon and adjacent brick shithouse, toward which our dishevelled antiheroes have seemingly beaten a careening retreat (a 'retreat' that, due to the protracted length of their stay, could be applied in the monastic sense of the word). The bus driver has therefore decided to utilise the time to fill up with gas. A pump is sought, and moments after the vehicle pulls away, an identical wagon takes its place, this being the hired property of rock legends Van Halen.

With the likely lads still having failed to reappear, the bus driver is dispatched to investigate the contents of their apparent sanctuary—which is now empty. The greasy spoon is searched, at which point the scene changes from *Paris, Texas* to *Priscilla Queen Of The Desert*, the diner being populated by alpha-male truckers with wrists like hams and mounds of cholesterol piled onto their plates. The idea of our two skinny boys, clad in their fetching baby tank tops, velvet flares, and electric-blue platform booties, their hair waxed and teased into punky spikes, finding themselves amid all that red-necked testosterone … well, it hardly bears thinking about. Still, the wayward ones cannot be found. Maybe they have been eaten?

The search party returns to the bus. There is nothing to do

now but wait and hope—at which point the Van Halen bus drives off toward its next port of rock'n'roll mayhem.

Oh no!

Yes, it is indeed entirely possible—nay probable—that the Van Halen touring party has suddenly been increased by two.

Our perplexed tour manager runs for the diner in a desperate last-ditch attempt to locate our AWOLs. The driver and I join in the search. No sign. The tour manager decides to phone the vehicle-hire company to inform them of the dilemma, and if possible get them to contact the Van Halen bus to check on the situation there. I return to the coach. The rest of the crew, exhausted from many nights with only little or no sleep, remains sweetly oblivious to our plight. I am the only one awake, until …

'*Where the fuck have you been?*'

It's Daniel, and as he helps the green-gilled Vampire Boy up the steps, I am made to feel almost guilty!

'Err, more to the point, where have *you* been?' I ask.

Apparently, upon emerging from the gentleman's convenience, he and Ian had been distressed to find a great gaping expanse of air where the bus had once been.

'The bastards!' cried Daniel. 'They've gone without us!'

In fact, what had happened is that, in order to get to the pumps, the driver had taken the most direct route, which involved making a circuit of the diner and accompanying rest room. For approximately three minutes, the vehicle would have been out of sight to anyone standing in front of the buildings. This, of course, was the precise moment the lost tribe of two re-emerged into the cruel light of neon.

Necessity being the mother of ill-advised invention, Daniel hatched a plan: they would venture into the diner, and proceed to charm the waitress into letting them stay over with her. Vampire Boy's eyes were showing only white as Daniel mopped the residue of vomit from the corner of his slack-jawed mouth.

'For God's sake, pull yourself together, and smarten yourself up! Come on, we've got work to do!'

It was at this juncture that Van Halen made their brief stop before rollin' on down the road. And so it could have happened—and very nearly did happen—but in the end, this case of mistaken bus identity was narrowly avoided due to unconscious bad comedic timing.

Having not surprisingly been given the cold shoulder by the waitress, our AWOLs then decided to try their chances at thumbing it. Vampire Boy resembled an imbecilic ape returning from a prolonged voyage in outer space as the two veered at ever more acute angles to the tarmac en route to the highway. With two dollars between them, our abandoned puppies were about to set forth on a scary hitchhiking adventure, when, glory of all glories, Daniel *saw the bus*. The rest, as they say, is misery.

* * *

In Chicago, we went into a studio to record our cover of 'Severance', which was shaping up to be a monumental track, and one we wanted to capture in full bloom. The recording turned out great. The atmospheric introduction slowly builds as Daniel's guitar swells in waves above a spare drum pattern that incorporates some shimmering electronic sounds and the bass lays a pulsing foundation. Peter's vocal is magnificent throughout, pulling in the listener with the intimacy of the verses and then soaring majestically on the bridge parts. Toward the end, the whole thing opens up and then falls into a great yawning abyss as great shifting tectonic plates of sound rise and crash to completion.

While we were in the studio we taped a radio interview, which did not go so well. Inexplicably, Peter had switched to paranoid Mr Hyde mode, and proceeded to snipe at Daniel, Kevin, and me throughout.

It was the first real show of the old demons, but they would be back in full force before long.

* * *

When the tour reached New York City, Peter asked if I would pen a biography for him to be used in conjunction with his next solo project. Biting on the bullet, I delivered it the next morning. Here is an excerpt:

> When Murphy treads the boards, it is an act of possession. I have stood next to him on stages of the world and felt the ferocity of psychic demarcation. Again, a big cat comes to mind and the emission of a potent territorial spray marking out the centre of the stage (his stage!) which, by definition, is wherever he happens to be at the time! That space becomes a vortex of primal force, a black hole of impacted energy into which one is either sucked, under violent protest, or tenderly allowed to enter in order to receive the blessed kiss of the Byronic mutant king.

* * *

Our New York shows—two nights at the massive Hammerstein Ballroom—were filmed for the production of a DVD that would eventually be released in tandem with a live album, both entitled *Gotham*. The film does capture something of the spirit of the tour, although the camera crew were most remiss to omit the essential 'Severance' section (they were apparently swapping film at this point on both nights). Still, in retrospect, it is strangely appropriate that this magical invocation/ evocation was not captured on film, as it remains occult and burning still in the imagination and memories of those who witnessed it live and in the flesh.

Following the US tour, we headed over to Japan. The shows were great, the audiences very vocal and quite abandoned, in marked contrast to those on our last visit in '83. They were also very young. These kids could have been—and probably were—the offspring of our original fans back in the 80s!

While in Tokyo, I made it down to the colourful area of Shinjuku in search of rare music-video booty. I found it in spades. One place was a real treasure trove, and after about thirty minutes I had a huge stack of delicious obscurities on the go: Tom Waits and Robert Wilson, Jacques

Brel, Ian Dury & The Blockheads, Mott The Hoople, The Residents, Suicide, Serge Gainsbourg, Scott Walker, The Rolling Stones, Bob Dylan, The Clash, and Massive Attack,[4] plus Love And Rockets and Bauhaus live shows from the early 80s, all now building blocks in a teetering VHS tower. The shopkeeper recognised me and proffered a deal: the tapes in exchange for a photo op. I happily agreed, posed with the grinning fellow, and left with my haul.

Back on the tour bus, we started to watch the Bauhaus tapes, until Peter suddenly pleaded for us to put something else on. He literally could not bear to watch the former incarnation of himself. It was a glimpse into a very vulnerable, guilt-ridden psyche.

Europe was our next destination, the tour kicking off in the beautiful old city of Prague. Over to The Undertaker:

October 23
The Green Spirit of Prague
Following a gruelling thirty-four hour journey from Japan, which preceded a strange, delirious concert at Prague's charmingly crumbling Lucerna Hall, the jetlagged Undead repaired to the elegant setting of Slavia, historical seat of Bohemian Cafe society and former den of insurrection. They say that the cloth from which the Velvet Revolution was spun, originated within its marbled walls. Here two of the Bauhausers, namely Mr J and Mr Ash, took recourse to the aperitif of the poets and found themselves in the soothing arms of the green spirit, Absinthe. What visions may come!

That night, I was indeed entertained by visions. The effects of absinthe are very different to most other alcoholic drinks. It is decidedly narcotic. I remember trying to find my way back to the hotel but having the hardest time trying to negotiate the narrow winding streets, which were crisscrossed with tram lines. I was entranced by the trams, their sparking cables triggering visions of exploding stars. By some miracle, I eventually made it back to where we were staying and collapsed onto the springy bed, which turned into a soft fluffy cloud on which I floated away, drifting in and out of a strange opiated sleep, and at one point was lying there in a state halfway between dreaming and waking consciousness when a floating apparition suddenly appeared above me. At first it was a vague, numinous swirling fog—a sickly white tinged with light green—and then, gradually, a more distinct form took shape. A woman! Her face was gauntly beautiful, with large green eyes that slowly blinked open and closed. A gentle seductive smile played about her lips. Her silky green body was undulating in the air above me, rising and falling in time with my breathing, which was quickening by the second. The phantom then levitated toward the ceiling, growing smaller and smaller in its slow-motion flight until it eventually vanished into the plaster.

When I related this story to John Van Eaton, gentleman roadie and scholar, he suggested that it was a visitation from the Green Fairy. At the time, I was not familiar with this spirit, often seen by imbibers of the green liqueur, so it was very interesting to have experienced such a classic manifestation. John's own experience with the powerful aperitif had not been so benign. He was apparently attacked by the most diminutive and mild-mannered member of the road crew who, having drunk an entire bottle of the stuff, went mad and exploded into unprovoked violence. Shortly thereafter, he collapsed, fully clothed, under the running shower in the crew bus, where he remained for the rest of the night.

Sparkling, snow-blanketed Vienna was the next port of call. The road trip from Prague had proven to be challenging, however. The Undertaker again:

October 24
The Hollow Hills Are Alive With The Sound Of Murphy

The mode of conveyance intended to transport their Byronic Majesties to the fabled environs of Vienna was dramatically downscaled when the black Mercedes luxury tour bus (formerly used by one Mr M. Jackson and Bubbles) was inexplicably turned back at the Czech border. In its place was a decidedly pre-revolution box-on-wheels, resembling the type of vehicle usually reserved for the conveyance of prisoners or the physically impaired. To add insult to injury, the driver of this sad can (in fetching pale blue) was victim to the unfortunate condition known as 'B.O.'. Bottles of eau de cologne and phials of essential oils were passed amongst the wilting flowers of the back seat in order to negate the effects of this severe olfactory affront. With four hours to go, it was definitely a case of 'pass the fragrant nosegay, and don't spare the horses!'

The gig at Rockhaus was distinguished by a pile-driving set that was abruptly curtailed when the power broke down completely during the introduction to 'She's In Parties' (coitus interruptus). The band held fast however, spontaneously striking a freeze-frame stance for several minutes until the electricity was fully restored, whereupon they resumed without missing a beat. The whole effect could be viewed as 'extreme dub'!

A blistering coupling of 'Passion Of Lovers' and 'Dark Entries' concluded matters most satisfactorily. The band then returned for a triple helping of encores to put the lid on a highly memorable Austrian debut. The hollow hills are alive with the sound of Murphy!

In Vienna, our new European merchandise turned up, but on closer inspection of the T-shirts, we discovered a problem.

October 27
Continental Drift or Collectors Item?
During the last few days, certain strange shifts in geological location have apparently occurred, as the denizens of Vienna suddenly found themselves enjoying their newfound citizenship of Australia, the good burghers of Deinze became German residents, and due to the outcome of what appears to be a bloodless coup, the former isolationists of Oporto surprisingly embraced their

newfound citizenship of Spain! All of the above being confirmed in black-and-white on the back of the official Bauhaus European Tour T-shirt. Then again, these phenomenal relocations could be traced to a certain individual possessed of a startling ignorance of geography and currently employed by the merchandising company, though probably and hopefully not for long.

From Vienna, we took in Munich and Milan, before making our way to the exciting city of Berlin. I have always loved the energy and artistic edge of the place. We took advantage of a day off to stroll through the streets. We were all in high spirits, and the following night held a wonderful surprise.

October 29
Der Tanz Von Bauhaus

As the spirit of October bowed out from the stage of seasons, and old haunted November prepared to enter, so the 'Tanz Von Bauhaus' returned to its early stomping ground of Berlin, and specifically the wind-wracked aircraft hanger that is Arena. A mercurial fire burned this night as a legendary performance was unravelled upon its stage. Afterward, der menschen von Bauhaus were received into the gracious society of the Turkish Modern Dance Company, a troupe of international esteem, directed by Mrs Beyhan Murphy, charming wife of The Singer. Kismet decreed a crossing of touring paths, and the night was made for dancing. Toasts were proposed as an informal soiree ensued. 'Lang lebe der tanz!'

The next day, we travelled by train to Hamburg, where I met up with my dear old pal Owen Jones, former drummer with The Jazz Butcher Group. Jones has been resident in the German port for many years, and after the gig we repaired to his local bierkeller for tall drinks and taller tales. I left him in the wee small hours, four sheets to the wind and sailing home to oblivion.

The City of Light was next. On the flight into Paris, we met up with Boy George, who was excited about the reunion. He told us that he still had all his old Bauhaus vinyl. We put him on the guest list for the show the following night at La Mutualite. This was one of the best, with the crowd singing loudly to 'All We Ever Wanted'. We stopped playing at one point to let them carry the end refrain: 'Oh, to be the cream.' It was beautiful.

When we returned to the hotel, there was a fax waiting for Mary Jo, our tour manager.

Mary Jo:
Thanks 4 the tickets. They (Bauhaus) were flawless. Tell Pete & Co. that I was mesmerised. What a fucking genius evening.
—Love, Boy George

The following week, George would devote his regular column in the *Daily Express* to a glowing review of the Paris concert, noting that as soon as he got back home to London, he had dug out all his old Bauhaus records and stayed up all night playing them. It was a nice pre-empt to our return to the home shores. We played Manchester first, and it was startling how much it had changed from the depressed, run-down, crime-riddled urban dump of old to a thriving, architecturally appealing modern city (albeit still crime-riddled). Here we were reunited with two old co-conspirators, Graham Bentley and Alex Green, the latter having put away his sax in favour of e-commerce ('It's the new rock'n'roll!').

The Undertaker wrote:

November 4
Still Weird After All These Years!

'Fifteen years and they're still weird!' came the anonymous cry from in front of the curtain on this the imminent eve of the return of the Caligari Crew to the inner city of Manchester, crime town central, previously the scene of duets with a velvet chanteuse and blatant daylight robbery.[5]

In feisty anticipation of a confrontational bout, the band came out fighting. They expected punches but received a bouquet of kisses. Then unravelled an evening of unprecedented boisterous revelry, characterised by a soccer-crowd-like bonhomie. Following a blistering set, the band encored with the usual glam-fest of 'Telegram Sam' and 'Ziggy Stardust', Mr J. sporting low-tech pyrotechnics in the from of a single sparkler taped to the head of his bass. (KISS, eat your hearts out!) Post performance, Mr Ash was handed the mobile phone number of a young lady in attendance at the show. Needless to say, this sophisticated ploy worked! The lady in question turned out to be an old friend from Mr A.'s notorious Brighton period. Backstage, many other reunions were sparked to flame.

A triumphant evening!

The first thing we saw when we pulled up outside the Brixton Academy in London was the graffiti legend 'All We Ever Wanted Was Your Money!' painted in large white letters on an adjacent wall.

'How, fuckin' typical!' Daniel muttered. 'England, cynical cunts!'

Some things never change, but then again, some things do. Writing for our old nemesis, the *NME*, Stephen Dalton gave the Brixton show a rave review in which he stated:

Bauhaus are only 'goth' like Radiohead are 'prog' … Murphy is a scream, but still too energised to qualify as a has-been pop clown. In his Robes Of Doom and Byronic sleeves, he's half Nureyev, half 70s Bowie on mime-troupe-casualty overload. Fittingly, then, the grand finale is a mighty collision of Dave's 'Ziggy Stardust' with the T.Rex classic 'Telegram Sam', a flame-thrower glam racket which burns itself out in a blue flame post-rock fury. Magnificent.

Considering the revival of interest in all things 70s glam that was going on at the time—as evidenced by the popularity of Todd Haynes's nostalgia drenched *Velvet Goldmine*—our timing for this tour, with its mood of slightly tongue-in-cheek decadent glamour, could not have been better. The 'Byronic sleeves' referred to in the review came courtesy of our tailor, William Hunt, then of Carnaby Street and now resident in Saville Row. Both Peter and I had taken advantage of his sartorial skills and replaced our old stage clothes, which had been stolen from backstage in Deinze.[6]

While in London, I met up with the poet Jeremy Reed. I had discovered his brilliant work one afternoon in 1995, while browsing in Compendium Books in Camden. I happened to pick up his book *Red Haired Android* and proceeded read it from cover to cover, there and then. I was astonished by the incisive beauty of the poetry, and remarked on this to the shop's owner as I bought it. He told me that Jeremy had been in the store about an hour beforehand, and that he was a friend. I told him that I would like to get in touch with him and enquired as to the best route. Much to my surprise, the shopkeeper said that he knew who I was and that he would give me Jeremy's phone number.

A few weeks later we were in a recording studio together. Elephant Studio in the East End resembled the red painted vision of Hell presided over by Peter Cook's Devil in the film *Bewitched*. ('Do you like it? Early Hitler!') We recorded two tracks there, Jeremy's words to my music, with wonderful assistance from Cathy Giles on cello and harp and Amrik 'the Sikh' on tabla.[7]

One of the pieces we recorded was called 'For Derek Jarman'. After finishing the mix, the engineer said, 'I suppose that you chose to do this here because of the association with Derek.' We responded with blank incomprehension. It turned out that Jarman had recorded the soundtracks to all of his films at Elephant. Although Jeremy had known the late director and planned to work with him before he died, in 1994, he was not aware that this was his studio of choice, and neither was I.

Following the session—which flowed effortlessly, to the extent that we felt as if we were being assisted by flights of angels from the great beyond—we staged a one-off live performance at the Freedom Cafe in London, Jeremy (in fetching leopard skin jacket and red beret) reading while I plinked and plonked on an antique miniature harp fed through various electronic FX pedals. At the conclusion of each poem, he would scrunch up the sheets and discard them onto the floor with indolent panache—a bit of stage flourish that I would shamelessly steal for my solo cabaret show in years to come.

* * *

Sitting at Heathrow Airport, looking out at the sheeting English rain and waiting for a plane to take us to sunny Spain, I scribbled down the following in the back of my tour book:

England Haiku #1
Pinched, pale
Sniffle, snarled
Miserable in drizzle

England Haiku #2
The exploding paint-box
Wings of gold
There will always be an upstart

In Barcelona, we all went out to the great Gaudi cathedral, La Sagrada Familia, which looks like it has been frozen after starting to melt. It is indeed, as the great art critic Richard Hughes, once put it, 'The architecture of delirium.' The four towers of this impossible structure grow very narrow, at the top and we had to take turns reaching the highest dreaming spire.

There was no gig that night, so I decided to go on an excursion into the old town. I asked Daniel if he would like to accompany me but he declined, which wasn't entirely surprising as the last time we had explored those wonderfully dark and winding streets, we had ended up endangered. It was a couple of years before the Resurrection tour, when Daniel and I were on a short European press junket.

One night, we decided to have a bit of a carouse. We wandered down a back street and were intrigued by the music coming from behind a huge wooden door. There was a small red light above it, but nothing to indicate that this was a public place. Feeling adventurous, we decided to investigate further, and tried the door. It was indeed a bar, very low lit, and serving only sherry and red wine. We ordered the former and parked ourselves at a corner table to take in the atmospheric scene. There were no tourists, only locals. Three guitarists were taking turns to play flamenco. They were all excellent musicians, and looked like they could be three generations of the same family.

We enjoyed the music, but after about hour we were ready to move on. This plan was immediately dropped, however, when the dank room was suddenly brightened by the appearance a drop-dead gorgeous Spanish girl, who was followed into the room by two young men. They settled in at a table across from our own, and soon Daniel and I both had our tongues on the floor. She was beautiful. More sherry was called for! Then Daniel hatched a plan.

'Hey, Dave. I've been working on this new song, and it's a bit Spanish, like. Do you reckon one of these guys would lend me a guitar so that I could play it for that bird? You know, serenade her, like!'

I answered most emphatically in the negative, and advised him to forget all about it.

'Aw, come on! It's worth a try. Which one of 'em do you think I should ask?'

I shot him a warning look that spoke of blood and bruises.

'The young one!' he continued. 'I'm gonna ask the young one. He'll understand! I can't speak Spanish, but I know a bit of French. Do you think they know French?'

I took a drink.

'Right, I'm going for it. Wish me luck!'

'Good luck, Dan.' I watched as the young gypsy guitarist embraced his instrument, holding it close to his chest while nodding a very definite NO.

A crestfallen and sheepish Daniel returned to the table.

'Well,' he said, 'he did speak French.'

'What did he say?'

'Well, basically, he said, *my guitar, my woman, my soul* … in other words, *NO! Fuck off, you bastard!*'

We ordered more sherry. It was very good—not too sweet, warming with a very pleasant aroma. It was at this point that the girl rose and walked up the winding stairs to the bathroom. We both took in the graceful ascent.

'Right,' Daniel said, 'I'm gonna ask the old man!'

'No, Dan, come on. Give it a rest!'

'David, don't be such a fuckin' defeatist!'

'More like *realist.*'

'Look. If I can get hold of a guitar before she comes down, then I'll be able to serenade her from the bottom of the stairs.'

Daniel was pretty plastered by this time, and the wind was in the sails. The next thing I knew, he was over in the corner, imploring the craggy old Catalan to part with his beloved guitar (*his woman, his soul*). The older man's refusal was even sterner than that of the younger. More sherry!

As we sat imbibing, we were quite astonished when the object of our desire sashayed over to our table, leaned in, and asked for a light. As she spoke, she slowly unzipped the fly of her jeans. Daniel fumbled with the lighter as her fingers played suggestively with the zipper. She cupped the flame and lit her cigarette, never averting the burning gaze of her massive green eyes.

'*Gracias!*'

She smiled, turned, and made her slinky way back to her two male companions, who were now shooting daggers at Daniel and me. A potential punch-up was averted when the big door suddenly burst open, and a swarthy, elegant woman, probably in her mid-fifties, strode in, accompanied by a large, noisy entourage. The manager of the bar swooped over to welcome the lady as the barman poured her a glass of the special reserve. The trio of guitar players joined the throng, bowing and placing their hands on their hearts. After a brief conference, they started to pick, strum, and clap, while the woman began to sing.

This grande dame had the most amazing voice: deep and throaty, but hitting the high notes with a piercing clarity. They finished one song, and after a flurry of loud applause immediately went into another. A slower, more intense piece that started with the singer and one of her group clapping out an intricate syncopated Flamenco rhythm. One of the guitarists also started to clap, and the older man then launched into a tumbling cascade of brittle notes. The pace picked up; the diva raised her hands imperiously above her head and drove her black heels down hard onto the wooden floorboards. It was magnificent and very infectious. *Duende!*

Caught up in it all, Daniel suddenly started to clap in 4/4 while shouting, 'All right, yeah!' His enthusiasm was met with silence—a stone dead *fool, if you think you're going to get out of here alive,* oxygen-sucking silence. All eyes burned in our direction. We suddenly became very interested in the floorboards under our feet. After what felt like an eternity, the singer threw back her head with utter contempt and slowly started to click her long bony fingers to initiate the resumption of the song. Once again, the complex rhythm started up, at which point we stealthily slipped away.

* * *

From Spain, we headed over to Portugal for the final two shows of the tour, in Lisbon and Oporto. The penultimate date, at the 9,000-capacity Pavilhao Multioso, was in the largest venue on the tour. The national radio station passed over the entire day's broadcasting to Bauhaus and Bauhaus-related recordings on the eve of what would prove to be one of the best shows of the tour. Everyone in the audience seemed to have a cigarette lighter, and every lighter was lit as we came back on to play the encore of 'All We Ever Wanted', which I introduced as a 'fado' song.[8] I swear that the temperature rose as a result of all those little flames.

We experienced more of the same at the final show of the tour, in Oporto, on November 16. At the end of the set, however, some idiot threw a lighter at the stage, catching Kevin in the head and drawing blood. The wound had to be attended to before we could play our final

encore of 'Bela'. Afterward, Murphy remarked that, in Sufi lore, this
bloodletting would be seen as a kind of blessing.

'That's all right for you to say,' Kevin exclaimed. 'It wasn't your head!'

When he was fully healed, I asked Kevin if I could have his bloody
Band-Aid. When he asked why, I told him that I wanted to stick it on the
back of my magickal journal.

'Be careful,' he advised me, sagely. 'That's my blood on there!'

At the very end of the concert, I had held up the two sets of stage
candelabra as a mirroring tribute to the flame-brandishing crowd. Slowly,
I blew out all six candles. Afterward, Peter remarked that he wished that
I had not done this, explaining that, according to his own superstition, I
should have left them burning, as now we probably would not continue
as a band.

This, in fact, would prove to be correct. But before it became apparent,
we went back into the studio to record a new track. The session came
about when we were approached to record something for the soundtrack
to *Heavy Metal 2000*, an animated movie based on the sci-fi graphic novel
(and the follow-up to the original cult film of the same title). For us, the
most interesting aspect was that the producer on the session would be
Bob Ezrin. This man was responsible for one of our favourite albums,
Lou Reed's *Berlin*, not to mention Pink Floyd's *The Wall* and all the early
Alice Cooper albums.

We entered Village Recorders in Los Angeles in June of 1999. The
place was formerly a Masonic temple, and was also the original centre
for Transcendental Meditation run by Maharishi Mahesh Yogi before
being converted into a recording studio in the late 60s. Assisting Bob
was the skilful engineer Joe Barresi.

Upon arriving at the studio, we received a nice surprise in the form
of a letter from Jeff 'Skunk' Baxter, the brilliant guitarist from Steely
Dan, inviting us to use his own private studio at the Village. In the note,
he said that he had always liked Bauhaus, and would feel honoured
if we were to take him up on his offer. I was somewhat taken aback
by this, as I had been a long-time admirer of his band, having been
first exposed to them in art school back in the early 70s.[9] We never

did get around to utilising his space, but it was a wonderful welcome nonetheless.

Here at the Village, we had decided to improvise a new song around a lyric of Peter's entitled 'The Dog's A Vapour'. It all came together very quickly, and we soon had a pretty epic track on our hands: dub bass, hypnotic elliptical electronic loops, tight but expansive drums, scorching guitar work from Daniel, and a great lead vocal that went from whispered nuance to searing, gut-wrenching drama as the track built to a climax and then returned to the atmospheric shimmer and haze of the intro.

The session was not all plain sailing, however, with the whole thing almost abandoned altogether after Daniel and Peter had a catty spat that involved a lot of verbal abuse, door-slamming, and walking out. Bob proved to be a good ambassador in this situation, employing humour to break up the fracas. He was also a great raconteur, delighting us with stories of the decadent 70s. As a producer, though, he was a bit too slick for us, and consequently we ended up staying behind late one night with Joe the engineer to work on our own, more rough-edged mix, which was the one that was ultimately used.

We were very pleased with the end result, and because of the success of the session—despite the usual indoor fireworks—we began to talk seriously about the possibility of a new Bauhaus album, and of approaching the great Tony Visconti, the producer responsible for making some of our all time favourite records sound as good as they did.[10] He was a true innovator, and the prospect of collaborating with him was very exciting. Following the completion of the Resurrection tour, he and I had had both been in attendance at a big music convention in New York City. After that, I sent him an email, broaching the idea of having him produce Bauhaus. I also mentioned that the first time Kevin and I made a recording was back in the early 70s, when we had played T.Rex records on our parents gramophone as I sang over the top of Bolan's original vocal while my brother bashed away on an upturned plastic flower pot, the whole racket being recorded onto an old two-track reel-to-reel. I also sent him a Bauhaus compilation CD, and a DVD of the band.

His response was enthusiastic:

Sat, Oct 30 1999
Hi David,
By the way, I was also one of the speakers at the recent IMX convention in New York, where I was fortunate enough to attend your panel. It proved to be the most stimulating session of the event. I shall be returning to NY on Friday, November 19, would you care to meet?
Of course! I always thought that Bauhaus was a great group and certainly left their mark in the 80's.
That was a very funny story about you and Kevin being T.Rex wannabes.
I loved the CD that you sent to me, with the videos included. I saw them on my Mac—very cool.
Yes, I'd love to produce your next record. Let's talk sooner than the 19th, even if it's via email.
All the best,
Tony

Three weeks later, I was on a plane to New York, where I met with Tony in a large office at the National Academy of Recording Arts and Sciences building overlooking Times Square. We had a most interesting discussion, during the course of which he played me some new tracks he had been working on with Bowie. He told me that he was seeing David that night, as he was playing a private show for his fan club and a few select members of the press. It was to take place in a little piano bar just off of Times Square.

'Would you like to go?' he asked.

'Oh, I'm not sure about that. I might have something on … no, no, I'm joking! Yes please!'

The next minute, he was on the phone sorting me out a ticket. That night, I sat with Tony and the legendary rock'n'roll photographer Mick Rock as they traded great stories about Mr Bowie. We had a table at the front of the balcony that spilled over with champagne and a cornucopia of fruit. Bowie was really on. The show started with just him on twelve-string acoustic and Mike Garson on piano for a goose-bump-inducing 'Life On Mars'. As the show went on, various other great musicians joined him, until finally a full band was blasting out from the small stage. It was the best Bowie concert I had ever seen—and in fact one of the best gigs, period.

I can almost hear that Visconti-produced Bauhaus album in my mind's ear, but sadly it was not to be. The unpleasant experience of working together on the *Heavy Metal 2000* soundtrack came to bear on this, as did the fact that Love And Rockets had finished our new album, *Lift*, which we were very proud of and wanted to take out on the road. Consequently, we would not play together again as Bauhaus for another seven years.

CHAPTER THIRTEEN
Yogi, Sidi, Sufu, Salim

Giant golden lotus petals bloomed atop the white domed walls, shaded by tall palm trees that swayed gently in the soft California breeze. In the winter of 1999, Annie, Joseph, and I moved to Encinitas, California, an unpolished jewel of a funky little beach town about twenty-five miles north of San Diego. One Sunday, we were out cruising along Highway 101 when we noticed this exotic-looking building standing proud up on the bluff. Upon further investigation, we discovered that it belonged to the Self-Realization Fellowship, founded by Paramahansa Yogananda in 1920. The swami had had a vision of this location while he was still in his homeland of northern India. The temple was built in the late 30s, and Yogananda's *Autobiography Of A Yogi* was written there in the study, which looks out onto the grand sweep of the Pacific Ocean.

I was oblivious to this history when we first discovered the place. We parked the car and walked through the large metal gates. The gardens were exquisite, bursting as they were with well-tended tropical plants, and with huge red, orange, yellow, and silver koi fish shimmering in the little ponds. At the top of a small hill was a sign stating that the hermitage was open. We entered this simple, elegant building, and I was interested to see an array of Indian classical musical instruments on display in the main room. On the wall above a large fireplace was a portrait of the yogi alongside various other saints and holy men, including Jesus Christ. Yogananda's comely countenance radiated peace and wisdom.

Annie ventured on and left me pouring over the picture. The eyes were so soulful! They pulled me into a deep pool of utter tranquillity. Finally, I broke away from the image and, guided by the saffron-robed sisters, proceeded up a small flight of steps and along a short corridor that led to the master's study. The sun-filled room glowed with a palette of peach, pink, and corn, and as I stood at the threshold, something extraordinary happened. I was suddenly overwhelmed by a sensation of pure bliss. It was like being enveloped by the wings of an angel. I felt suffused with spiritual warmth. Then I felt my legs begin to give way, and I had to steel myself in order to remain standing. It was positively transcendental.

One of the sisters gave me a gentle tap on my elbow, and I became aware that there were other people lined up to view the room. Somewhat stunned, I wandered out into the blazing sunshine of the upper-level lawn. Annie asked if I was all right, and I told her what had just happened. She then showed me a testimonial that she had been reading in some of the SRF literature, written by a lady who had had a very similar experience to myself.

I purchased *Autobiography Of A Yogi* that day. Tearing through those pages, so full of revelation and insight, I was delighted to discover an unexpected and wonderfully cheeky sense of humour. I had found my guru—or, more accurately, he had found me. As the old Buddhist saying goes, 'When the student is ready, the teacher will appear.'

* * *

Despite this supernal awakening, I still found myself vacillating between the light and dark. The angels were singing, but still there were devils on my shoulder, dishing out death metal and the blues. A black psychic undertow threatened to pull me under at any given moment into a swirling eddy of malevolence. I felt shadowed and forlorn. They say that when the forces of spiritual good are on the rise, those of the opposite disposition will try their damnedest to kick back and reclaim dominion. Under the black cloud of those early years of the twenty-first century, I would become estranged from my wife and move to LA, and I hit the bottle hard while couch-surfing, or holed up in some cheap motel. The simplest old pop song on the radio would reduce me to a sobbing wreck. It was during this troubled time that I wrote and recorded a new solo album, appropriately entitled *Estranged*. I was also stone broke.

One early September day in 2004, I was driving up through the Hollywood Hills on my way to an agent's office, to pick up a $500 paycheque. I turned on the radio to *Fresh Air*, the long-running NPR show hosted by Terry Gross. The interviewee was speaking. His voice was imbued with sincerity, evenly modulated, humble and wise. He was talking about his spiritual path, that of the Sufi's, and how his teacher—the head of the High Sufi Council in Jerusalem, Sidi Muhammad al-Jamal—would be appearing in Lake Arrowhead that weekend. His reverence for this master was evidently genuine, deep and profound. He spoke of how there was no division between this man and God, and how he was a direct descendant of Mohammed and is regarded in no lesser a light by his followers.

It was strange and impulsive, but at that moment I knew that I had to be there for this communion. The man went on to talk about his previous life as a highly successful doctor specialising in the treatment of addiction, and how he had contracted a viral infection in his eyes and lost his sight. The condition was considered to be incurable by the medical profession. Then, after he became frustrated and angry while on a prolonged meditative retreat, he had a sudden epiphany, and his sight was restored. He abandoned his conventional practice and took up a new path as a spiritual healer. The man's name was Dr Robert Ibrahim Jaffe. Reaching my destination, I picked up the cheque and sped back down the hill to book my reservation.

While driving north on my way to Lake Arrowhead, I was pulled over by a cop and given a ticket for an out-of-date registration sticker. I had been putting off getting a new one, as I simply did not have the funds, and now I would have a fine to pay. With a sigh, I continued on my way. The road started to ascend. I had not realised that Lake Arrowhead was on the top of a mountain. I reached the summit and pulled up in the parking lot of the hotel where the gathering was to take place. The place was thronging with people, most of them Muslims. I confirmed my reservation for the event and wandered into a big room, where they were serving lunch. Following this, we were advised to attend a briefing about what was to come. This proved fairly alarming, as we were informed that Sidi's power was such that it was common for new initiates to become overwhelmed and sometimes angry, as repressed emotions were released in the presence of his spiritual power. We were told that the master works on a very deep level, and that while his words are powerful, there is also a subconscious psychic effect operating simultaneously. We were advised to look deeply into our hearts to intuit whether we were ready for our encounter with him, which was scheduled for the following day.

As I drove away from the hotel in search of a place to stay for the night, the devils on my shoulder piped up, and they were loud.

'Fuck this! It's bullshit! New-age fucking bullshit! Give it a miss, why don't you? Let's get back to the city! It's still early! Fun times await! Delicious dark delights!'

I felt the pull away from the light. Those dangerous swirling eddies again! I shook off the taunts and made a sharp turn into the driveway of a lodge behind a young couple who were about to check in. From the way they were dressed, I took them to be Muslims, no doubt intent on a good night's sleep before the big day. They had their backs to me, but the man looked vaguely familiar. Before I could ascertain if I knew him, though, I was called to check in.

I did not have anything like a good night's sleep that night. In fact, I was up all night, caught up in a raging battle, those old angels and devils, duking it out. It was relentless. (In the words of the old Clash song: 'Should I stay or should I go?') It was a tug of love and hate, and my very soul was the rope. Then I was seized by a rather odd notion, which had to do with the ticket that the cop had given me. *Where is it?* I wondered. I needed to contemplate it. I didn't know why, but somehow it was important. I ploughed through the contents of my bag in search of the citation, starting to feel like I was going a bit mad. Still, I laid out the sheet of paper on the bed. So, what was it that was so significant about this scrap of bureaucratic ephemera?

The voices were hammering hard now, the devils doing their damnedest to drown out the angels urging me to enquire within. What was it? What was it? Then, all of sudden, a spark of perception. I had been given this ticket because I had been putting off getting a new registration. What else had I been putting off—putting off for many years? Spiritual enlightenment, that's what. Now, here I was in this place on the top of a mountain, with a very real chance of obtaining exactly that. I kissed the ticket, blessed the cop, and told the demons to fuck off.

* * *

I was ready bright and early for the events that were to unfold the next day. While wandering through the milling crowds, which had grown from the previous day, I felt a light tap on my upper arm.

'David?' It was the young man who had checked in before me at the lodge. 'David, right?'

'Uh, yes. Hey, wait a minute! Edie?'

'Yes! This is incredible! How come you're here?'

Back in 1991, I had fallen in with a young band, based in Brighton, called Rose Madder. They were fresh and talented, and in John Tribe they had a prolific and visionary songwriter. I had decided to take them under my wing and pay for the recording of their debut album, as well as producing the thing. I also played bass on it. The lead guitarist was a brilliant musician but he was also something of a fuckup—a pretty boy with an androgynous wardrobe and a taste for Class-A drugs. Unfortunately, the unreliable behaviour that always comes with the latter was seriously undermining the band's potential to succeed. It was an agonising decision, but in the end I strongly suggested that he be sacked. And he was.

People called him 'Edie' due to his resemblance to Warhol's beautiful wayward muse, and now here he was, fourteen years later, talking to me on top of a bloody mountain in California! He looked great, his hair cut very short and his huge blue eyes glowing with health and vitality. By his side was the girl who had checked in with him at the lodge. He introduced her as his fiancée and then reminded me that his real name was Malcolm.

He had come to the States to consult with Dr Jaffe in a desperate attempt to be cured of his addiction. The subsequent treatment was successful, and he and the doctor became friends. When the good doctor discovered his spiritual path, Malcolm stayed with him as a student. He was eagerly anticipating the communion with Sidi and told me that this moment would be the culmination of seven years of study in the Sufi way.

A meal was to be served before the main event, and Malcolm and I sat together for it, fondly remembering our old friends back in Brighton. I brought up the difficult subject of his sacking, and with great dignity and compassion he assured me that, although he was angry at the time, he had grown to understand very well the reason why it had to happen and that, ultimately, it had helped him on his road to sobriety. We hugged, and shortly after that the gong was sounded for the great gathering. As we made our way in, we saw Dr Jaffe. Malcolm introduced me to him, generously explaining that I was a great musician. I shook the doctor's hand and instantly felt a warm surge of wonderful positive energy.

'You feel like a healer,' I told him.

'And you feel like a musician,' he replied.

Smiling, we all made our way into the great hall. There was an electric crackle of anticipation in the air as everyone located their seats. Malcolm told me that, following the master's talk, we would be given a chance to take a pledge of allegiance to the Sufi way. He said that he would certainly be taking the pledge. At this, I felt a jolt of panic. I was not ready to become a Muslim! In Paramhansa Yogananda and the SRF I had found something that resonated with my spirit in a very deep way, and I was not about to relinquish it. I was also somewhat alarmed to find out that the slips of paper that we had been handed out on the way in were for donations. In my mind, whenever money enters into the picture, the red flags are unfurled and blazing.

As these thoughts were going through my mind, a middle-aged woman called out to Malcolm and came over to greet him. We were introduced, and I felt an immediate strong connection with her. Malcolm whispered that she was a spiritual healer, and old friend of Dr Jaffe. Acting on impulse, I asked her if I could talk to her in private. She agreed, and we made our way outside. I told her about my reservations. On the issue of money, she assured me that all funds went directly to the poorest people of the world; that Sidi personally oversees this and travels to those impoverished places in need, and that this was a very important part of his work. I also briefly told her about my experiences with magick, and the spiritual tussle of the previous night. She said that yes, indeed, magick is fraught with dangers, but that there can be also be a spiritual aspect to the path, albeit on a low vibratory level.

What about Paramansa Yogananda, I wondered? Smiling compassionately, she reassured me that by pursuing the Sufi path I would only be adding to the spiritual treasure that I had found in Yogananda, and that I would certainly not be expected to deny him, quite the contrary. 'Your head might not be ready,' she said, 'but your heart is.'

That was all I needed to hear. I thanked her from the bottom of that heart and made my way back in. Sidi was about to arrive, and the energy level was rising. Then, without ceremony, a small white-bearded old man appeared at the rear of the hall. He was dressed all in white, and as he made his way down the centre aisle, the devoted fell down on their knees, bowing before him like scythed blades of grass. All the while, Sidi raised his hands in a gesture of humility. I had been in the presence of great charisma before, but this was something beyond that. It was like being witness to Christ's entry into Jerusalem.

Eventually, Sidi climbed the steps to a raised stage and took his seat in between Dr Jaffe and another man. There was some unheard discussion between them, and then it was announced that the translator was late. We waited for a further five minutes, and then after another little confab we were told that Sidi had decided to begin without the missing interpreter. He then proceeded to speak in perfectly eloquent English, expounding on his theology, with particular attention paid to the perversion of religion in the world: the distortion of the Koran, and how religious extremists and terrorists were living in a way that was completely contradictory to its essential message of inclusive love. He spoke about the second coming of Christ, and how this, in great part, would manifest itself as an elevation of consciousness in the human race, although he did also say that a man possessed of the *Christos* was alive and living in England at this time as well.

Sidi spoke with the rolling oratory skill of a Martin Luther King. It was riveting. Finally, the interpreter turned up, full of profound apologies. If ever anyone was redundant, it was he. Still, for the remaining ten minutes of the talk, the interpreter sat at Sidi's feet and performed his role. Then the assembled were told that if they wished to make a donation, they should fill in the paper slips that had been provided. The amount could be anything from a nickel to $500—500 bucks being the maximum. It was suggested that whatever one put in would be returned a thousand fold in kind, if not in cash. If the donator wished to be helped with a problem or had a prayer to say, then this could be written on the back of the slip. Sidi would then give these issues his full attention. One of the suggested entreaties was, interestingly, 'protection from the negative effects of magick', which is exactly what I wrote down, before filling in the other side to the tune of 500 greenbacks (leaving me with a measly $50 in the bank).

It was then time for the laying on of hands. A great wave of humanity surged toward the stage, all of them bowed down, and the person at the very front held Sidi's hands. Someone behind him put her hands onto his back, the person behind her did the same, and so on, until everyone who wished to partake of the blessing and the oath was linked to the sacred source that was invested in the little old man dressed all in white sitting in the middle of the stage. Malcolm was beaming, delighted to be able to take part in all of this, but also because I had decided to join in.

What I felt next is hard to explain. It was like being connected to an awesome spiritual generator. The room and everyone in it went away. There was blackness, and then white—white light suffused with glacial phosphorescent colours. There was Love. Following this mass blessing, everyone who wanted to was allowed to come to the front and line up to meet Sidi. When I walked up to him, it was like I was floating on air, and as I looked into his ancient, watery, milky-blue eyes, I had the sense that he knew everything about me in an instant. That he was entirely present in the moment, and yet removed from it, off communing with a higher power and the essence of the cosmos.

I held his hands and thanked him.

'Don't thank me,' he said. 'Thank God.' He placed a string of wooden Rudraksha beads around my neck, and gave me my Sufi name, *Salim*. Then, in his native tongue, he said, 'This name means *peace*, and you shall be a peace-bringer. Very pure soul. I am sure that God gave you this name.'[1]

I walked away in a daze. Following Sidi's departure, Dr Jaffe held a session in one of the smaller rooms. This talk acted as a kind of debriefing and a grounding exercise. It helped one absorb the monumental shared experience that had just come to pass. Come dusk, I was driving back down to LA, fiscally poor but spiritually rich, a beaming smile slapped across my mug.

* * *

True to the promise, a few months later my donation to the Sufi's would be multiplied many times over following a late-night phone call from Paul Tollet. Paul is the head honcho at Goldenvoice, the promoter responsible for the highly successful Coachella Music & Arts Festival, which is held annually on a sacred Native American site-cum-polo field in Palm Springs.

Paul wanted to know if Bauhaus would entertain the idea of being one of the headlining acts at the next event. He said that he was looking for something really special, and that we were the band. We would be given complete freedom to stage the show in any way we thought fit, and would receive a guarantee of a quarter of a million dollars, as well as a separate production budget of $50,000.

At this point, I was still eking out a living by hustling DJ gigs and writing the odd magazine column, so this was all very enticing to say the least! I told Paul that it was a very interesting offer, and that I would speak to the others. Six weeks later we were in rehearsal.

A couple of months prior to this agreeable turn of events, I went to see Genesis P. Orridge and Psychic TV perform at the Knitting Factory in LA. Genesis had undergone a lot of plastic surgery since the last time I saw him as part of the 'pandrogeny' project through which he and his wife Jackie were attempting to become 'one'—a self-constructed hybrid third sex. As well as the major reconstruction of his face, Genesis had even gone so far as to have breast augmentation. His lips were bee-stung with collagen, and his hair was died platinum blonde and cut in a Brian Jones pageboy mop. He looked *very* different.

Halfway through the set, a girl in the audience shouted out, 'I love you!' Without hesitation, Gen responded with a sincere 'I love me, too!' I immediately thought of what that weird voodoo doll had said to him in his dream: 'I came to make you love yourself.' All that expensive surgery, and the attendant shift in psyche that I am sure had helped in great part to engender this self-love; it would all have been impossible without the court settlement that he had received. The potency of voodoo!

PART THREE
Some Lonesome Devil's Row
2005–06

Why you gotta be so out of space?
Why you gotta wear those different faces?
Why you getting sucked into that void?
What's it gonna be, the horns or the halos?
Damien Youth, 'Man In The Middle (A Pusher's Theme)'

A broken arrow in a bloody pool
The wound in the face of midnight proposals
Bauhaus, 'Who Killed Mister Moonlight'

CHAPTER FOURTEEN
The Hanged Man

Peter was hanging upside down in the storage closet at Swing House Studios in Hollywood. This was a daily training exercise in preparation for the planned opening of our set at Coachella. At the start of 'Bela Lugosi's Dead', he would appear from behind a screen, upside down and suspended from a rope, with his head some seven feet from the stage floor.

We had been trying to think of an astonishing set piece—something that would wow the crowd and be talked about for a long time following the concert. One idea was to release hundreds of live bats into the audience, but this was a non-starter, as apparently a 'bird release' is illegal after 5pm, and bats are evidently labelled as 'birds' in such circumstances. (There were also the twin perils of rabies and bat shit to consider.)

Then Peter came up with the hanging man idea. Brilliant! We knew that this stunt would be perceived as a depiction of Gothic bat-like vampiric iconography, but Murphy had a whole other esoteric slant. It was very interesting. In alchemy, the hanged man symbolises the penultimate stage of the transfiguration of the soul, from base material into spiritual gold. It is the intermediate stage of pestilence and decay—the darkness before the light.

On the large whiteboard listing the various tracks we might incorporate into our set, Peter wrote the following:

Inverted hanging man corresponds to Hermes in alchemical archetype and is the state of putrification (sic) prerequisite to the base metal's transformation to gold (easy action)

Following his suspension in the rehearsal room, he would be lowered and released by a member of our crew.[1] Peter would then lay prostrate and pray to Mecca, and this would be repeated four more times during the day. On the first day he asked if he could borrow my leather jacket to kneel on. I complied, and was later informed that the jacket was now holy.

He certainly looked holy. With his grown-out hair dyed silver-white, a matching straggly beard, and a seven-foot-long wooden staff, which he would slam down onto the stage, Peter now resembled an Old Testament prophet returned from the wilderness and ready to lay down God's Law. And lay down the law he did, but it was the law of Murphy, and not the Almighty. As he had on the last tour back in 1998, he made certain changes to the lyrics of our songs to reflect his commitment to Islam, rather than Lucifer. As a consequence of this, 'The pangs of dark delight' became 'No more pangs of dark delight'; 'In my yearn for some cerebral fix' became 'in my yearn for some spiritual fix'; 'Searching For Satori' was altered to 'Searching For The Sufis'; and so on. (The rest of us conceded that he was being authentic to his own core belief, so we let it go.)

The rehearsals went very well. We even started to work on some new material, but we abandoned this for now in favour of focussing on the live set. Coachella was a huge event, and we wanted it to be stunning. We worked hard, and by the time we hit the stage on the night of April 30, we were a force to be reckoned with—a gleaming black juggernaut revving up in the cool desert air.

As we took the stage, the flashing lights from the cameras were dazzling, and the crowd seemed to stretch up to the outer rim of the vast Coachella Valley. One thing that we had been concerned about was the use of big video screens, which can look a bit too *rock* for our liking. We wanted to scrap them altogether, but the organisers insisted on having them. This dilemma was solved one night after rehearsals, when I was watching the old German Expressionist classic *The Cabinet Of Doctor Caligari* on DVD. What if we used the screens, but stuck exclusively to black-and-white? Goldenvoice liked the idea, and it looked great, perfectly suiting the vibe of the band. We added a few extra touches, such as making the image negative on 'Silent Hedges', and throwing in the occasional splash of green or red. We were always a band that would rise to the big occasion, and this one saw the ascent of a rocket. By the time we left the stage, there was a palpable glowing buzz in the air. As Peter shouted out, just prior to our departure, 'Now you can say that you were there!'

The 'inverted man' ploy paid off, and the next day, photos of the suspended singer were plastered all over the papers and internet. We were immediately inundated with requests from promoters to play more big gigs. We were well up for it, too, and had soon committed to an autumn tour of the USA.

In the interim, Peter returned to Turkey, and very sadly succumbed to a nervous breakdown—perhaps, in part, a manifestation of that alchemical process he had initiated. Suddenly, the tour was in jeopardy. It was touch and go right up to the week before rehearsals were due to start in LA. In the end, he agreed to come out, but only on the condition that he would be able to take a buddy on tour with him. 'The Sufi' was a gentle soul Peter had met at the Sufi Center in Philadelphia. He clearly had a calming effect and would act as a kind of nurse-cum-grounding force to our fragile frontman. We agreed to this, of course, but we were still genuinely concerned about his ability to handle the rigours of the tour.

The day that he arrived, Peter told us that he had consulted with his spiritual teacher in Istanbul. The master had told him that there were three men waiting for him in the West, and that it was his true calling to go and join them. When Peter explained about the band, he was told that his role as a singer, performing before people of the world, was essential to his spiritual path. That clinched it.

The rehearsals were hard work. Our old friend was very, very quiet. The crackling energy of the inverted man of Coachella had apparently dissipated. He was sullen and morose. A shadow. We were very worried.

The Near The Atmosphere tour started with a sold-out gig in Vancouver. The reception was ecstatic, but there was something lacking in Peter's performance. He sang wonderfully well—probably better than ever, with more nuance and control—and hit all the notes, high and low, with precision and aplomb, but his movements were stiff and introverted. He was subdued.

As the tour progressed, so Peter's self-confidence receded. He was retreating into himself. He would sit on the bus, staring into space for hours on end, unresponsive to anything around him, never saying a word. We would all try to engage with him, but this would be met only with a weak smile or near catatonic indifference. Daniel was concerned that Peter was suicidal and, in a laudable gesture of self-sacrifice, volunteered to give up the sanctuary of his own hotel room so that he could keep a watchful eye on his beleaguered old school pal.

At the end of October, we arrived in Los Angeles to play three nights at the beautiful Art Deco Wiltern Theatre. For the first time, the show would be taped, with the recording then sold immediately at the end of the night. It was an exciting concept.

Listening back to those recordings, they certainly benefit from Peter being focused on his singing. He was losing himself in the world of the songs. It was an escape rather than an exorcism. The band was playing with ferocious intensity. We were intent on lifting Peter out of his depressive funk, and each night we would try harder. We would play as if our lives depended on it. 'Bring him back! Bring him back!' became our war cry, as brothers-in-arms answering a rallying call to retrieve our wounded captain from the battlefield. It was, alas, to no avail.

'What is this demon that's got into him?' Daniel wailed in the dressing room, following another 'storm the ramparts' show. The pain that he felt for his friend was etched across his face. 'I want to help him, but I don't know how.'

With this, Daniel, who can be quite lachrymose at times, burst into tears. I put my hand on his shoulder, and a tsunami of pent-up emotion flooded out. He then rose from his seat like a launched bottle rocket and smashed every mirror in the room. I got up slowly and slipped out of the door, the sounds of carnage continuing as I walked down the hall.

Daniel, Kevin, and I would often stay up and play music to each other on the bus following a gig. We would take it in turns to pick a track. It was a good way to unwind. Peter rarely joined us, as he tended to turn in early.

One night, we were having a few drinks, unwinding and playing music, when Peter suddenly appeared in the gangway like Cesare's ghost from *Doctor Caligari*, a haunted, pale somnambulist.

'What's that?' he enquired.

'What's what, Pete?'

'That singer. Who is that?'

'It's Richard Hawley. It's a track called "Tonight".'

A long silence followed, and then, 'That's a singer!' With that, he turned in a slow-motion stupor and stumbled back to his bunk.

I shrugged at Daniel and stared at the endless flash of the lights of the highway.

Tonight, I got it really bad, Hawley crooned, as the stars disappeared behind hanging black clouds.

One morning, Peter came and sat beside me on the bus. He said that he wanted to ask me something, and that it was important that I answered honestly. He said that he had been lying awake in bed listening to the music that we were playing, and that he knew that everything that we had played was about him—that we had planned the sequence so that it told a story about his life, and that every song was intended as a knife in his back.

I was astonished. I told him the truth: that we were just letting off steam, having a bit of fun, playing music we liked. He nodded silently, but I could tell that he was not convinced.

On October 31, we played a special Halloween show at the Fillmore in San Francisco. We had already played two sold-out shows at the Warfield Theatre a few nights earlier, but this Halloween event was also an instant sell-out. We had been trying to think of something special as an opening but were stumped for ideas until five days before the event when I had a sudden flash of inspiration while listening to a classical music station on the radio. *How about a string trio on 'Bela Lugosi's Dead'?*

The others liked the idea a lot, so I was left with the task of assembling the players with very little notice. My starting point was Tom Vos, an excellent violinist with whom I had collaborated in the past. Unfortunately, Tom, who was always in demand, already had a concert on the 31st. He gave me some recommendations for other players, but they too were booked up. They in turn suggested some other string players, and on it went. We cut it close, but by the day before the show we finally had a trio of three young women: Lila Sklar on first violin, Alisa Rose on second violin, and Jessica Ivry on cello. With their long flowing Pre-Raphaelite locks and Romanian Roma leanings, this trio could not have been more perfect. They were dressed in Victorian funeral garb and wore white masks as a finishing touch. We had one run-through at soundcheck, and that was it.

The eighteen-minute version of our signature song that announced the start of the set that night was epic. The ladies took the stage on their own for the first few minutes, weaving a wonderful improvised fabric of sound around the theme. Then we joined them, one by one, starting with Kevin, then Daniel, then me, and finally Peter. It was one of the high points of not just this tour but our entire career. The interplay between classical acoustic musicians and avant-dub-rock electric playing was intoxicating. The crowd, dressed to the nines, went wild.

At the song's conclusion, the trio slipped away like sylphs into the shadowy wings, and Daniel started the glistening rumbling intro to 'In The Flat Field'. The energy level soared to new heights. This was the one night where some of Peter's old spark returned. He was still restrained, but the overall effect was dignified and sophisticated. ('So cool, like a Gothic Frank Sinatra,' as one friend in attendance remarked.) The whole thing was recorded to tape and once again made available fifteen minutes after the end of the set. My friend David Jude Thomas also captured the performance of 'Bela' on film, shooting it guerrilla-style from a balcony at the back of the venue. We had wanted to film the whole concert, but were told by the management that in order for that to happen we would have to pay through the nose. We could, however, shoot one song, with one camera, for free. David also managed to operate another camera, cunningly concealed in the hip pocket of his overcoat. He then made a brilliant edit that effectively utilises overlaid images and really captures some of the magic of the event.

Once we were back on the bus for our overnight drive to San Diego, Peter slipped back into zombie mode while the rest of us partied up front until the small hours, when the energy finally became more subdued. I love this time. There is something quite magical about being awake when most of the world is asleep. Riding shotgun up front, getting to know the driver, tuning into some obscure country or soul station on the radio, or else sitting in silence as the bus sucks up the endless parade of painted white lines. It's more about leaving than arriving—a state of stasis in transit. Freedom.

* * *

The tour rolled on, the enthusiastic audiences oblivious to the private drama that was being played out on and off the stage. It was a roiling, poisonous pressure cooker, and by the time we reached Boston, some five weeks in, Daniel and I were in desperate need of a release.

That night, we played at the historic Orpheum Theatre, a beautiful old variety hall. Two individuals in the audience stood out. Shone, in fact! In stark contrast to all the other members of the crowd—who were, of course, liberally draped in black—this couple were all in glowing white. Two pearls set in a sea of black velvet. I could well imagine the light-bulb moment when they came up with this little stunt: *Hey! What if we …* She had even painted her eyelashes white to compliment her antique embroidered Suzie Wong number, while he sported a radiant white suit, shoes, shirt and tie all topped off with matching bowler. Yes, Amanda Palmer and Brian Viglione, aka The Dresden Dolls, were in the house.

I had met Amanda the previous year, when the duo performed for the first time in LA, at the Viper Room. That day, I happened to be driving down Sunset, listening to the excellent *Morning Becomes Eclectic* on KCRW. The Dolls were the featured live act. I had not heard of them before, but the music instantly caught my ear. The conversation was intelligent and interesting, too, so when it was announced that they would be appearing live that night, I knew exactly where I would be spending my evening.

At the time, I had been asked by the management of the Knitting Factory to put together an alternative cabaret night at the club. The Dolls' self-proclaimed 'Brechtian Punk Cabaret' fitted the bill perfectly. I called the club's managers and suggested that they should join me that night in order to check out the band. What had not been so evident as I listened to the radio was the electric, sexually charged rapport that existed between the pair. They built their set from a whisper to a gut-wrenching scream that climaxed with a thunderous cover of Black Sabbath's 'War Pigs'. Brian's bombastic drumming was incredible. He could also be extremely subtle and nuanced when the song called for it. Similarly, Amanda alternately tickled and slammed, her throaty voice sexy and authentic. Every word rang true. The sometimes witty, sometimes touching, always powerful rock-meets-vaudeville songs were quite brilliant as well. We were wowed!

After the set, I took Amanda aside and we spoke outside the club in the balmy SoCal night. I was intrigued by her eyebrows, which were like tattooed arabesque swirls. It turned out that they were painted on daily over the shaved flesh canvas. I told her about the cabaret idea, and she was excited by it. We exchanged email addresses, and we would meet up whenever the Dolls came back through town (always playing larger venues, their following growing and becoming quite fanatical).

That summer, I received a commission to write and record some music for a couple of Samuel Beckett plays to be staged at the Piano Factory Theatre in Boston, and Amanda kindly let me stay in her apartment there while she was out on tour. On my last night, she arrived back from the Dolls' show in New York, with Brian and tour mate Regina Spektor—the petite and hugely talented Russian émigré songstress—in tow. After helping them load in their gear on that icy cold night, we all repaired to Amanda's rooms, where Regina entranced us by playing Chopin Études on the baby grand.

It was to this same apartment that Daniel and I returned at Amanda's invitation following Bauhaus's Boston gig. Casa Del Palmer is situated on the sketchy south side of town. The building is a place of magic and wonder. A huge ancient wisteria vine clings to the front of the house, its gnarled stems like arms wrapped lovingly around the walls. You have to duck down to get in the front door, as part of the vine hangs right across the threshold at chest height. She shared the place with various other artists and an avuncular landlord and gentleman philosopher named Lee.

Amanda's nest lay on the second floor, and as we made our ascent up the rickety old staircase we passed various found objets d'art like Dadaist Stations of the Cross. Once inside, Amanda exchanged the blanc for noir, donning black T-shirt, stockings, and suspenders, while Brian slipped into one of her slinky little dresses. A few of our hostess's friends also tagged along—a nice, friendly little group. I volunteered to mix up some cocktails while someone rolled a spliff, and we were treated to some tracks from the Dolls' forthcoming album *Yes, Virginia*. It sounded very strong, with excellent production.

Amanda then asked Daniel and I if we had any musical requests. 'Anything at all!' Daniel's choice was Michael Jackson's 'Billy Jean', which was instantly manifested via the wonder of iTunes, inevitably followed by 'Thriller' and a spontaneous re-enactment of the famous video. We all turned into zombies right there and then. Mad fun! When it was over, I grabbed the passing Amanda and pulled her onto my lap. Daniel whispered into my ear that he was ready to go, so I told him that I would make my own way back.[2]

Following Daniel's departure, we all went up another floor to the 'Cloud Club', a marvellous attic space full of overgrown jungle plants and stargazing windows. I sat in a big leather chair opposite Amanda on the couch, and every now and again her stocking'd toes would do a seductive little walk up my thigh. I would raise my eyebrows, smile, and take another sip of vodka.

The room gradually thinned out, leaving Amanda, Brian, another guy, and me. After the drummer and his pal announced they were going to call it a night, Amanda put on Antony's *I Am A Bird Now* and climbed into an old rocking chair. We sat back and got lost in the beautiful music, smoking cigarettes and sipping our drinks. My eyes were inexorably drawn to that creamy expanse of flesh between stocking top and hem. The music was pulling us both in. Lou Reed's spoken intro to 'Fist Of Love' came on, and the stars came out. As the soulful track built and built, I could stand it no longer. I slid across the floor to where Amanda was rocking back and forth, stopping before her on my knees.

'Amanda,' I announced, 'I have to go to bed with you!'

I held her lovely face in my hands. A big smile beamed across it, and we kissed as the music hit a crescendo. I slipped my hands under her shirt and cupped her breasts. She scrunched my hair and my glasses fell to the floor. I climbed on top of her, the creaking rocking chair suddenly whipped to a canter.

Fumbling with the intricate mechanics of her underwear, I exclaimed, 'I can't work this out!'

'It's complicated, isn't it?' she replied, before taking my hand and leading me downstairs.

When we reached her room, Amanda climbed the little stepladder that led to her big raised bed. The T-shirt was flung, then the stockings and suspenders, followed smartly by her knickers, which amusingly struck me in the face. I stripped off and climbed the steps for a sojourn in paradise.

At a crucial point during the ensuing romp, Amanda stopped to ask, 'Aren't you married?' I answered in the affirmative, before telling her about the recent understanding that I had entered into with my wife—namely that, certain caveats notwithstanding, liaisons such as the one that we were having were permissible without fear of reprimand. No one would be cheating.

'If that's true,' she said, 'then it's beautiful.'

I explained that this was the first time I had chosen to act upon this new liberty.

'Really? Well, now I feel really weird.'

'Come on,' I said. 'It's OK.'

Copulation was tentatively resumed, but then she whispered, 'You know what I really want?'

'No, tell, me.'

'I just want you to hold me.'

With poignant resignation, I kissed her softly on the lips and acquiesced. She snuggled in close and then started to cry.

'And now I feel like a fool,' she sighed.

I put my finger to her lips then held her closer still. We fell asleep in each other's arms.

I arrived back at the hotel the next morning, fifteen minutes before the bus was due to leave. Montreal was our next port of call. We had a night off, so I drifted through the old cobbled streets until I found a snug little bar with a huge portrait of Jacques Brel on the wall. I asked the bartender if he had any music by Brel, and once again our old friend iTunes came to our aid. I sat at a table by the window, sipping cognac and basking in Brel while writing a heated poem of infatuation to the 'Sphinx in a rocking chair, all snowflake lashes and complicated underwear'.

* * *

On November 21, we were scheduled to play the Starland Ballroom in Sayreville, New Jersey, but after the gig was cancelled the promoter offered the band and crew top-flight tickets for Bruce Springsteen's solo concert at the Sovereign Bank Arena in nearby Trenton.

The Boss kicked off this home-turf show in dramatic style with a riveting performance of Link Wray's great instrumental 'Rumble', in tribute to the recently deceased guitarist. It was one of the most powerful things I have ever witnessed on a stage: Bruce harnessing a preternatural power that conjured up the primal spirit of rock'n'roll. Having struck the final chord, he set his electric guitar on its stand, leaving a wall of awesome feedback to wring out and ricochet off the sides of the cavernous venue.

What followed was spare and compelling. Achieving intimacy in an arena is a hard trick to pull off, but Springsteen achieved that desired effect with seasoned aplomb. Strangely, Daniel was not into it at all, and ended up leaving after the first couple of songs. He waited outside the venue until the concert was over—two and half hours later! Apparently he spent most of that time talking and bitching with the janitor, who was also not a great fan of the Boss.

On November 30, the tour reached Mexico City. Our previous show there, in 1998, had ended with anarchy at the opera house when the guttersnipes stormed the gates. Perhaps in consideration of that incident, we were placed for our return visit in the 26,000-capacity Palacio De Los Deportes, home to the 1968 Olympics. The sound was awful, the ten-second delay that bounced off the concrete at the rear of the stadium making syncopation impossible. You couldn't hear the vocals, there were brawls in the audience, and Peter resembled a consumptive aesthete dazed in the midst of an absinth binge. The biggest headlining gig that we had ever played, and it was somewhere between tragedy and farce.

The notion of farce brings to mind an incident that happened the last time I had been to that great poisonous city, with Love And Rockets in 1996. My wife joined me after the show at the Teatro Cine Opera, and as we were getting into the car to go back to the hotel, an audacious young Mexican woman climbed in next to us—or next to me, to be specific.

'I'm going back with him!' the woman exclaimed.

'No, *I'm* going back with him!' Mrs Haskins retorted.

At this, the girl snorted and hooked her arm around mine, in response to which my wife put her hand on my leg.

'I'm his wife!'

This caused the girl to relax her grip—and then tighten it. I found the whole thing highly amusing. Eventually, with the intercession of our tour manager, we managed to ditch the predatory senorita and made it back to our room, in serious need of a stiff drink. We had tequila but no ice, so off I went down the corridor, bucket in hand. I left the door slightly ajar as we had been having a problem with the key-card, which more often than not would fail to open the lock. There was no ice machine on our floor, so I had to go down a level, but the dispenser there proved to be empty, so down I went again. I finally located what I was looking for, but on the way back I became somewhat confused about which floor my room was on. The potent local marijuana was not helping matters.

I got out of the lift on the tenth floor, saw the open door, and entered what I thought was our room, and sat down on the bed, suddenly feeling very stoned. Then the bathroom door opened, and out came a Mexican bride in a voluminous white wedding dress. She saw me sitting on the bed and screamed. I rose to my feet, apologised, and shot out of the room … only to bump into the groom!

'Excuse me.' I blurted. 'I uh … made a mistake!'

With that, I hurried back to the elevator and up to the eleventh floor, where a large tequila on the rocks was sunk without trace.

Meanwhile, back in 2005, what happened in San Diego, on December 13, was more *fierce* than farce. Following a wonderful tough-love pep talk from The Sufi—in which the names of inspirational avatars both secular and sacred, from Elvis to Jesus, were cited—something clicked, and Peter, resplendent in a long flowing red-velvet coat, reclaimed his wings. His wings, and also his fire. It was the last gig of the tour, rescheduled from November 2 as a result of the fact that construction of the venue, the 4th & B, had not been completed in time for the original date. The show crackled with renewed energy. The roaring boy was back at last!

When we left for London to rehearse for a European tour in late January of 2006, it was a very different Peter Murphy that boarded the jet, a wildly aggressive Mr Hyde having replaced the introverted Dr Jekyll. God only knows what had gone on during the forty days and nights since the end of our US stint, but he was certainly back from the wilderness—and back with a vengeance.

The first gig of the tour was in Dublin at the Ambassador Theatre. Extraordinarily enough, it was also the first time we had ever played in Ireland. The first thing that I did was call up Gavin Friday to invite him to the show, but unfortunately he was busy in the studio. He gave us his blessing, though, which in my book is far better than one from the Pope. The benediction kicked in, and the gig was a cracker. At one point, I remember glancing over at Daniel, and the two of us nodding to each other. Yep, Murphy was back in full effect, and we were elated.

That night, one song re-emerged as a charged centrepiece. 'Rose Garden Funeral Of Sores' was once again transformed into a mini opera, a psychodrama played out with Daniel down on his knees, his mirrored guitar slung low and flashing under the strobes as Peter encircled and anointed him with rose petals. It was like a homoerotic passion play, with Daniel cast as martyr and Peter the sadistic scourge. 'Severance' was also inspired, with Peter singing his heart out.[3] A great addition to the set was the coupling of Joy Division's 'Transmission' with 'St Vitus Dance', with its allusion to epilepsy-induced ecstatic vision. Post-show, we were all up for the craic, Peter included, so we took off on a pub crawl in search of scratchy fiddles and creamy Guinness. (We found both in spades.)

The intensity built from gig to gig. There was a meaner, keener attitude abroad, and the staging of the opening number, 'Burning From The Inside', really set the scene. A single white pencil-beam spotlight would come up on Daniel as he coolly picked the opening chord progression, looking great in his long black leather trench coat. Another white spot would then blaze down on me as I came in with the bassline, then another on Kevin as he kicked in the beat, and then finally The Singer, and the drama of the epic song would unfold.

Emboldened by Peter's soaring recovery, we felt like a real band again—a band of brothers, tough and up for the prizefight, or at least the thorn and the rose. With each successive show we cranked it up another notch. We were playing at the top of our game, with Peter very much back in the thick of the action. One of the best gigs was at the Birmingham Academy. We did several encores, one of which was 'Ziggy Stardust'. At the end of the song, during the pause that precedes the last word of the climatic line ('And Ziggy played …'), Daniel whispered in Peter's ear to leave it at that. Peter took his cue, and we left the stage on that very pregnant pause. It proved extremely effective, especially when we returned some ten minutes later to deliver that final word, plus the appropriate power chord, without missing a beat. You can only be that cheeky and that audacious when you are brimming with the confidence that comes from being shit hot.

By the time we got to London, to play at Brixton Academy, we were on fire. In the audience was Orian Williams, who had recently produced *Control*, Anton Corbijn's film about Ian Curtis. Anton himself could not attend that night as he was filming. Before we played 'Transmission', I informed the crowd of this fact, mentioning that they were filming in Nottingham, as it apparently bore a resemblance to the run-down Manchester of the late 1970s (the real thing now being a bit too posh). After the gig, Orian came backstage and asked if I would be interested in playing the part of the punk poet John Cooper Clark in the movie. I said that I would indeed, but they eventually had the gangly man play himself, and you can't argue with that!

* * *

As well as his Promethean reclamation of fire, Peter had also regained his sparkling wit and disarming charm, and would keep us entertained with the adoption of a new character of his own invention: an old thespian queen, outrageously camp and sexually predatory. In a plummy velvet purr, he would intone such gems as, 'Kevin, tonight it will be your turn to admire my marvellous member. Report to my room after the show, and don't forget to bring your drumsticks.' Or, 'Have that man washed and oiled and brought to my boudoir immediately!' Or, 'Daniel, may I request that you shave your testicles and join me in the Turkish bath? It's time for my rub down, darling.' And so on.

Backstage, Peter would entertain guests with old world charm and gentlemanly grace. He could flip in an instant, however, and the old horns would come out, along with the malevolent, castigating scourge. Being of an easy-going disposition, Kevin would often bear the brunt of his master's spleen. On one occasion, we were waiting for a flight when Peter suddenly announced in a great booming voice, 'Listen everybody, Daniel, David, Mary Jo, can I have your attention? From now on, I veto Kevin's input on all group matters. He is no longer to be included in any group discussions concerning band business. Understood?'

The reason for this outburst was that, faced with Peter's bullying, Kevin had finally begin to stick up for himself. Well, that certainly went against the grain! In response to the 'veto', a fuming Kevin remarked, quite rightly, that this was yet another example of bullying. Peter ignored him and went off to sulk in the corner behind his laptop. The next day, he would revert back to Prince Charming, and Kevin would be the pampered object of affection.

Despite such vicissitudes of temperament, the tour continued into Europe with stellar gigs in Brussels, Paris, Cologne, Copenhagen, and Berlin. The outrageous Peaches came to see us in the latter (her home town.) We had met prior to this night, when she had appeared in San Diego, where I had written a preview of her show for a local paper. She had ended up using the piece as part of her official press kit because, she told me, 'It was so mad!' Milan, Barcelona, Madrid, and finally Oporto followed, and every show was a stormer. Suddenly, the prospect of recording a new album was very real and exciting.

CHAPTER FIFTEEN
Djinn, Petal, And Thorn

At the start of the last tour, I had stuck a photo of a maniacally staring John Lydon to my amp as an inspirational icon—a little reminder of my punk rock roots. It was still there on the amp when we started work on our new album eight weeks later.

Prior to this we recorded an atmospheric little piece entitled 'With Gravity Comes A Broken Heart' for a major exhibition at the Tate Gallery in London. We had been invited to contribute an installation to the show, which was called *Gothic Nightmares: Fuseli, Blake, And The Romantic Imagination*. We were pleased to do so, and came up with what we felt was a very interesting concept.

The band's instructions to the gallery organisers were as follows:

The room to be very low lit to evoke a dusk-like atmosphere. A passageway consisting of twenty-four white Romanesque pillars (i.e. two parallel lines, twelve pillars to a line, with enough space for one person to pass through) to be placed at the entrance to the room and ending at the back wall with enough space for the person to exit right or left. The pillars should be approximately seven feet tall. A bar (black) to be placed across each set of two pillars. From this, a black box containing a playback system to be suspended with the speaker face down so that the sound is above the person's head. The sounds (water drops on water, fire raging, earth thrown onto coffin, flapping of bird wings) to be placed at random. The pillars and the bars to be covered in dead dried roses (red). These to be arranged in serpentine spirals bunching at the top. The boxes to be completely covered. Four white Romanesque pillars to be placed in each corner of the room. A speaker mounted on top of each. The main audio soundtrack to be played through these speakers. The whole installation is intended to convey a feeling of disquieting melancholic beauty as in a painting by De Chirico or early Dali.

What we actually got was entirely different, and fell so far short of our original idea as to be laughable. Basically, the Tate set up a Formica table on which were placed half a dozen CD players wired up to headphones, with the soundtrack looped and playing at low volume.

We wrote a letter of bitter complaint to the organisers, but they were evasive and unapologetic. In 2002, the brilliant graffiti artist Bansky had spray-painted the phrase 'Mind The Crap' on the steps leading into the Tate before the Turner Prize ceremony. It was a warning we should have heeded.

* * *

On April 20 2006, we entered the Zircon Skye studio in bucolic Ojai, California, to start work on the first new Bauhaus album in twenty-three years. We had no songs whatsoever. The idea was to put ourselves on the spot—to improvise, and to roll tape as soon as something started to come together—the idea being to catch that exciting seminal spark. Lightning in a jar!

We had come up with a few tracks like this in the past, but the majority of our songs were tried and tested on the road before being committed to tape. In 2006, however, we needed a challenge, and the idea was exciting. We did have a whole bunch of lyrics that Peter, Daniel, and myself had written over the preceding six months, and these were taped to the walls of the vocal booth, so that Peter could select at will.

The first day was spent setting up gear and getting sounds. We also received a surprise phone call that day from Chris Martin from Coldplay. His band had appeared on the same bill as Bauhaus at Coachella the previous year, and on the day, he had been taken to task by the influential DJ Mike Halloran after confessing, when asked how he felt about having to follow Bauhaus, that he was not familiar with the band. Having been put to rights by the impassioned DJ, Chris had become something of a late-coming fan. He had exchanged phone numbers with Peter, and was calling to wish us good luck with the recording. It was a generous gesture on his part, and welcome, too—as it turned out, we would need all the luck we could muster. We were at least very fortunate to have two skilled engineers, Jeff Evans and Ken Eros, present for the sessions. They were genuinely excited about the prospect of working with us, and about the daredevil approach to sessions, which added a lot to the band's own confidence.

Also on that first day, Peter presented Daniel with Jimi Hendix's own original Vox wah-wah peddle. Daniel was speechless, but his eyes spoke volumes. This totemic wobble-box was a rock'n'roll heirloom that had been passed down from Jimi to Stevie Winwood, who in turn gave it to Jim Capaldi, who then gave it to his guitar player, the renowned session musician Pete Bonas, who had worked with Peter on several of his solo works. It was then passed on again, Peter being the next recipient. It needed something of a tune-up, however, so Ken extracted his trusty screwdriver and slowly opened it up with the care of a bomb-disposal expert. After he had reassembled it and plugged it in, it was like the spirit of Hendrix was surging out of the thing. Daniel would use it selectively throughout the sessions.

We had booked the studio for eighteen days. Time was tight, as we were scheduled to start a US tour as special guests of Nine Inch Nails the following month, with rehearsals for that due to start a few days after we finished recording. We were all booked into a cheap motel about a mile from the studio, and we each had our own distinctive modes of travel. Peter would pedal in on an ape-hanger handlebar bicycle he had borrowed from Daniel, who in turn would roar in on his Harley. Kevin drove his hybrid, and I would take the trusty Shank's pony.

This diverse individuality would also be apparent in temperament and work ethic. At best, it would result in creative sparks; at worst, blood and flying feathers. I tend to be very spontaneous in the studio, picking up on the accidental and turning it into inspiration, whereas my brother is highly methodical, head down with earphones on, beavering away in the corner, meticulously refining loops. When he is playing the kit, he will always come up with something unexpected but just right. He really is one of the most innovative drummers around.

Daniel is a dynamo of wired energy. A tireless worker, he will craft a part for hours, multi-tracking and honing until the rough jewel gleams. Peter works in explosive bursts. Like me, he errs toward spontaneity: Wham! Bam! It's in the can, and he's out of there!

This can be exciting but also maddeningly frustrating at times. Our MO for these sessions was that all of us would play together at the same time while Peter sang live in the vocal booth. Daniel, Kevin, and I would feel that we needed to play the track over a few times in order to really make it cook, but Murphy would call it after one or two takes and simply walk out of the booth, don his little flowerpot pixie hat, and leave for the night.

'I've done my bit,' he'd say. 'Now it's time for you girls to do some work!'

We needed him there so that the songs could evolve through changes, but when we tried to explain this to him, it would be met with a 'talk to the hand' attitude. Consequently, some tracks were abandoned or resigned to half-cocked takes.

The edgy atmosphere in the studio was exacerbated by an ongoing debate about the prospect of a fly-on-the-wall documentary film that Steven Cantor and Mathew Galkin, the makers of *loudQUIETloud: A Film About The Pixies*, were keen to produce. They had wanted to follow us on the previous tour of Europe but were denied, mainly due to Daniel's strong objection. Now they were proposing that they document the making of the album. Peter was 100 percent for it, Daniel 100 percent against, and Kevin and I somewhere in the middle.

Peter's belligerent manager continued to push for the film to happen, and we had several heated conference calls with her and the filmmakers. Daniel's point was that the presence of the cameras would be a huge distraction, potentially interfering with the music-making process, and that the music was the most important thing. This was a valid point, especially in Daniel's case, as he has always detested the intrusion of the photographer's lens. In the end, Kevin and I sided with him, much to Peter's chagrin.

Following a final long-distance confab with Peter's manager and the filmmakers, Daniel and Peter actually came to blows. At one point, Daniel was on his back in an upturned office chair, with Peter kneeling on top of him. In his hand was an old style telephone receiver. He held it high in the air, threatening to smash Daniel's face in.

'Yeah, go on then, Peter! Let me have it, kill me, you cunt!'

Fortunately, he ended up throwing it across the room instead, smashing it into pieces against the wall.

Just like the old days, this aggression would be channelled back into the music. We recorded 'Adrenalin' soon after this outburst, and it shows.

* * *

One explanation for poltergeist activity is that it is, in part, the result of psychological stress and pent-up sexual or aggressive emotions.

My Ampeg bass rig was set up in a small isolated room adjacent to the main studio, where I would play alongside the other band members. We were working on a track called 'Saved': a long, sinewy atmospheric piece with a motorik Can-like drum part. I thought that I would try something very simple over it: a one-note pulse that would harmonise with the chord changes. It wasn't quite working, but I decided to persist. Suddenly, I lost power.

'What happened?' Jeff asked over the intercom.

'No idea!' I replied.

Ken dashed into the empty iso-booth to check out my amp.

'Did someone turn this off?'

'No!'

'Well, it's not on now!'

The amp had a large, heavy switch that sometimes required two hands to flip it, so this was very strange. Ken raised an eyebrow, shrugged, and switched it back on. Peter then came out of his booth to work with me on the part. Five minutes later, the same thing happened again. No power. The amp had been switched off.

Ken's voice crackled over the intercom. 'This is weird, guys!'

We decided to take a break. Peter suggested that we were being visited by a djinn—an Arabic term for a mischievous and perverse elemental spirit. It was my birthday a couple of days earlier, and Peter had presented me with some rare incense from Mecca. Now, I decided to burn it in the iso-room. I placed a dish on the floor in front of the amp, lit the coal, and sprinkled the pungent incense. I sat down and spoke to whatever it was that had gained our attention. I told it that I wished to make peace and that, if it had anything to say, I was listening. *Is there a message here?* I thought.

Back in the main room, I reconsidered what I was playing. We ran through the song again, and instead of the original part, I started to play notes all over the shop, not an anchoring bassline but more a spiralling arabesque. It worked very well, and the amp stayed on. After laying down the part in two takes, I went back into the isolation booth, lit some more incense, and thanked the wise old djinn. I would repeat this action every day after that. The only time I did not, having removed the dish so that I could clean it, the amp once again switched itself off.

One day, I rolled into the studio and was greeted by a wonderful and mysterious sound echoing down the hallway. A resonant sustained 'ping'. *What was that?* I wondered. I followed the source and crept into the main room. Daniel had his sax stuck into the guts of the grand piano and was blowing clipped notes into the metal sound-holes. The natural reverb made the notes open up like sonic blooms. These were then sampled, processed, and dropped into a rhythm track built around one of Kevin's subtle loops and a sitar, played (again by Daniel) as a percussion instrument.

Inspired by this innovation, I picked up a National Dobro guitar, a metallic instrument with an in-built resonator. I put it in an open tuning, fed it through some effects pedals, and sawed away with a violin bow. Once the instrumental soundscape had been laid down, Peter added a rich, multi-tracked vocal, ending with the refrain, 'Loves me, loves me not.' True words indeed! At times the very soul of charm but more often than not simply an insufferable prick, Peter Murphy would slip in and out of our collective affection like sand through a sifter.

One of the strongest tracks to come out of the sessions was 'Endless Summer Of The Damned', an eco-rant set to a gothic-surf soundtrack. I had recently seen the great Dick Dale live. Halfway through his set, he had jumped offstage and walked down the aisle of the theatre and out into the street before proceeding to stop traffic as he stood in the middle of Highway 101, still playing his guitar. It was magnificent! This was in my head when I borrowed Daniel's Telecaster to lay down the big descending surf guitar lines.

This was a final overdub, though the track was, at one stage, in danger of never being completed. As usual, we had been working it up, jamming it through, until we felt ready for a first take. It was sounding great. I complimented Peter on his vocal, and we gave the thumbs up to Jeff to roll tape. Suddenly, Mr Murphy stuck his head out of the booth.

'Yes, I am sounding excellent,' he announced. 'Perhaps, David, you have finally learned to appreciate me!'

This preceded one of his outrageous soapbox harangues. This one was all about an interview I had done back in 1984, where I had apparently described Peter in less than glowing terms. I was speechless, but Daniel cut in, 'Peter, what the fuck are you talking about, man? That was over twenty fuckin' years ago!'

'Yes, so it's taken him that long to know what a good thing he's got in me!'

Finally, I found the words. 'You can't be serious?'

'Oh, yes I can!' he snapped. Then, addressing Daniel but referring to me, he added, 'He knows what I'm talking about. Him, with his clever little mind, always ready to have a go!'

'Peter, what are you talking about?' Daniel replied. 'We were all ready to do a take here.'

'Yeah,' Kevin added, 'it was sounding really good. Why'd you have to dredge up all this nonsense?'

'No one asked you, young 'un!' Peter continued.

At this point, Jeff chimed in over the intercom. 'Uh, guys, are we going to roll?'

'NO!' we replied en masse.

The session was abandoned, and we left that night convinced that the whole thing was over—not just the recording but The Band, full stop. The next day, Daniel, Kevin, and I arrived early to discuss the disaster at hand. We had funded the sessions out of our own pockets, so that was now money down the drain. We would have to cancel the NIN tour, too, and as we were under contract we would potentially end up being sued by the promoters. On top of this, the good music that we had made thus far would, in all likelihood, never be heard. It was a nightmare.

Finally, Murphy breezed in, and the air turned thick with rancour. He then did something that I will never forget as long as I live. As we stood in the narrow hallway that led to the kitchen, he spat red rose petals into each of our faces. It was pure Zen—brilliant in its conception and execution. There was nothing that we could say after that, so we simply went back in, picked up our instruments, and nailed the fucker in one take.

The first thing we had recorded for the album was the track 'Mirror Remains'. The lyric was Peter's spontaneous Burroughs-style cut-up of a poem I had written some twenty years earlier. The recording starts with the ad-libbed camp exclamation 'But I'm marvellous already! No, I'm exhausted!' This is followed by a personal favourite moment. During an instrumental passage, the following can be heard:

PETER: Solo … right, that's a solo there of some kind.

DANIEL (*sounding laconic*): This is the solo!

PETER (*with a laugh in his cigarette-scratched voice*): All right! That's good!

The reason that this kind of thing was left on the record was that, during the NIN tour, Trent Reznor asked if he could listen to what was at the time considered to be the rough mix of the album. We lent him the CD, and he listened while in flight. He was waiting for us when we disembarked from the plane, full of praise for the urgency and vitality of the sound, and strongly suggested that, instead of going back in to smooth things out, we should leave it as it was.

After some consideration, we decided to go with Trent's advice. Ultimately, there would be another practical aspect to this decision, as by the end of the Nails tour, the knives would once again be out, and the idea of the four of us being holed up in the studio together would be about as appealing as getting sent to the gallows.

CHAPTER SIXTEEN
Coffin Nails

I hardly recognised him. Gone was the slim, androgynous aesthete of yore, and in his place stood a muscular, alpha-male athlete. The man was ripped, but he was still as quietly charming and engaging as ever.

'Hi, David, how's it going?'

'Hi, Trent. Good, thanks. Pleased to be on the tour.'

'Oh, very pleased to have you!'

We were standing in the wings at the Gorge Amphitheatre in George, Washington, home of the Sasquatch Festival. Wolfmother had just taken the stage, but while these young turks were rockin' out righteously, the audience seemed more interested in looking at their cell phones or throwing Frisbees. *This is going to be a tough one*, I thought. And then I had an idea.

When Bauhaus were finally up, following in the wake of some four other bands—all of whom had been met with varying degrees of disinterest or derision by the hard-core NIN fans—we began our set, rather than launching straight in, by standing, stock still, and staring out into the crowd. The buzz of chatter slowly dissipated, turning instead into a combination of abuse, cheering, and mute incomprehension. We held our ground and the tension built further. As at our very first Resurrection gig in LA, back in 1998, we were due to start with 'Double Dare', so it was once again my call to kick things off with the fuzz-bass intro. I waited some more, stretching out the pregnant pause to an excruciating extreme. Finally, a hole appeared in the atmosphere, and we dived in.

It worked. We got the fuckers' attention that night, and we would repeat the same trick for the rest of the thirty-two-date tour. As well as the old favourites, we were playing two songs from the new album, *Go Away White*: 'Endless Summer Of The Damned' and 'Adrenalin'. The former really clicked in the stadium heat, and the latter grew into a Stooges-like pile driver, with Peter screaming the repeated motif of 'Shift, crank, pull', which I had first spotted on a trucker's T-shirt during a pit-stop on the previous tour, to great visceral effect.

Between shows with NIN we played our own headlining gig at the Town Ballroom in Buffalo, New York, and it was one of the best ever. We had some nineteen gigs with NIN under our belts by this time, so we were running like a well-oiled machine—but a machine with heart and soul. We relished the idea of playing for our own fans, who had travelled from all over the country for the gig. The reception they gave us was vocal and inspiring. There was a very strong connection between us and them on this night—to the degree that it really felt simply like 'us'. There were many memorable moments during the ninety-minute set, but one that stands out was when some young kid in the front row was enveloped and swallowed up by Peter's voluminous black coat during 'Bela'. When he finally re-emerged, he looked ashen but deliriously happy, despite having possibly lost a little blood!

A few days later, we found ourselves in Cleveland, Ohio. We had a day off before the show, so we decided to visit the Rock and Roll Hall of Fame. On the way to the museum, we bumped into the members of NIN, who were just returning from a visit to the same establishment. They strongly advised us to enquire after the weirdest item: a mysterious object they said was not on public display but housed in the vaults at the back of the building. We had been promised a tour of this inner sanctum by the managers of the Hall, and upon our arrival were ushered directly there. Our guide wore special white gloves, and we were politely advised that it would be inappropriate to touch any of the hallowed memorabilia without them.

Huge silent steel doors parted at the push of a button, and we were inside. It was like something out of a James Bond movie. On our way to the 'weirdest of the weird', we passed by a row of Beatles attire, including

292 • David J. Haskins

John Lennon's green satin suit, as worn on the cover of *Sgt Pepper*, and Ringo's grey suit with black velvet collar, circa 1964. I was struck by how tiny this gear was. There was also a rack of Bowie garb from the early 70s, and again it was all extremely diminutive. Another item that caught my eye was Gene Vincent's black leather biker's jacket, and here I must confess to an illicit fondling of the hem, in the hope that a pinch of its mojo would be imparted. Finally, we arrived at a vault of sliding drawers for the great unveiling. I held my breath as the white gloves located the container in question, and there it was: Bob Marley's dreadlock! A clump of thick, matted dark-brown hair, preserved under temperature-controlled glass like some holy relic in a reliquary. You could probably get high from sniffing the thing!

After this we took a tour of the regular museum. I especially enjoyed the 'Story of The Clash' section, which included Paul Simonon's smashed bass from the cover of the *London Calling* album. They also had Strummer's original handwritten lyrics for the album's title song. Before we left, the museum's managers requested that we send them some Bauhaus memorabilia for future display. *God!* I thought. *Whatever happened to those old Ray-Bans?*

One of the delights of the NIN tour was the opening band on the first leg, TV On The Radio. I had caught them once beforehand, when they had played at the Mayan Theatre in Downtown LA, but they were really hitting their stride on this tour with a very interesting collision of avant-rock and soul. Strangely, no one else in my band was into them, but I would catch some of their set whenever I could. It was original stuff, and they were very nice guys to boot. Another great thing was that Trent would organise special live events for fan-club members and radio show contest winners. These would take the form of collaborations by musicians drawn from all three bands and would take place either on the stage or backstage before the start of the official concert. For the most part, though, it would be just Trent and Peter performing. They came up with some brilliant duets that were broadcast live on the radio. I recall great versions of NIN's 'Hurt', The Normal's 'Warm Leatherette', Iggy Pop's 'Nightclubbing', 'Pere Ubu's 'Final Solution', and our own 'Sanity

Assassin', as well as a brace of Joy Division covers. On one occasion, TVOTR joined Trent and Bauhaus for 'Bela Lugosi's Dead', which was a real kick!

Speaking of which, the World Cup tournament was once again taking place at the time, and we had the match schedule printed out in our tour book. We would try to watch as many games as we could, usually on the bus TV. Our tour manager for this run was the personable Carlos Donohue, who, being of Brazilian decent, would don his country's yellow-and-green jersey whenever they were playing. Carlos would also fly a large Brazilian flag from his production office. This all made for some good-natured rivalry and beery badinage.

* * *

In the meantime, Peter's transformation into Hyde was now complete. He had a gentleman-werewolf air, greatly aided by the huge mutton-chop side-whiskers that he had sprouted. He had also taken to wearing enormous jewelled rings, ascots with opulent pins, an electric-blue velvet drape coat, and drainpipe trousers. He looked pretty great, in a decadent aristo dandy kind of way.

Daniel's sartorial display, however, was upsetting in the extreme. He had taken a shine to an awful white rabbit-fur vest thing that would malt and leave great chunks of tat all over the dressing room floor—and, inevitably, the stage. Worse, while travelling through airports, he would wear nylon running shorts and flip-flops. (Oh, the horror!) Kevin and I attempted a fashion-police intervention, but alas it was all to no avail. Comfort over style is all very well, but the two are not necessarily exclusive. (Out of sheer embarrassment, I would endeavour to keep a distance of at least one hundred feet when walking through airports.)

The fire that had been lit under Peter's arse continued to burn voraciously, and he would take on the role of provocateur with maniacal glee. Sometimes, this would be levelled against an audience member who had got his goat; at other times it would be one of us. When we played at the spectacular Red Rocks Amphitheatre in Denver, Colorado, Daniel came in for a thorny rose-stem-lashing that drew blood and much anger. He was also slammed hard in the chest with Peter's wooden staff. A blazing row followed in the dressing room afterward, and when I tried to diffuse the situation by playing Lou Reed's 'Vicious'—'Vicious, you hit me with a flower'—on the boom box, it did not go down too well with Daniel, who exploded into a fit of rage levelled in my direction.

'Come on, Dan,' Kevin pointed out, 'Dave was just trying calm things down with a bit of humour.'

'Well, I don't see the fuckin' joke!' the wounded guitarist screamed, before blazing out of the room.

'Such a fuckin' Mary!' was the rose-wielder's only comment.

Tension was also building between Peter and the crew, especially Carlos. On one occasion, the tour manager was sitting at his laptop in the production room, which was being shared with the NIN management team, when Peter nonchalantly dropped a bag of cocaine onto the keyboard.

'Look after this until after the show, all right?' He chirped. Astonished, Carlos grabbed a towel and covered the drugs, hoping that no one had seen the incident. Since getting sober, Trent had a strict 'no drugs' policy on tour, and this incident could have seriously jeopardised Carlos's job and our continuing involvement on the tour. Over the weeks that we had been on the road, I had heard Peter repeatedly calling out to various crewmembers for 'socks'. *He's getting through a lot of laundry!* I naïvely thought. Then I discovered that 'socks' was code for cocaine. Peter Murphy in full-on manic bastard mode is bad enough, but when you factor white powder into the equation … look out!

I have to confess that I had also fallen off the coke wagon on this tour. It was only one night, but that was one night too many, as no one on the wrong side of middle age should be 'marching to Bolivia' like that.

One day, toward the end of the tour—which by now was feeling very long indeed—we had just pulled up in front of our hotel when Carlos received word that a close friend of his had died. He was understandably shaken, and was being commiserated by the bus driver (who also knew the deceased) when Peter, riding in the passenger seat upfront, incomprehensibly launched into the most insensitive tirade.

'Look, if you girls want to natter to each other, why don't you go to the back of the fuckin' bus and do it there?'

Carlos was flabbergasted—as was everyone else within earshot.

'That's really out of line, Peter!' I exclaimed, but this was met with haughty indifference as he stared out of the window, exquisite nose tilted skyward. A seething Carlos climbed down from the bus, resigned to quitting the tour. Having found themselves in the singer's line of obnoxious fire on previous occasions, some other members of the road crew had expressed the same desire.

The situation was exacerbated by Peter's insistence that his young nephew be given a job as a roadie. This act of nepotism proved to be calamitous, with the kid's lack of experience leading to a doubling of our usual load-out time. Sometimes he would be found chatting up girls when he should have been hauling crates, which did not go down well with the other highly professional members of the crew; on another occasion, the tour-bus TV screen was mysteriously cracked when only the aforementioned nephew and Peter's brother were present on the vehicle, but neither owned up to it, and Peter's defence of his family members was vehement.

Carlos decided to tough it out until the end of the US tour, but he made it clear that he would not be working with us on the subsequent European dates. Later on, Peter claimed that he had sacked Carlos, to which I replied, 'No you didn't, he left of his own volition because he couldn't stand your bullshit!' Peter insisted that Carlos had been acting in a very underhand manner, but when I asked him what that meant, he could not or would not answer.

Carlos was one of the most professional and personable tour managers we had ever worked with. Three of us were very sorry to see him go.

* * *

We had sadly lost another member of the old team in 2005 when our ex-manager, Charlie Hewitt, overdosed on OxyContin. It was a complete shocker, as we'd had no idea that he was using. His lodger had apparently discovered him bent over on the floor of his house, the needle still in his arm.

We had parted company with Charlie after the Resurrection tour, but on amicable terms. His replacement, Pete Reidling, came into the picture in 2005 at the enthusiastic suggestion of Mr Murphy. We all felt that we needed an injection of new blood, and we were impressed by Pete's track record, especially in regard to his continuing tenure at the helm of the very successful US band Tool. An old punk rocker—his LA office was resplendent with Jamie Reid's original Sex Pistols art—he was a true music lover, and we liked his progressive thinking, energy, and Cockney élan.

While we were out on the road, Pete had been doing the rounds, touting the new album to prospective labels. There were several bites, but the most intriguing came from ANTI-, a sister imprint of Epitaph Records, both of which were run by Brett Gurewitz, the founder of the seminal punk band Bad Religion. ANTI- is a great label—one of my personal favourites—with a select roster that trumpets good taste. Among its acts are Tom Waits, Nick Cave, Elliott Smith, Neko Case, Tricky, Marianne Faithfull, Merle Haggard, and Betty Lavette. One of Gurewitz's specialities was the smart and hip reinvention of established older acts, making the label potentially the perfect home for the contemporary Bauhaus. We were excited by the prospect of working with the label, not least because, when it came down to the nitty-gritty of greenbacks, they were also very generous—even proving agreeable when Kevin suggested we ask for an increase on their original six-figure offer. We had a really good deal on the table.

In July 2006, Brett came to see us play the penultimate show of the NIN tour at the Shoreline Amphitheatre in Irvine, California. Also in attendance that night was the male porn star Ron Jeremy, quite possibly lured by the presence of the opening act on this second leg of the tour: the sex-positive and provocative Peaches.[1] During our set, Mr Jeremy was standing by the mixing desk at the side of the stage when Peter strode toward him, brandishing his staff. I watched from the other side of the stage as he screamed something into The Hedgehog's hairy face and then slammed the staff down hard in front of him before storming off to stalk the front row.

When we came offstage, I asked Peter what he had said. Apparently, he had admonished Jeremy with the words, 'You! Get off my stage, and furthermore, clean up your act!' I suggested that if Ron Jeremy were to clean up his act, he really wouldn't have an act left.

Later, back in the dressing room, we heard a knock on the door.

'Who is it?' Daniel asked.

At this, the door swung open, and there, standing in the jamb, was an indignant Ron Jeremy.

'Hi,' he began, 'is Peter here? Cos he shouted something to me when he was on the stage, and I couldn't quite make it out, so, if he wants to say it again, then he can say it now and to my face.'

Peter was getting changed in the bathroom at this point, which was probably fortunate. Seeing the potential for a punch-up, Daniel shot to his feet and shook hands with Mr Porno. 'Hey, man!' he exclaimed. 'Wow! You're a fucking legend, you are!'

Daniel then led Ron out of the room for a placatory drink. Ten minutes later, Peter came out of the bathroom and slumped down next to me. Suddenly, the door opened, and a head peered into our space.

'Hi guys! That was great! Can I come in?'

'NO! You can't!' Peter blurted.

The head retracted, and the door softly closed.

'Hey, Pete,' I said. 'It would be funny if that was the bloke from the record company.'

'Well, if it was, he should fuckin' know better, and give us some time to come down.'

I nodded in agreement. Twenty minutes passed, and the room was opened up to guests and well-wishers. Pete Reidling came in and introduced us to the CEO of ANTI-, and yes, it was indeed the same early bird who had previously been given his marching orders. Then someone from our merch company appeared, wanting our opinion on a new T-shirt design.

'I think it's cool!' Mr Gurewitz piped up.

'Fuck off!' Peter replied. 'Who asked you?'

A black frown corrugated across Gurewitz's brow. Charley led him over to the drinks table, and what was left of the vodka after a certain guitarist had laid into it. Then came the knockout punch, when a sozzled Daniel pinned the poor label man against the wall in a corner.

'Listen, man! If we sign with you, then you've gotta fuckin' pay us, right? And pay us good, cos we've been fucked over in the past, and it ain't gonna happen again, got it?'

The guitarist punctuated every other word with a short sharp stab of the finger to the chest, and each one was a nail in the coffin of the deal. By noon the next day it was all off.[2]

CHAPTER SEVENTEEN
Territorial Pissing

Mmmmmmwah! Mmmmmmwah!

Peter Murphy was blowing kisses, and his reflection was blowing them back. His gleaming, bald pate was plastered with heavily waxed strands of lank thinning hair, his stratospheric cheekbones dusted with white powder and rouge, his full, puckered lips mashed with blood-red lipstick.

Twenty minutes to show time. Outside, the rain smacked down hard on the old cobbled streets; inside, the air in the club was thick with cigarette smoke and expectation. We were in Utrecht, Holland, at Club Tivoli, and the crowd was growing like bacteria in a petri dish.

Thanks to the positive response generated by our last, trailblazing tour of Europe, we had been persuaded to return for a seven-date summer tour, which included several headlining spots at festivals. Unfortunately, this jaunt would be plagued by technical problems and emotional meltdowns, and would ultimately result in the band's demise.

It started in London. We were playing the first of two nights at the Forum in Kentish Town when Daniel's guitar went down during 'Stigmata Martyr'. A backup was plugged in only, for that to crash and burn as well, so off he stormed for the rest of the set. I kicked the bass into fuzz mode in an effort to compensate for the loss, but the band's sound had been reduced to a rhythm section and vocals, and you can only do so much with that. Toward the end of the truncated set, the guitars were coaxed back into partial life for an impromptu tribute to the recently deceased Syd Barrett and something approximating 'Interstellar Overdrive' meets 'Bela Lugosi's Dead' was achieved, but the sonic pallet was still seriously compromised by this failing of the axe. But at least our new guitar tech, on loan from Primal Scream, had the whole of the next day to fix it.[1]

On the second night, I struck the opening notes to 'Double Dare', the opening song. It sounded like two strings had broken. I looked down to see that all four were still intact—intact but horribly out of tune. I had no option but to stop and tune up. The night went down hill from there. Daniel's guitars were still up the shoot, cutting out and howling all over the place. Somehow we finished the set—which included an unrehearsed cover of Bowie's 'The Bewlay Brothers'—winging it with the jets full of bloody feathers. Despite this, the crowd was still shouting for more at the conclusion of the set, but when we came back on for an encore I found that my bass had inexplicably disappeared. I ended up playing imaginary air-bass until one of the road crew found the instrument and handed it over. Jesus![2]

The next show was in Brussels, at the Lokeren Festival. We were headlining, and the gig was sold out. This was Super Roadie's last chance to get it right. Suffice it to say that he failed, and was promptly fired on the spot.

'Sorry mate,' he muttered, sheepishly, as we came offstage. 'It won't happen again.'

'No, it fuckin won't!' said I.

We now had twelve hours to find a replacement and get him to Holland. Fortunately, Bernd the monitor engineer knew the answer to our prayers: namely Dirk Schulz, a fellow Kraut, who specialised in electrics and miracles. Dirk flew in from Dusseldorf and proceeded to take everything apart—guitars, effects pedals, amps and cables, the lot. The wizard discovered many wiring problems, and true to his reputation he fixed every one. We were all set to get back on track.

* * *

'OK guys,' Dirk announced, 'everything is up and running. Have a great show!'

'Ten minutes to show time,' Mary Jo added, before escorting us to the stage.

We waited, concealed in the wings, up for it at last. Tonight was a chance to reclaim our pride and badly bruised self-confidence. There was just one problem: Murphy had the knives out. A handful of them, in fact, like a knife-throwing circus act gone psycho—and, as usual, the rest of the band were tied to the spinning wheel. *Thwwack!*

> PETER: We've got the wrong lighting tech on this tour. We really should have gone with my choice.[3]
> DANIEL: Peter, we discussed this, and the reason we went with *A* was because he's reliable. *B* is not: he gets on the sauce and that's it, everything is all over the place.
> PETER: No, you've got it wrong, as usual.
> DANIEL: Dave, is *B* erratic?
> ME: Yes.
> PETER: Look, you guys, you don't have a fucking clue when it comes to lighting. (*Thwwack!*) I design my own lights with *B*, and they're brilliant. You really should listen to me a lot more. You just don't appreciate me for what I am, which is the Main Man. There's a hierarchy in this band, and I'm at the top! (*Thwwack! Thwwack!*)
> DANIEL & ME: *What?!*
> PETER: Yes, I'm the Main Man here, and you would be nothing without me! Love And Rockets, ha! You thought that was cool but it wasn't cool really. You have one fluke hit and you think you're really something. It's a joke really! (*Thwwack! Thwwack! Thwwack!*)

With that, we were on. The Main Man made a beeline for his mic stand and threw it aside, then picked up Daniel's stand and slammed it down in the centre of the stage. He then strode over to Daniel's monitor and sat down on it in an apparent black sulk. There he remained for the next hour, not making any attempt to engage with either audience or band. At one point, I glanced over to Kevin and gave him a perplexed look. Kevin slowly shook his head from side to side.

The small club was getting hot. At last, Peter stood up to remove his velvet jacket, which he tossed to the rear of the stage.

'What the fuck's going on?' I shouted, as he brushed past me.

'Someone needs to be taught a lesson!' he replied. He then retreated into the shadows at the back of the stage to sing into his armpit.

We finished the set, stormed offstage, and exploded into the dressing room.

'Peter,' I asked, 'what the fuck was all that about?'

'Tonight I proved that nothing happens without me.'

'This is supposed to be a band! Everyone has a job to do. Each of us is as important as the other.'

Peter had other ideas.

'You see, that's where you're wrong, and if you would only wake up to the fact that I'm the Main Man, you might start to learn something! Once again, I proved that this band would be nothing without me—and, also, Daniel needed to be a taught a lesson, and he knows what I'm talking about. That's my space out front, and when he keeps wandering into it and getting in my way, I can't do what I need to do. It's like me going over to your backline and fucking with the settings. The front of the stage is my backline, and you have got to understand that. Anyway, tonight I gave him the opportunity to come up front and be me—and, as we now know, it just can't happen. Nothing happens without me being there.'

Daniel stared back at him, shaking his head. To his great credit, he had not risen to the bait. So Peter dug the knife in deeper and twisted the blade.

'Look at you!' he continued. 'You want to be the frontman, but when I give you the chance to step up you don't know what to do with it. You hang around with groupies and rock'n'roll scum. The dregs of society. And cos they're all over you, you think you're something special, but really you're just pathetic.'

'Whew! Hold on a minute,' Daniel replied. 'What are talking about? *The dregs? Rock'n'roll scum?* Do you mean my friends?'

'Your *friends?* Ha! Scum, man, scum. And that girlfriend of yours! Mutton dressed as fuckin' lamb, or what?'

Now he really had gone too far. I was expecting Daniel to explode, but once again, with great dignified restraint, he took it on the chin. He glared an oxyacetylene torch glare then quietly packed away his things and left the room. With a deep heavy sigh, Kevin followed suit, leaving only Murphy and me.

'Who the fuck do you think you are?' I asked.

'I know who I am, and I'm right, and what's more, he knows it, too.'

'Jesus!' Now it was my time to go. I slammed the door solidly. I found a perch in the upper regions of the club and resorted to the taking of strong drink.

Back at the hotel, many inter-room phone calls were made between Kevin, Daniel, and me. We all agreed that we could not go on, and even the idea of completing the three shows that remained felt like an extremely daunting prospect—let alone the planned world tour that would take us well into 2008. Even if, as promised, we would all be millionaires by the end of it. Some things just aren't worth it.

We called Mary Jo to ask how we stood contractually, regarding the current tour, and were told that we would face enormous fines were we to pull out now. We simply could not afford to do so. It was a matter of biting on the bullet and soldiering on.

Two days later, the atmosphere backstage at the M'era Luna Festival in Hildesheim, Germany, was poisonous. The dressing room was a huge temporary enclosure with an open top. The open top was good psychologically, at least, as it felt like the black cloud had somewhere to go—and it was, indeed, black. Daniel, Kevin, and I were at one end, Peter at the other. We were not talking. The air was toxic, and the gig was flat and anaemic. I felt that we were letting down the 25,000-strong crowd. It was very sad.

In Venice, a small motorboat took us over the gently lapping jade-green water to our hotel. It felt like a ride across the Styx with Charon, the ferryman of the Underworld, and what awaited us on the other side was certainly a kind of death. Having crossed the water, we checked into the opulent Luna Baglioni Hotel. Following the upheaval of the last few days, Peter and I were at least in agreement that we should talk in private about the dire situation.

As soon as I got to my room, I called him to request that he join me there. He was in the bar with a lady friend, and suggested that I join them. This would obviously not have been at all appropriate, so I insisted he come to my room, alone.

There were two loud knocks at the door. He came in blazing.

'OK I'm here. Let's fucking talk!'

'Yes, Peter, let's.'

'You killed me! You killed my spirit! That night in Holland—you, Daniel, and Kevin—you destroyed my spirit and my love for this band. You lot killed the band!'

'Peter, if anyone killed the band then it was you! And if you and your spirit have been killed then it was suicide and not murder!'

'No, that's where you're wrong. You're the ones who've committed suicide. You simply don't realise how important I am to you. You're so arrogant, David!'

'Uh … ever heard of the pot calling the kettle black?'

'No! See, that's where you're wrong, and I want an apology.'

'An apology!? For what?'

'Your soul is so cold. You're as hard as nails. I quit, and don't ever say that you sacked me!'

'Peter, there's nothing left to quit. It's over! We had a chance to pull it all back but you blew it. When things are going fine, it's like you have to create aggro and chaos. You purposely disrupt things. You seem to feed off of that.'

He wouldn't have it. He insisted that the territorial pissing that had taken place in Tivoli had all been very necessary, as Daniel needed to 'learn his lesson', and all of us had to learn to appreciate what a gem of a frontman we had. Well, actually, we did. Yes, the gleam from that jewel was hardly lost on us, but neither was the flaw. And it was this that was increasingly occluding the sparkle and flame.

* * *

We played the penultimate gig at the Arena Alpe Adria in Lignano, Italy, truly like a troupe of the undead. The fire had gone out, and we were

305 • ?Moonlight Mister Killed Who

now counting the hours until the end of the tour. Until … The End. We all felt it. It was as inevitable as rain in Manchester.

The final show was in Portugal, at the Paredes De Coura in Odemeira, and that predictably filthy Manc weather had travelled south. It was sheeting down. We were headlining a festival bill that also featured The Cramps, who had always been a firm favourite of mine. They were great when we played with them back in 1981, and they were still great now, in 2006. The very essence of feral rock'n'roll.

Returning to the Nissen hut that served as our dressing room, Daniel, Kevin, and I were vocal in our enthusiasm about Lux Interia's band, having just witnessed their explosive set.

'TAXIDERMY!' hollered Mister Murphy.

'What?' Daniel asked.

'TAXIDERMY!'

'What do you mean?'

'The Cramps. Fuckin' taxidermy, man! Dead and stuffed and over!'

The three of us protested, but predictably this was met with supercilious derision. He was still going off when we finally took the stage at one in the morning.

'TAXIDERMY!' came the booming non-sequitur announcement over the PA.

The rain-sodden crowd of Portuguese die-hards looked on nonplussed as we kicked off what we knew would be our very last live set. Not every band knows when it is their last stand, but we certainly did, and because of this, each song took on an added poignancy.

This reached its emotional zenith at the end of the set, with 'All We Ever Wanted Was Everything'. When the huge throng started to sing along with the final refrain—'Oh, to be the cream'—we all stopped playing and let it ring out in a big a-cappella soccer-crowd crescendo. On and on and on they sang, as the skies opened up once again.

Endnotes

Prologue

1 Reggae was the first music that I was seriously into. When I was thirteen, I would sneak into a local skinhead discotheque with a couple of mates and listen as the DJ spun vinyl imported direct from Kingston, Jamaica. All reggae, all night. These were records that you could only hear in a place like that. It was the first time that I had heard music played that loud in the dark, and in the edgy society of the 'bovver boys', it was intoxicating. We would lurk in the shadows, dressed in our two-tone Sta-Press strides and Ben Sherman shirts, and watch as the skins drank lager, teased the girls, and did the Moonstomp and the Skank. They were mildly amused by us young tykes and would buy us beers and scoff at our distaste for the stuff, not to mention our inability to hold it.

2 Apparently, Daniel had no idea that Peter even *could* sing. His motivation to start a band with him was based purely on his looks and the outsider camaraderie that they had shared at high school.

Chapter 1

1 At the time, Northampton had a large Rastafarian population, centred around the Matta Fancanta Youth Movement, which had its base at the old Salvation Army Citadel on the corner of Sheep Street, just across from Derngate Bus Station. It was run by Trevor Hall, whose uncle had started the famed Count Shelly sound system, which Trevor inherited. They would hold monthly events featuring two outfits competing against each other, spinning dub plates—instrumental tracks direct from Jamaica—and blasting them over the huge speakers while their respective 'toasters' took turns freestyling over the top. They would really go to town, painting up the entire place in the red, green, and gold of the Ethiopian flag and wearing suits and outsized hats to match, while the women would dye their hair. There were quotations from Haile Selassie all around the walls, and the air was thick with ganja smoke and the gamey aroma of goat's head soup. It was a true 'temporary autonomous zone', to quote the anarchist writer and poet Hakim Bey, and the police would wisely keep their distance. Daniel, Kevin, and I would be the only white faces in the throng, but there was never any trouble—quite the opposite—and the amazing music that we heard in that place became a big influence on us, 'Bela Lugosi's Dead' being a good example.

2 Daniel told me that he once brought Peter along to see me perform at one of these shindigs. I was doing a sort of spontaneous, William Burroughs-type cut-up, reading out random lines from a newspaper while walking on a heavily distorted, cheap electric guitar, which I had placed on the floor. According to Daniel, they agreed that I was genuinely 'weird'—especially as I was wearing a suit, and had the top button of my shirt done up!

3 *Withnail & I* is a black comedy cult movie about two unemployed actors set in London in the late 60s. Withnail (played by Richard E. Grant) is a flamboyant alcoholic quixotic character.

4 I recently received a Facebook friend request from Mr Stewart, which I accepted. Were we to meet now, I would like to think that we could share a laugh about the obnoxious arrogance of youth—a foible that I myself was not devoid of.

5 The resulting recording was eventually released in 1997 as a free CD included with *Bauhaus / Beneath The Mask* by Andrew J. Brooksbank.

6 Peel's slogan was 'John Peel: right time, wrong speed', as this kind of endearing mishap was a common occurrence.

7 Stock's script preceded Anton Corbijn's *Control*, but the film was never made. Michael had wanted me to compose the score, hence the loan for inspiration (at my request) of these heartbreaking missives.

8 The possibility that this sexual overture was directed exclusively at thirteen-year-old Taiwanese girls was not yet public knowledge.

Chapter 2

1 'The gods' is a theatrical term, referring to the highest areas of a theatre, such as the upper balconies. These are generally the cheapest seats, and tend to be occupied by the poorest of the poor. One reason for naming them 'the gods' is because older theatres often have beautifully painted ceilings, often with mythological themes, so the cheap seats really are up near the gods.

2 Worse still, this arrangement would be held over and applied to subsequent releases by Love And Rockets, as well as solo recordings.

Chapter 4

1 Nico: 'I kept telling him, Lou, it is *farrrrm*, not *fem*, but of course he was stubborn and would not listen.'

2 Shortly after this, I would swear off coke forever after seeing it for what it is: a nasty, mean-spirited drug that only brings out the egotistical worse in people, and results in awful depression and psychosis.

3 I originally adopted 'David Jay' as my stage name and later abbreviated it to David J., J being my middle initial (for John).

4 The old surrealist parlour game in which a piece of paper is folded into four, with someone then drawing the head of a figure, extending the neck line over the folded line; this is then passed to the next artist, who supplies the body, and so on, until a complete figure is revealed.

5 Bauhaus did exactly the same thing a couple of years later, although the victim of our crime was a music store in Northampton, not a gang of crazy gun-toting rude boys.

6 Gysin was a close friend of William S. Burroughs, and had introduced to him the cut-up technique that would become so central to his work.

7 This I did. The machine was very effective, and I found myself falling into a vortex of red and green spirals. It had been broken when I first arrived, but Gysin came down and fixed it with gaffer tape! I also saw him read at the 'talk' that he had mentioned. This turned out to be the Final Academy event curated by Genesis P. Orridge at the Ritzy in Brixton. Also on the bill were William Burroughs, John Giorno, Psychic TV, and our old pal Z'EV.

8 I have always been somewhat sympathetic when it comes to bootleggers. I believe that they provide a valuable service in making available interesting and rare recordings of music that would otherwise be lost on all but those who attended the actual gigs, and even in the old days, when record sales were relevant, the damage to the bootlegged artists' royalty income was negligible if non-existent, while today, with the prevalence of free recordings available via the internet, it really is a moot point. Perhaps here I should fess up that I bootlegged the first concert that I ever went to: The Kinks at the London Palladium in 1974. It was a wonderful show, and Ray Davis was on top form—the very personification of the witty English fop. After the gig, a couple of mates from Northampton and I waited behind in the rain, like proper little stage door Johnnies. Eventually, the object of our devotion appeared, resplendent in the white suit that he had worn onstage, plus a shaggy fur coat and straw boater. He was clutching an opened bottle of champagne, and was evidently a bit tipsy. I persuaded him to say a few words into my illegal tape recorder. I still have the cassette, as well as the crimson opera glasses that were tucked into the backs of the seats—the words 'Not to be taken away' inscribed on them. (As has already been revealed, I was something of a 'tea leaf' back in the day!)

9 We recorded a new version of 'Bela' for the movie. The classically trained Howard Blake was the musical director and producer on the session. At one point, he requested 'More trill' from Daniel. 'Trill?' Daniel asked. 'What are you? A bloody budgie?'—Trill being the name of a popular bird food.

10 These songs would eventually surface on my first solo album, *Etiquette Of Violence*.

Chapter 5

1 The resulting recording was later flown in over a dubbed-out deconstruction of 'Silent Hedges',

a song that spoke of 'going to Hell again'. This mix was done in Peter's absence, which probably exacerbated the negative situation.

2 When the Berlin Wall came down in 1989, we were briefly hounded by an opportunistic team of East German lawyers— one of a wave of wolves, chancing a stake in western tender in the slipstream of Perestroika, and in this instance a law firm with an intimidating roll call of four long German Jewish names at the top of their official letterhead—who had chosen now to seriously questioning our plagiarism. Action would be taken! Fortunately, it never was. As for that other act of grand larceny, the good Mister B. never said 'nay', and the image remained as a perfect graphic description of its subject. Hail to the thief!

Chapter 6

1 Burroughs's birthday was actually on August 2, but the event was more in observation of the year than that of the day.

2 'In researching occult conspiracies, one eventually faces a crossroad of mythic proportions (called Chapel Perilous in the trade). You come out the other side either stone paranoid or agnostic; there is no third way. I came out agnostic. Chapel Perilous, like the mysterious entity called "I", cannot be located on the space-time continuum; it is weightless, odourless, tasteless, and undetectable by ordinary instruments. Indeed, like the Ego, it is even possible to deny that it is there. And yet, even more like the Ego, once you are inside it, there doesn't seem to be any way to ever get out again, until you suddenly discover that it has been brought into existence by thought, and does not exist outside thought. Everything you fear is waiting with slavering jaws in Chapel Perilous, but if you are armed with the wand of intuition, the cup of sympathy, the sword of reason, and the pentacle of valour, you will find there (the legends say) the Medicine of Metals, the Elixir of Life, the Philosopher's Stone, True Wisdom and Perfect Happiness. That's what the legends always say, and the language of myth

is poetically precise. For instance, if you go into that realm without the sword of reason, you will lose your mind, but at the same time, if you take only the sword of reason without the cup of sympathy, you will lose your heart. Even more remarkably, if you approach without the wand of intuition, you can stand at the door for decades never realising you have arrived. You might think you are just waiting for a bus, or wandering from room to room looking for your cigarettes, watching a TV show, or reading a cryptic and ambiguous book. Chapel Perilous is tricky that way.' (Robert Anton Wilson, *The Cosmic Trigger*)

Chapter 7

1 Rumour has it that on the first day of recording at the Manor residential studios, Peter turned up first and claimed the master bedroom, leaving his suitcase on the bed. He went for a stroll around the grounds, and when he returned found that the case had been flung down the hall, its contents strewn, and Mick Karn's luggage placed on the bed instead. Not an auspicious start!

2 Apparently, just prior to this, Daniel had contacted Peter about reforming Bauhaus, only to find that the latter wasn't interested. I only found out about this recently, and to be frank, I would not have been into it either.

Chapter 8

1 I had brought along *The Book Of Copulations* and asked Aaron to write something in it. Intuitively, he wrote, 'An absence of cuts.'

2 During rehearsals earlier that day, Alan's girlfriend, Melinda Gebbie, had taken a photo of the two of us running through our routine. When the picture was developed, we were astonished to see a spectral figure standing behind us. It appeared to be a woman dressed in Victorian clothing, holding a fine, gauze-like veil that billowed out over Alan's seated figure. Alan had locked the negative in a drawer in his house, but when he went to retrieve it, he found that it had vanished. (The Theatre of Marvels, the show that never ends!)

Chapter 9

1 The witches' alphabet, aka the Theban script or the Runes of Honorius, is an ancient system of ciphers used in witchcraft to encode writings and spells.

2 According to Aleister Crowley's *777*, tobacco corresponds to Mars.

3 The repetition of the phrase 'Red Hex' put me in mind of that extended performance of 'Antonin Artaud' in Chicago. Somehow, that past event was also part of this working.

4 During one of these experiences, when I was about six, my father had taken me from the parental bed very much against my will and put back into my own cot. I felt guilty, confused, and angry. Frankly, I wanted to kill him—and therein lay the archetypal myth. I still have deeply disturbing Oedipal dreams to this day.

5 In a review of the Bridewell Theatre performance, the writer D.M. Mitchell had described me as 'Ariel to Alan's Prospero'.

Chapter 10

1 Later, I was told that the place used to belong to an old lady, and that one night the tweakers who dwelled illegally in the basement of the mansion had made a raid on her. They had tied her up and tortured her in the back room for days.

2 A couple of weeks after the fire, we remembered the video that Howard had shot during the Cinematic performance. We wanted to look at the film, and more specifically at the point where the woman came onstage and wrestled Gen to the ground. Did she have the doll? When we played the tape back, however, it was blank, even though the red *record* light had been on throughout the show. Is it possible that the dramatic events at the Steinway Mansion could have been the result of a kind of occult intersection with chicane? As previously mentioned, former residents included David Bowie, Mick Jagger, and Jimmy Page, all of whom have dabbled in the occult. It is also rumoured that Rick Rubin had been heavily into the black arts back when he was planning world domination from his student dorm at NYU in the

early 80s, and that his walls there had been daubed with inverted pentagrams. Add to this bubbling bouillon Genesis's long-time emersion into sorcery, plus my own magickal experiments and those undertaken with Alan Moore, and you have the makings of an especially volatile witchy brew.

3 Xochitl, pronounced 'Shoh-chee-tuhl'.

Chapter 11

1 For the rehearsal, Peter wore blue jeans, an old T-shirt, a waistcoat, and Turkish slippers.

2 Malena told me that in order for the crystal ball to become 'active', I would need to enclose it in a metal container that resembled an atomic structure. Clever Ken Elwell eventually constructed just such a structure, creating a thing of beauty that was designed so that it could fold down flat, thus enabling the insertion of the ball. It sits on my desk as I write. The athame is now buried somewhere in the Mojave desert following my decision to ceremoniously relinquish my magickal tools in 2006.

Chapter 12

1 That night, we finished with the Bowie staple, as usual. Then, while deciding what to play as an encore—something we always called just before going back on—I suggested that we go and play the same song again. We all shared a look, like, *that's nuts, but I like it*, and did precisely that. It was a gloriously jarring moment that hinted at Warholian replication.

2 Speaking of dogs—and madness—Daniel once accused me of employing black magick to expedite the remote assassination of his puppy, which is frankly absurd! But you gotta love him.

3 This was the first time we took a hair stylist on the road with us. It was at the instigation and insistence of Daniel, who was still very concerned about the follically challenged Murphy's visage. Kevin and I were against the idea at the start, but it has to be said that the boy worked wonders with some hairspray, a comb, and a pair of scissors—not to mention a lick of boot polish!

4 In September 2006 I saw Massive Attack at the Hollywood Bowl, with TVOTR also on the bill. I later met Robert '3D' Del Naja from the band, who told me that it was great shame that Bauhaus had split up as Massive had wanted us to play at the upcoming Meltdown Festival in London, which they were curating. Seeing Bauhaus in Bristol in the early 80s had a profound effect on him and his bandmate Tricky, he said, especially as we were utilising dub in an original way. That, he added, was really the start of Massive Attack.

5 I was later advised that I had misheard this exclamation, and what the punter had in fact shouted out was, 'Fifteen years and we're still waiting!'

6 We were caught quite literally with our pants down, as B12 shots were being administered by a dodgy local rock'n'roll doctor. 'Anything else you guys need?' he whispered. 'And I do mean … *anything*!'

7 I had met the latter two days earlier, while attending a dance music all-nighter at Brixton Academy. High on MDMA, I was transfixed by a white turban bopping amidst the crowd. Seeking out the Sikh, I asked his opinion on a strange phenomenon that had occurred that day and was all over the papers. 'The Day The Gods Cried Milk' ran one headline. Apparently, in Hindu temples all over London, statues of deities had been producing milk tears. There were lines around the blocks as people of the faith clamoured to witness this miracle. Anyway, this enquiry became the entree into a very interesting discussion about spirituality, religion, and hysteria. Eventually, I asked Amrik if he by any chance played tabla. He showed up for work the next day.

8 Fado is the traditional form of melancholy music, sometimes referred to as 'Portuguese Blues', a common theme being the concept of 'saudade', which speaks of a deep longing for a lost person or place—a bittersweet ache that is beyond nostalgia.

9 I had been introduced to Steely Dan by Andy Keightley, the resident teenage guitar god, who lent me two cassettes and his chunky mobile cassette player (with headphones) on a bus trip to the coast. For the duration of the journey, I was lost in *Pretzel Logic* and *Countdown To Ecstasy*, the band's second and third albums, respectively. Their sophisticated yet funky music was heavily jazz-influenced, and as tight as a duck's arse under water. The lyrics were extremely 'adult', full of sardonic wit and wry observations of modern life. I really liked Donald Fagen's dry delivery, and 'Skunk's' guitar solos always seemed to grab you by the lapels.

10 Namely, T.Rex's *Electric Warrior*, and all the Tyrannosaurus Rex albums before that, plus Bowie's groundbreaking trilogy of *Low*, *"Heroes"*, and *Lodger*, as well as *Scary Monsters (And Super Creeps)*, *Young Americans*, *The Man Who Sold The World*, and *Diamond Dogs*.

Chapter 13
1 I briefly considered the idea of legally adding the name 'Salim' to my own, but on second thoughts, getting through airports post-9/11 was enough of a hassle as it was.

Chapter 14
1 We were fortunate in that all of the old guard were available, including Martin Phillips on lights, Chris Rawley doing sound, and Mary Jo, tour manager extraordinaire.

2 He had looked a little crestfallen earlier on in the evening when Amanda responded to his enquiry as to whether there was any cocaine to be had with an emphatic, 'No, there are no hard drugs in this house!'

3 We had just received a note of approval concerning our recording of this song from Brendan Perry, the composer.

Chapter 16
1 At her own enthusiastic request, Peaches joined us that night for a memorable encore of 'Dark Entries', during which she straddled and dry-humped a floored Murphy.

2 After calling ANTI- repeatedly for weeks, we finally heard back, and they confirmed the

obvious: Daniel's behaviour following the show had blown it. *Go Away White* was eventually released on our own independent label, Bauhaus Music, in 2008, distributed in the States by Red Eye and in Europe by Cooking Vinyl. It did moderately well but—thanks to rampant illegal downloading, general lack of promotion, and no touring—nowhere near as well as we had hoped. In 2010, the distributer trashed thousands of CD copies of the album.

Chapter 17
1 Our regular man, the stalwart Troy Stewart was off working on another tour to which he had already committed before the Bauhaus offer came through.

2 Richard Hawley had been all set to sing 'All We Ever Wanted' with us for the encore, but due to lack of organisation on our part he had failed to make it to the theatre, which was probably a good thing in retrospect. A few days prior, I had gone with Peter to see Richard introduce his favourite film, *Zulu*, at the Curzon Cinema in Soho. He also performed a great short acoustic set, after which I introduced Peter, and the proposition of joining Bauhaus was made and accepted. Apparently, Richard had been a teenage Bauhaus fan back in the early 80s.
3 Our regular lighting tech, the very brilliant Martin Phillips, was another member of our team who, due to other touring commitments, was unavailable for this eleventh-hour tour.

Discography

Singles, EPs, Downloads
David Jay & Rene Halkett
'Nothing' / 'Armour' (4AD AD112, w/ lyric sheet insert, 1981; Urbane Music limited edition CD reissue w/ bonus tracks, 2001)

The Sinister Ducks
'March Of The Sinister Ducks' / 'Old Gangsters Never Die' (Situation Two SIT25, 1983)

'Joe Orton's Wedding' / 'Requiem For Joe' / 'The Gospel According To Fear' / 'Point Of Departure' (Situation Two SIT26T, 1983)

'The Promised Land' / 'Saint Jackie' / 'A Seducer, A Doctor, A Card You Cannot Trust' (Glass Records GLASS 0310, 1983)

V For Vendetta EP (Glass Records GLASS 032, w/ comic strip insert, 1984; Plain Recordings PLAIN 123, reissue w/ extra tracks, 2006)

'I Can't Shake This Shadow Of Fear' / 'War Game' (Glass Records GLASS 039, 1984)

Blue Moods Turning Tail EP (Glass Records GLAEP 101, 1985)

'Crocodile Tears And The Velvet Cosh' / 'Rene' / 'Elegy' (Glass Records GLASS 042, 1985)

'I'll Be Your Chauffeur' / 'I'll Be Your Chauffeur' (original version) / 'The Moon In The Man' (Beggars Banquet BEG 243, 1990)

'Fingers In The Grease' (remix) / 'Fingers In The Grease' / 'This Town' (RCA 2717-2-RDJ, 1990)

'Candy On The Cross' / 'Antarctica Starts Here' / 'Memphis Ghosts' / 'Antarctica Starts Here' (reprise) (MCA 54424, 1992)

'Some Big City' (edit 1) / 'Some Big City' (edit 2) / 'Some Big City' (extended) / 'Some Big City' (album version) (MCA promo 5P-2261, 1992)

'Space Cowboy' (edit 1) / 'Space Cowboy' (edit 2) (MCA promo 5P-2473, 1992)

'The Trees In Silence Sing' / 'Empathy' / 'I Can't Shake This Shadow Of Fear' / 'War Game' / 'Journey To The End Of Faith' (Urbane Music download, 2001)

'The Guitar Man' / 'The Dope Show' / 'Mickey Rourke Blues' / 'The Auteur' (Heyday Records HEY053-2, 2002)

'Mess Up' / 'Goth Girls In Southern California' / 'Good To Be Loved' / 'Jeanna Fine' / 'Mexican Drugstore' (Heyday Records HEY054-2, 2002)

David J. & The Glossines
'The Bottle, The Book Or The Dollar Bill' / 'The Bottle, The Book Or The Dollar Bill' (demo) (Andromeda Records AND002, coloured vinyl w/ DVD, 2007)

The Devil's Muse EP (Urbane Music, limited to 100 copies, 2008)

David J. & Shok
'Tidal Wave Of Blood' / 'Blood Sucker Blues' (Saint Rose Records SRR04, 2010)

David J. with Ego Plum
'In The Temple Of The Id' / 'Indelible Blue' (Bare Bones Version) (Custom Made Music W000-0038, 2011)

David J. with Jill Tracey
'Bela Lugosi's Dead (Undead Is Forever)' (download, 2013)

'You Suit A Rainy Day' (download, 2014)

'Toxic' (download, 2014)

Albums
Etiquette Of Violence (Situation Two SITU 8, 1983; SITL 8, reissue with extra tracks, 1990; Cherry Red CDBRED604, reissue with bonus disc, 2011)

Crocodile Tears And The Velvet Cosh (Glass Records GLALP 010, 1985; Plain Recordings PLAIN 121, 2006)

On Glass (Glass Records GLALP 017, 1986; Cleopatra CLP 0210-2, alt. tracklisting, 1998; Plain

Recordings PLAIN 122, with extra track, 2006)

Songs From Another Season (Beggars Banquet BEG 112, 1990)

Urban Urbane (MCA 10616, 1992)

Estranged (Heyday Records HEY 056-2, 2003)

Embrace Your Dysfunction (Heyday HEY 061-2, 2003)

January 08 2003 David J.'s Cabaret Oscuro Live At DNA Lounge (Urbane Music, hand-numbered/signed private pressing limited to 200 copies, 2003)

Silver For Gold: The Odyssey Of Edie Sedgwick (Music From The Original Stage Production) (Urbane Music private pressing, 2008)

David J. & Ego Plum
The Devil's Muse (Music From The Motion Picture) (HALO EIGHT H825, 2008)

Not Long For This World (Starry Records / Saint Rose SR101-SRR011, 2011)

An Eclipse Of Ships (Sorted! Records, 2014)

Missives From The Burning Stage (Private pressing issued to funders of *An Eclipse of Ships* Kickstarter campaign, 2014)

Further Listening
Alan Moore / David J. / Tim Perkins
The Birth Caul (Charrm Records 22, 1995)

David J. / Alan Moore / Tim Perkins
The Moon And Serpent Grand Egyptian Theatre Of Marvels (Cleopatra 96882, 196)

Various Artists
Very Introspective, Actually (Dancing Ferret Discs 061-01, 2001; Pet Shop Boys tribute album featuring David J.'s 'Being Boring')

Three
Evocations (Arena Rock Recording Co. ARE0048-2, 2005)

Basic
Splinters Of The Cross (Reverb Records RR015CDX, 2005)

Jarboe
The Men Album (Atavistic Records ALP167CD, 2005; David J. appears on 'Angel David')

Various Artists
2. Contamination (Fail To Communicate Records FTC005-2, 2006; David Bowie tribute album featuring David J.'s 'Time')

Strange Attractor
'Sleaze' / 'Quietude' (Music For Speakers M4S 31 S1, 2007; David J. co-wrote and appears on 'Sleaze')

Various Artists
Nation Of Saints: 50 Years Of Northampton Music (included with *Dodgem Logic* issue one, 2009; features David J.'s 'Light Years From Gold Street')

Darwin
Five Beats One EP (Download only; vocals by David J. on 'Ghosts Are People Too')

Strange Attractor
Anatomy Of A Tear (Music For Speakers / Big Blue Records 8483502, 2011; David J. wrote and sings on 'The Corridor')

George Sarah
Who Sleep The Sleep Of Peace (Pusan Music Group 215179, 2012; David J. co-wrote and sings on 'Spalding Grey Can't Swim')

David also contributed production, songwriting, and/or instrumentation on the following: The Jazz Butcher Conspiracy *Illuminate*, 'Sixteen Years' (both 1995); Stranger Tractors *Vibration* (1995), *Point Blank* (unreleased); Max Eider *The Hotel Figueroa* (2001); The Centimetres *Help Is On The Way* (2001); Panoptica *She's In Fiesta's* (2002) Jane's Addiction *Strays* (2003); Pepe Mogt/Roberto A. Mendoza *Desierto* (2004); Renata Youngblood *Weightless* EP and *The Side Effects Of Owning Skin* (2005); Mount Sim *Wild Light* (2005); Don C. Tyler *Sonic Scenery* (2006); Music For Collections *Stars And Eyes* (2006); Michael Berg *Run Away* (2008) and *Lights Down* (2009); *Repo! The Genetic Opera Movie* soundtrack (2009); Vinsantos *A Light Awake Inside* (2009); Armed Love Militia *Stormwinds* (2010); Jajouka Sound System *Salahadeen* (2011); Voltaire *Riding A Black Unicorn Down The side Of An Erupting Volcano While Drinking From A Chalice Filled With The Laughter Of Small Children!* (2011); The Moog *The Passion Of Lovers* (2011); Amanda Palmer & The Grand Theft Orchestra *Theatre Is Evil* (2012); The Dandy Warhols *This Machine* (2012); Darwin *Starfishing* (2012) and *Souvenir* EP (2014); Dub Gabriel *Raggabass Resistance* (2013); Stellarum *Heart Of Glass* (2014)

Compiled by Andrew J. Brooksbank

Photo Credits

The majority of the photographs used in this book come from the author's archives. All efforts have been made to contact copyright holders, but if you feel there has been a mistaken attribution, please contact the publishers. **Jacket** Circle23 **1** Mitch Jenkins **2** Anton Corbijn **27** Mitch Jenkins **213** *bottom* Ann Greenaway **215** *bottom* Eugene Merinov **216** Anton Corbijn **217** *middle* Dawn Hurwitz *bottom* Stella Watts **219** Mitch Jenkins **220** Melinda Gebbie **221** *top* Kerry Colonna *middle* Howard Rosenberg *bottom* Pat Fish **222** *bottom* Cathryn Farnsworth **223** *top* Mary Jo Kaczka **224** *top* Judy Lyon *bottom* Richard Peterson **265** Richard Peterson.

Index

Unless otherwise noted, words 'in quotes' are song titles, and words *in italics* are albums.

Also available in print and ebook editions from Jawbone Press